DATE DUE

Demco, Inc. 38-293

Critical Criminological Perspectives

The Palgrave *Critical Criminological Perspectives* book series aims to showcase the importance of critical criminological thinking when examining problems of crime, social harm and criminal and social justice. Critical perspectives have been instrumental in creating new research agendas and areas of criminological interest. By challenging state defined concepts of crime and rejecting positive analyses of criminality, critical criminological approaches continually push the boundaries and scope of criminology, creating new areas of focus and developing new ways of thinking about, and responding to, issues of social concern at local, national and global levels. Recent years have witnessed a flourishing of critical criminological narratives and this series seeks to capture the original and innovative ways that these discourses are engaging with contemporary issues of crime and justice.

Series editors:

Professor Reece Walters
Faculty of Law, Queensland University of Technology, Australia

Deborah Drake
Department of Social Policy and Criminology, The Open University, UK

Deborah Drake
PRISONS, PUNISHMENT AND THE PURSUIT OF SECURITY

Maggie O'Neill and Lizzie Seal
TRANSGRESSIVE IMAGINATIONS
Crime, Deviance and Culture

Critical Criminological Perspectives
Series Standing Order ISBN 978–0–230–36045–7 hardback
(*outside North America only*)

You can receive future titles in this series as they are published by placing a standing order. Please contact your bookseller or, in case of difficulty, write to us at the address below with your name and address, the title of the series and the ISBN quoted above.

Customer Services Department, Macmillan Distribution Ltd, Houndmills, Basingstoke, Hampshire RG21 6XS, England

Transgressive Imaginations

Crime, Deviance and Culture

Maggie O'Neill
Durham University, UK

and

Lizzie Seal
Durham University, UK

First published 2012 by
PALGRAVE MACMILLAN

Palgrave Macmillan in the UK is an imprint of Macmillan Publishers Limited, registered in England, company number 785998, of Houndmills, Basingstoke, Hampshire RG21 6XS.

Palgrave Macmillan in the US is a division of St Martin's Press LLC, 175 Fifth Avenue, New York, NY 10010.

Palgrave Macmillan is the global academic imprint of the above companies and has companies and representatives throughout the world.

Palgrave® and Macmillan® are registered trademarks in the United States, the United Kingdom, Europe and other countries.

ISBN 978–0–230–57784–8

This book is printed on paper suitable for recycling and made from fully managed and sustained forest sources. Logging, pulping and manufacturing processes are expected to conform to the environmental regulations of the country of origin.

A catalogue record for this book is available from the British Library.

A catalog record for this book is available from the Library of Congress.

10   9   8   7   6   5   4   3   2   1
21 20 19 18 17 16 15 14 13 12

Printed and bound in Great Britain by
CPI Antony Rowe, Chippenham and Eastbourne

To Steve, Patrick and James
To Damien

Contents

List of Figures   viii

Acknowledgements   ix

1 Exploring the Transgressive Imagination   1
2 Children as Victims and Villains: The School Shooter   20
3 Violent Female Avengers in Popular Culture   42
4 Transgressing Sex Work: Ethnography, Film and Fiction   64
5 Madness and Liminality: Psychosocial and Fictive Images   83
6 Serial Killers and the Ethics of Representation   100
7 Outlaws, Borders and Folk Devils   119
8 Crime, Poverty and Resistance on Skid Row   138
Postscript   155

Notes   160

References   163

Index   179

List of Figures

4.1 John Wayne and Angie Dickinson on the set of the movie 'Rio Bravo' in 1959 in Tucson, Arizona   75

4.2 Tips of the Trade   78

4.3 Tools of the Trade   79

7.1 Photo: The 'othering' of asylum seekers. What's the story? Article 19 and Cardiff School of Journalism   122

7.2 Photo: A culture of disbelief. What's the story? Article 19 and Cardiff School of Journalism   123

7.3 Sketch of a map. *Sense of Belonging* project of 2008   127

7.4 Sharing a walk   127

7.5 Home away from Home   131

7.6 Home-made   133

7.7 Escape to Safety. Storyboard from workshops with unaccompanied young asylum seekers   134

8.1 Research participant taking a photograph of the Megaphone Office   141

8.2 April and Hendrik of AHA Media   144

8.3 AHA citizen journalist's media team Christmas 2011   145

8.4 Patrick Doyle. Megaphone vendor   147

8.5 Levi Holland. Megaphone vendor   148

Acknowledgements

Thanks to Helen Cook, Conrad Lodziak, Janice Haaken, Rosie Campbell, Kate Green, Mary Bennett, Leslie Kemp, Jessica Numminen, Karenza Wall, Louise Painchaud, April Smith, Sean Condon, Kerry Porth, Ken Lyotier, Aria Ahmed, Heather Connelly, Chris Gledhill, Janice Haaken, and the artists, groups and people Maggie worked with on the various projects: Charnwood Arts, Soft Touch Arts co-operative, Long Journey Home Artists, Nottingham City Arts, Walsall Youth Arts, Walsall Community Arts, the Community Arts Council of Vancouver, Megaphone, United We Can, PACE society, Atira Women's Resource Society and AHA Media.

1
Exploring the Transgressive Imagination

Introduction

Transgressive Imaginations focuses upon the breaking of rules and taboos involved in 'doing crime', including violent crime, as represented in fictive texts and ethnographic research. Here transgression is understood not only as exceeding boundaries or limits (Jenks, 2003, p. 7) but as resistance, protest and escape. Particular emphasis is placed upon the spatial, temporal and sensory dimensions of 'doing crime', 'deviance' and 'social control' in an era of globalisation, as well as 'the mediated construction of crime and crime control' (Ferrell 1999, p. 395) and the portrayal of 'heroes' and 'villains' in different cultural forms.

Building upon our own research on and with marginalised and criminalised groups, this book seeks to facilitate better understanding of transgressive acts and how they are perceived through critical, cultural criminological analysis. We explore contemporary and historical 'transgressive imaginations' in relation to the 'outsider', the 'criminal' and the 'deviant' through the genres of art, film, literature and ethnographic research. A key feature of the book is to examine the various ways in which 'outsiders' are re-presented in these genres.

In addition to deconstructing restrictive portrayals, including the way that some of those who transgress societal norms are labelled as mad, bad and abject, we also look for the radical democratic possibilities that certain cultural representations and criminological analysis can offer, whether this is through research that challenges restrictive stereotypes and normative assumptions, or the means through which

1

those labelled 'outsiders' defy their marginalisation. Therefore, we do not assume that cultural representations of 'crime' and 'deviance' are always and automatically supportive of culturally dominant or conservative positions – and we highlight in the following chapters the radical democratic potential of cultural criminology.

This introduction sets the scene for the book and contextualises the chapters within the field of critical and cultural criminology, including concepts such as 'the carnival of crime' (Presdee, 2000); transgression as a mode of protest and escape; the 'glamorisation' of crime in contemporary society; crime, deviance and social control (Redhead, 1993, 1995, 2004; Ferrell and Sanders, 1995; Young, 1999, 2004a, 2007; Ferrell, 1999; Ferrell et al., 2004; Greer and Jewkes, 2004; O'Brien, 2005) and the social and moral construction of 'abjection' (Kristeva, 1982). Topical subjects are explored that portray different examples of transgression in order to gain an understanding of the multiple ways in which moral boundaries are transgressed by people of different ages, genders, ethnicities and socio-economic positions. In this chapter, we introduce the theories and concepts used to undertake analysis of cultural representations of those labelled deviant, criminal or outsiders, and provide an account of the theoretical underpinnings of the book.

Transgressive Imaginations adds to the literature in the field of cultural criminology by developing cultural criminological analysis of discourses and representations of 'outsiders' in fictive and ethnographic texts. In doing so, it identifies the ways in which 'imagining deviance' works to construct or challenge 'moral boundaries' in society and the ways in which fictive texts contribute to popular understandings of 'folk heroes', 'folk devils' and 'moral panics'. Crime and deviance are culturally embedded both in the imagination and in material practices. The book explores the organisation, operation and consequences of some of the agencies of social control, such as schools, psychiatric hospitals, border control agencies, the criminal justice system, and their intersection with popular understandings and lived experience. The concepts of transgression and imagination are pivotal to the work we present here, and are outlined in the next two sections.

Transgression

Transgression is a key feature of contemporary life – whether it is to transcend limits, to engage in edgework or in the carnivalesque

(Jenks, 2003). Transgression may result from a desire to transcend the everyday and the culturally prescribed, or it may be a consequence of being perceived to evade established categories. Writings by Bakhtin (1984), Foucault (1977) and Stallybrass and White (1986) have been particularly influential in foregrounding transgression as an analytical category. Jenks (2003, p. 7) defines transgression as

> a dynamic force in cultural reproduction – it prevents stagnation by breaking the rule and it ensures stability by reaffirming the rule. Transgression is not the same as disorder; it opens up chaos and reminds us of the necessity of order. But the problem remains. We need to know the collective order, to recognise the edges in order to transcend them.

From Jenks' definition, it is clear that transgression can have both liberating effects and severe consequences. It can be liberating to 'break the rule' and to find and go beyond the edges of acceptability. To do so potentially offers new ways of constituting social identities and new ways of living and engaging with others. This is exemplified by Lyng's (1990) notion of 'edgework', where individuals voluntarily participate in risky activities, such as skydiving, in order to negotiate 'the boundaries between chaos and order' (p. 855) and to 'test the limits of body or mind' (p. 858). Engagement in such transgressive activities can be exciting, but it can also be a moment of resistance. Ferrell, Milovanovic and Lyng's (2001, p. 180) ethnography of BASE jumping (illegal parachuting) highlights how edgework 'offer[s] a glimpse of alternative, nomadic ways of being that emerge and become visible inside, but to some degree outside, an actuarial order'. Located within the risk-averse culture of twenty-first century America, the BASE jumpers 'experience brief, sensual visceral and adrenalin intensities' (p. 181) that create moments of transcendence.

Presdee (2004) utilises Bakhtin's (1984) concept of the 'carnivalesque', acts or events that turn the world upside down and reverse established hierarchies, enabling the questioning of the 'supremacy of any authority' (Presdee, 2004, p. 41). As carnivals were officially sanctioned times of revelry, they did not represent the overthrow of the established order but did allow 'those normally excluded from the discourse of power [to] lift their voices in anger and celebration' (p. 42).

According to Presdee, the carnivalesque has largely disappeared from the dominant mass culture of the present day and consequently emerges instead in criminal behaviour such as joyriding (taking cars and racing them), which is 'a challenge to death and to authority' (p. 50). Joyriding turns the world upside down as unemployed, working-class young men race highly expensive prestige cars of the kind they could never afford. Participation in racing teams demonstrates group belonging and constructs 'an identity of excitement and opposition' (ibid., p. 51).

The concepts of edgework and the carnivalesque highlight the excitement of transgression and its possibility as a form of resistance. The participants in BASE jumping and joyriding have chosen to engage in these activities and understand that they are breaking the rules – this is their appeal. However, crossing boundaries and exceeding limits is not something that groups and individuals perceived as transgressive always want or intend, but is something which occurs when they are seen as 'out of place'. Drawing on Stallybrass and White (1986), Cresswell (1996, p. 9) argues that 'the margins can tell us something about "normality"', as the attempt to keep things in their right place highlights the otherwise taken-for-granted discourses and ideologies that underpin the normative. For Cresswell (1996, p. 10) 'transgressive acts prompt reactions that reveal that which was previously considered natural and commonsense'.

In the early 1980s in New York, the mayor introduced an 'anti-loitering' law (which was subsequently overturned), targeted at homeless people using Grand Central Station as a place of shelter. Speaking in defence of the law, the mayor, Ed Koch, stated use of 'commonsense' made it obvious who the homeless people in the station were, and that they were not there in order to travel. As Cresswell (1996) argues, there were many reasons why people not intending to travel might be in Grand Central, such as admiring the architecture or buying flowers from a stall. Mayor Koch's assertions about homeless people revealed that they exceeded the limits of whose presence was considered acceptable in public space. However, the homeless people were not intentionally resisting society's dominant values and most of their actions were 'simply strategies for survival' (ibid., p. 4). Indeed, their inability to be other than out of place augmented their transgression and, unlike the BASE jumpers and joyriders, being homeless was not an identity of group belonging (this is not to suggest homeless people are without identity or culture; on this see Ferrell, 2006).

Transgression entails crossing the boundaries of acceptability but it does not necessarily connote edgework and the carnivalesque, as useful as these concepts are. Transgressors do not always choose to be seen as such, or employ transgressive behaviour as a mode of resistance. They may not even recognise their own transgression (Butler, 1997). As Jenks (2003, p. 8) states, transgression more often 'resides within the context of the act's reception'. Clearly, too, the transgressive are often not attractive or easy to sympathise with, particularly when their behaviour is violent and harmful to others (Hall and Winlow, 2007). However, this type of transgression is also worthy of examination for what it reveals about the values of the collective order.

If we further unpack the earlier quote from Jenks (2003, p. 7), the flipside of transgression is the reaffirmation of the shared values of the social order. Through exceeding social and cultural boundaries, transgression completes them (ibid.). However, the values that constitute the boundaries are not universally agreed and accepted. They shift and change over time, and are to some degree porous (Walkowitz, 1992). Seal (2010) examines transgression in relation to gender representations of women who kill – who, in committing fatal violence, contravene norms of femininity. This violation of gender boundaries highlights norms such as violence as an attribute of masculinity, and femininity as connoting 'nurturance, gentleness and social conformity' (ibid., p. 1). Analysis of particular cases reveals how they can become sites of contention over the meaning of not only gender, but also sexuality, family, nationality and respectability. Cases highlight anxieties about shifting cultural boundaries, but also demonstrate that change is taking place (Shapiro, 1996). Women's 'deviant' sexuality was often significant to their representation in murder trials in 1950s Britain, which can be understood as the criminal justice system reaffirming the dominant contemporary gender norm of the married mother. However, attempts to shore up this idealised version of femininity reveal the mid-twentieth century undercurrents of social and cultural change in relation to, for example, women's sexual behaviour and their increased presence in public space (Seal, 2010). Therefore, transgression only partly reaffirms the rule. It also shows that the rule is not fixed and is open to change.

A related concept to the cultural constructions of transgression documented above is the 'abject'. For Kristeva (1982, p. 2), the abject has to do with what 'disturbs identity, system, order. What does not respect borders, positions, rules. The in-between, the ambiguous, the composite.' It constitutes the horror of a breakdown in meaning whereby there is a loss of distinction between subject and object, or self and other. Kristeva highlights the pile of shoes at Auschwitz which draws attention to a breakdown in order and rule but also highlights the fragility of the law. And, deeply implicated with the abject is 'jouissance', for understanding the concept of the abject also brings awareness that we are drawn to the abject by a mix of both fascination and desire. 'One does not know it, one does not desire it, one joys in it [*on en jouit*]. Violently and painfully. A passion' (Kristeva, 1982, p. 9).

For example, Chapter 2 examines the liminality of children who kill, who evade the boundaries of childhood by outraging notions of innocence. Its particular focus is the school shooter, who occupies the liminal category of adolescence, in-between childhood and adulthood. In Chapter 4 we find that dominant representations of the prostitute in cultural texts include a focus upon the prostitute as body-object and as abject-body operating in liminal spaces and places at the margins of legality – the street, alleyways, industrial areas and brothels. This chapter argues that such representations, particularly of street 'prostitutes', are maintained through and by a set of relatively self-sustaining discourses and images linked to the commodification and aestheticisation of the female body in prostitution. These representations, found in the mass media and in filmic texts, serve to reinforce the stereotype of the prostitute as a sex object – a body-object symbolised by certain images and tropes in the public imagination. The prostitute is the salesperson and commodity in one; she is both an organic body (a subject) and a commodity (an object). In the public imagination the prostitute as abject-body symbolises dirt, decay, corruption *and* is also an instrument of pleasure, of thrill, frission and (illicit) desire. Stallybrass and White (1986, p. 137) argue '[i]t was above all around the figure of the prostitute that the gaze and touch, the desires and contaminations, of the bourgeois male were articulated'. We find in the cultural history of prostitution that the prostitute is a body-object symbolised by liminality, abjection, commodification and desire. Moreover, this sets up a bifurcation around the bad, fallen, lower-class/under-class, polluted, diseased body in contrast with the good, pure 'woman', who is a loving wife, partner and mother. Around this binary the whore stigma is built and sustained and these contradictory discourses have led to the ongoing regulation of prostitution and the bodies of prostitutes (Corbin, 1990). Transgression, abjection, pleasure and desire are of course intimately related to the power of the imagination and the imaginary.

Imagination: Towards a radical democratic imaginary

Our focus on re-presentation in art, fictive texts and ethnographic research means that what Young (1996) terms 'imagining crime' is central to our analysis. Young (1996, p. 16) defines the 'imagined' as 'the written and the pictorial: the linguistic turns and tricks, the framing and editing devices in and through which crime becomes a topic, obtains and retains a place in discourse'. She highlights the need for criminologists to pay attention to the representation of crime, particularly given the ubiquity of its images and stories (Young, 2008). As Clarke (2001, p. 72) points out, the news reporting of crime is 'outweighed by the huge range of fictional representations of crime that circulate in television drama, films and books'. Rafter (2007) terms these representations 'popular criminology', which has a bigger audience and therefore greater social significance than academic criminology. The scope of these popular representations is also larger, as they can engage simultaneously with the psychological, philosophical and ethical aspects of crime and criminality. Crime is therefore represented and consumed as part of popular culture. Psychosocial analysis explores how crime as entertainment satisfies the need for emotionality and excitement (Gadd and Jefferson, 2007). Analysis of the seductions of crime and 'those moments of voluntary illicit risk taking' (Ferrell, Milovanovic and Lyng, 2001, p. 177) reinforce that transgression can be exciting and pleasurable, which is especially relevant to the consumption and enjoyment of crime as popular culture. As stated before, the carnivalesque symbolises rebelliousness and resistance, the world turned upside down (Presdee, 2004). Cultural representations of crime and deviance offer a vicarious means of experiencing this.

There is an urgent need to think through the 'implications of the cultural fascination with crime' (Young, 2008, p. 19). Crucially, criminologists must acknowledge that 'everyday life is lived in the imaginary' (ibid., p. 27). The reactions of a viewer or reader to representations of crime, deviance and transgression are part of their everyday lived experience of these phenomena (ibid.), and 'draw on and add to the repertoire of images, ideas and meanings that are available to us about crime' (Clarke, 2001, p. 73). The ways in which we imagine the 'outsider' are imbricated in the various measures of social control and sanctions that society employs to deal with them (Rafter, 2006; Melossi, 2008), and these measures become particularly acute when outsiders are imagined to be dangerous or polluting. We examine this inter-relationship in the chapters in this volume with particular emphasis upon children, women, the mad, the bad and the outlaw as outsiders. We also make a case for the importance of cultural criminology in developing a radical democratic imaginary, in enabling us to think otherwise, and in facilitating public scholarship on these cultural issues.

For Cornell (2006, p. 31) 'the imaginary domain is a moral and psychic space that is necessary in order to keep open and rework the repressed elements of the imaginary'. O'Neill (2010b) has argued, drawing upon Cornell (1995, 2006) and Smith (1998), for a radical democratic imaginary in our work as critical and cultural criminologists. It is crucial to open and keep open the space for 'the circulation, radicalisation and institutionalisation of democratic discourse' (Smith, 1998, p. 7) and 'knowledges of resistance' (Walters, 2003, p. 166). O'Neill argues that methodologies incorporating the voices of citizens through participatory methodologies can enlighten and raise awareness but also crucially create and sustain spaces for democratic discourse, uncover hidden histories and produce critical reflexive texts that may help to mobilise social change. Methodologically, the doing of cultural criminology examines how crime is constructed, made, understood and experienced whether through historical analysis and uncovering hidden histories, ethnographic and participatory research, or analysis of media and cultural forms and practices. In the following section, we explore the emergence and development of cultural criminology, and review the contribution it has made to the wider discipline. We outline its methodological and analytical toolkit, and consider some of the critiques of cultural criminology.

Crime, deviance and cultural criminology

We understand cultural criminology as 'the many ways in which cultural dynamics intertwine with the practices of crime and crime control in contemporary society' (Ferrell, Hayward and Young, 2008, p. 4). There is a focus on the everyday meanings of crime and crime control – as they emerge in the media, city and urban spaces, and as part of globalisation (Ferrell et al., 2004). Methodologically, historical, archival, ethnographic, textual and visual analyses are most commonly used. What we find in this literature is the argument that crime is produced or constructed through social relations and that cultural expressions can themselves be criminalised (Ferrell, 1993). As discussed, there is a major focus upon transgression and transgressive acts and the ways in which boundaries shape and constrain us, meaning that 'transgression' and 'limit' are central concepts. Through a range of examples, *Transgressive Imaginations* examines where boundaries are crossed and how deviance is created.

Cultural criminology is a relatively young sub-field in the discipline. Its intellectual roots can be found in the work of the Birmingham Centre for Contemporary Cultural Studies (Hall and Jefferson, 1976; Hall et al., 1978; Willis, 1978; Hebdige, 1979), particularly in terms of the focus on subculture and style; the National Deviancy Conference, which sought to radicalise British criminology (Cohen, 1971; Taylor, Walton and Young, 1973); and the subsequent tradition of critical criminology, which also incorporated feminist, anti-racist, queer, postcolonial and postmodern approaches. In the US it emerged out of symbolic interactionist and ethnographic approaches to crime and deviance, particularly the work of Jack Katz (1988, 1999), Stephen Lyng (1990, 1998) and Jeff Ferrell (1993, 1999, 2001). In the 1990s, a distinctive 'cultural criminology' emerged at the intersections of postmodernism, ethnography, critical/theoretical criminology and subcultural theory. Ferrell and Sanders (1995, p. 297) offered a 'prospectus for an emerging cultural criminology', which was born out of the 'cross fertilization' of criminology with other disciplines and approaches rooted in Ferrell's earlier work.

The cultural turn in sociology and criminology can be charted by looking at the importance of Marxism to the development of British cultural studies and the means by which ethnography emerged as an effective and popular approach to researching cultural processes (see Hall, 1982). It is also important to acknowledge that cultural criminology shares a methodological and epistemological focus with postmodern and critical criminologies. This includes a primarily phenomenological approach to understand the processes and practices of our sociocultural worlds, and the everyday lived experiences and meaning making practices we engage in. In *Empire of Scrounge* (2006, p. 27), Ferrell describes the evolution of what he termed 'cultural criminology' from his background of critical criminology and cultural studies and the fact that his research and publications focus upon symbolism, style, labelling and the need for 'deep immersion in the situated meanings and emotions of crime' (ibid.). As Ferrell states, 'cultural criminology has from the first incorporated issues of risk, edgework, and existential autonomy in its commitment to exploring the cultural and phenomenological margins of the contemporary order' (ibid.).

Framed by the theoretical and methodological orientations of the development of a distinctive cultural criminology in North America, the UK and Australia, cultural criminological analysis has hence developed through subcultural theory, media analysis, the cultural construction of crime and ethnography, all of which we outline next.

Subculture

The concept of subculture has had a profound influence on cultural criminology. Deviant cultures and behaviours are understood as meaningful responses on behalf of marginalised groups to combat their marginalisation (Ferrell, Hayward and Young, 2008). In subcultural theory, crime is viewed as 'a sub-cultural phenomenon organised around symbolic communication, shared aesthetics and collective identity' (Ferrell, 2005, p. 75). As an embodied and collective experience, 'crime is given meaning within shared vocabularies of language' (ibid., p. 76). Style and collective aesthetics are central to the organisation and status of subcultural groups. This focus on style displays cultural criminology's intellectual inheritance from the sociology of deviance and British cultural studies outlined previously, but also reaching back to earlier social and cultural anthropology (Ferrell, Hayward and Young, 2008), and is something that distinguishes it from other contemporary criminological perspectives. In Ferrell's (1993, 1995) work on graffiti, we see distinctively that crime is culture and that culture can be reconstructed as crime. He examines how graffiti, as part of hip hop subculture, expanded culturally and spatially from New York City in the 1970s across the United States and further afield to Europe, Japan, Australia and New Zealand by the 1990s (Ferrell, 1998). Graffiti writers 'operate in opposition to and on the run from police officers and private security personnel' (p. 602) and hip hop can be understood as a deviant subculture, which offers forms of resistance, its 'illegal images' achieving a 'temporary triumph' over prescribed meanings and structures of social control (p. 603). The global expansion of this subculture means that its images and style are also packaged in commercial forms removed from their original cultural contexts, although these mass media appropriations can also 'cycle back through the subculture' (p. 603).

Recently, some cultural criminologists have argued that subcultural, ethnographic studies need to pay closer attention to the 'background' of criminalised activities – the structural forces that shape the criminalisation process, such as class, inequality, place and locality (Webber, 2007; Martin, 2009). Martin (2009) contends that cultural criminologists must analyse how the aesthetics of rule breaking interlock with political economy. For Martin (2009, p. 132), a key aspect of the contemporary 'background' is the 'exclusive nature of consumer culture in late modernity'. At the level of aspiration, this culture is inclusive, but it is economically exclusive. In response to Hall and Winlow's (2007) criticism of cultural criminology's argued lack of attention to the structuring force of capitalism, Ferrell (2007, p. 92) states that 'capitalism is essentially a cultural enterprise these days', where lifestyles are sold more than the products themselves. Understanding both consumerist appropriations of image and style, as well as capitalism as a dynamic rather than solely oppressive force, is essential for a contemporary critical/cultural criminology, which must explore not only the wreckage of rapacious capitalism, but also the ingenuity of those who survive and resist their cultural and economic marginalisation.

Media construction and analysis

The mediated constructions of crime and its control are an important focus of attention in the field of cultural criminology due to the argued importance of analysing how the symbols, images and meanings of crime are imagined. Examining the processes by which certain activities come to be constructed as 'criminal' or 'transgressive' is vital in understanding crime and deviance as both threat and entertainment. This also applies to constructions of victimisation, particularly in terms of who is and is not represented as a 'worthy' victim. Why is it that Madeleine McCann's disappearance in Portugal in May 2007 generated enormous media coverage, yet as Greer, Ferrell and Jewkes (2008) recognise, drawing on Woolf's (2007) article in *The Independent*, more than 600 children have been missing in the UK for as long as Madeleine and are also still unaccounted for? Many of these other children disappeared from local authority care, 'have no parents to launch an appeal', and were not necessarily British, white and middle class (Greer, Ferrell and Jewkes, 2008, p. 5). Analysis of the media representation of the McCann case is complicated by the vilification of Madeleine's parents, Kate and Gerry McCann, with a virulence that could be described as 'trial by media' (Greer, Ferrell and Jewkes, 2008; Machado and Santos, 2009). Therefore, although Madeleine was portrayed as an 'ideal' victim, her parents and her mother in particular, were constructed as objects of suspicion. We pay particular attention to this issue of the relative social and cultural value placed on the victims of crimes of violence in our discussion of serial killers in Chapter 6.

As Greer (2003, p. 90) points out, 'the relationship between media images and popular consciousness is complex and notoriously difficult to unpack'. He goes on to suggest (drawing upon a range of literature, including Hall et al., 1978; Cohen and Young, 1981; Soothill and Walby, 1991; Maguire, 1997; Thompson, 1998) that the mass media are first, 'instrumental in the orchestration of moral panics'; second, employ 'important symbolic mechanisms used in the construction of ideology'; and third, 'inform the political processes aimed at dealing with social crisis' (Greer, 2003). Moreover, the mass media representation of social issues is central to the ways in which we make sense of them and to where they fit into our everyday lives. Different forms of media are 'spaces in public life where the meaning of crime and punishment is created, consumed and recreated' (Phillips and Strobl, 2006, p. 307). Phillips and Strobl (2006) analyse the representation of justice in American comic books, finding that the restoration of the social order is an important theme, although this is usually achieved via extralegal, vigilante justice. In addition to dominant themes of retribution and revenge, certain comics had stories which included counter-hegemonic themes of restoration, diplomacy and peacemaking (ibid.).

Cultural constructions

That crime and transgression are culturally constructed and lived is a central tenet of cultural criminology and key to its rejection of straightforward positivist accounts of lawbreaking (Young, 2011). The cultural construction of crime, particularly in relation to marginalised groups such as sex workers, the homeless and asylum seekers, needs to be understood through analysis of the relations of 'power, control and resistance' (Ferrell, 2005, p. 76). The liminality of the street, massage parlour and brothel, or the spaces and places at the margins of citizenship and belonging, such as camps and transit zones, sets limits to the notion of social order. This highlights liminality and abjection and the way that the marginalised, the outsider can be indexical. For example, Chapter 4 analyses the cultural construction of prostitution as a social problem. The making of prostitutes as an outcast/abject group in the Victorian period exposes the fictive nature of the construction of sexual identities and sexual politics within patriarchal capitalism and the British Empire, and at that particular point in history. The problem of prostitution was dealt with by regulating the poor women involved through a combination of legal and medical discourses, which shaped legislation and social practices that controlled women's bodies, sexuality and their access to public spaces. Here 'deviant identities become the basis of law reform rather than the social factors that construct those identities in the first place' (Phoenix, 2009, p. 160).

In *Framing Crime* (Hayward and Presdee, 2010), a number of authors unpack cultural criminology and the image by focusing specifically upon visual representations of 'crime, transgression and punishment' and the power of 'visual culture' (p. 3). In this edited collection, Hayward and Presdee (2010) ask criminologists to 'be closely attuned to the various ways in which crime is imagined, constructed and framed within modern society'. They also argue for 'new methodological orientation towards the visual that is capable of encompassing meaning, affect, situation, symbolic power and efficiency and spectacle in the same "frame"'(ibid.). For them, cultural criminology is a distinct theoretical, methodological as well as interventionist approach that 'situates crime, criminality and control squarely in the context of cultural dynamics' (ibid.) and fuses phenomenological analysis of transgression with theoretical analysis of late modern culture. We consider the shifting constructions of young people as late modern 'folk devils' via an analysis in Chapter 2 of perceptions of 'school shooters'. *Framing Crime*'s chapters deal with photography, film, artworks, contemporary advertising, documentary film-making, internet violence studies and atrocity images, and map the terrain of cultural criminology which is marked by ambiguity and contingency underpinned by the critical analytic research. Certainly, in this text, cultural criminologists are further forging an identity based on the importance of cultural constructions of the image and visual culture as it pertains to crime, violence and society. In Chapter 5, we discuss examples of images of madness and liminality found in different types of representation, such as a documentary, feature films and psychosocial analysis. Methodologically the use of visual and multi-sensory methods documented in Chapters 5, 7 and 8 are rooted in ethnographic and participatory approaches that engage with the everyday lives of marginalised groups and in so doing are involved in both challenging and constructing visual cultures of transgression, crime and deviance.

Ethnography

Ethnographic work is a major focus in cultural criminological literature. It has enabled research which explores the cultural and symbolic meanings that are created by and circulated among different groups, as well as producing rich data on the subjectivities and lived experiences of the members of these groups. Examples that explore crime as a central means of doing masculinity for men who are unable to access hegemonic masculinity, albeit mediated by race, class and age, include Winlow and Hall's (2006) *Violent Nights* and Winlow's (2001) *Badfellas: Crime, Tradition and Masculinities*. In O'Neill's ethnographic research with female sex workers (2001, 2010a) and asylum seekers (2010b), biographical and narrative approaches are used alongside participatory and arts-based methods to constitute what she calls ethno-mimesis, which we discuss in more detail in Chapters 4, 7 and 8. Ferrell's (2006) year spent living and working as a dumpster diver, trash picker and street scavenger is an excellent example of ethnography drawing upon 'the work of labeling theorists like Howard Becker and British scholars like Dick Hebdige, Stan Cohen, and Stuart

Hall' (Ferrell, 2006, p. 27). He states that 'cultural criminology has from the first incorporated issues of risk, edgework, and existential autonomy in its commitment to exploring the cultural and phenomenological margins of the contemporary order' (ibid., p. 27).

What we find in much of the literature is a clear focus upon ethnography and participant observation inspired by ethnomethodology. Brotherton and Barrios' (2004) work with one of the most notorious street gangs in the US is a notable example. The field research undertaken with the Almighty Latin King and Queen Nation by the research team at the Street Organisation project, John Jay College of Criminal Justice, produced sensitive ethnographic research on the lived experiences and life worlds of the gangs, adding greatly to criminological understanding of gangs' organisational structures and experiences of agency, resistance, power and politics. And as Walters (2003, p. 166) has shown 'knowledges of resistance' are incredibly important not only in relation to the way that criminological knowledge is produced but to the potential impact on politics and policy. We explore the production of such knowledges in Chapter 8, which discusses participatory action research carried out with communities in Vancouver's Downtown East Side (skid row).

These theoretical and methodological orientations that have contributed to the development of cultural criminology interlock and overlap. The influence of subcultural theory has inspired ethnographic research that prizes the subjectivities and worldview of the 'researched'. It has also guided cultural criminology's attention to the importance of analysing transgression and its focus on marginalised and non-mainstream groups to excavate hidden histories, knowledges and ways of life. Both subcultural analyses and ethnographies, as well as media analyses, examine the creation of meaning and the production and circulation of symbols and images. It is through diverse forms of global media that constructions of crime, criminality and transgression are both widely circulated and reinterpreted by different audiences. Therefore, connecting cultural criminology's other theoretical and methodological orientations is an overarching attention given to cultural constructions and imaginings.

Accompanying cultural criminology's prioritisation of the symbols, images and lived experiences of transgression and marginalisation is its attention to counter-hegemonic possibilities and resistance. Challenging derogatory and stereotypical representations is an important part of this, whether through the deconstruction of popular culture or through working with members of marginalised groups and subcultures. In addition to countering derogatory portrayals, the theoretical and methodological toolkit employed by cultural criminologists enables them to offer newer, more open readings of transgression and deviance, or to help previously silenced voices to be heard.

Critiques of cultural criminology

Criticisms of cultural criminology have questioned what is particularly cultural about it (O'Brien, 2005) and what is particularly criminological about it (O'Brien, 2005; Carlen, 2009). We do not intend here to set out a programme of, or manifesto for, cultural criminology. Our aims are more modest: namely, to explore different ways in which transgression is imagined and to analyse the normalising and restrictive aspects of these imaginings, as well as their counter-hegemonic potential. We examine processes of resistance to, and reclamation of, images of transgression. Employing a postmodern lens, we view cultural representations as polyphonic and multiple (Bakhtin, 1986), but also as shaped and constrained by the sedimented relations of power in the wider society (Laclau and Mouffe, 2001). In answer to why culture, we follow Williams' (2001 [1958]) dictum that 'culture is ordinary', found in the everyday and that it involves the making, contestation and remaking of meaning. Our particular focus in this book is on cultural representation, which can be understood as 'processes of discovery and creative effort' (ibid., p. 11), but, like Williams, we also view culture as a collective, lived experience. The inter-relationship between these two renderings of 'culture' is exemplified by O'Neill's (2010a, 2010b, 2011b) participatory, ethnographic work with sex workers, asylum seekers and skid row residents. We do, however, in this volume address an important criticism of cultural criminology: that there has, to date, been a lack of attention to gender. We discuss constructions of femininity in relation to sex workers and female avengers, and understandings of masculinity in relation to school shooters and serial killers.

Our analysis in the chapters that follow shows how cultural representations can reflect, critique, destabilise, reproduce and remake the cultural understandings found in wider society, and which are constituent parts of the operation of institutions of power. In answer to why criminology, we examine 'why certain people routinely fall foul of the law ... and are then routinely rounded up and officially clobbered for it' (Carlen, 2009, p. 575), in addition to paying attention to the cultural boundary maintenance that underpins these processes. Rather than glorying in transgression in and of itself, we ask how different cultural representations allow criminologists to think through the meanings, effects and responses to transgressions of gender, ethnicity, sexuality, age, nationality and social class. In particular, we seek out examples that reimagine transgression in non-stigmatising, ethical and liberatory ways in order to understand the ways that cultural criminological analysis might support a radical democratic imaginary.

Our analysis is informed by the theoretical and methodological orientations that we have outlined here, although we do not engage directly with questions of subculture. The chapters that follow take as their theme various transgressive identities, which are boundary-breaking in different ways. We do not conceive of these various identities as subcultures or 'tribes', although we do highlight counter-hegemonic reimaginings and knowledges of resistance. *Transgressive Imaginations* is transdisciplinary, drawing on elements of film, gender and cultural studies, literary criticism, history, visual culture and psychosocial analysis, as well as sociologically based criminology. This is consistent with our pluralistic understanding of cultural criminology, which we see as holding the possibility for diverse and eclectic analyses of crime, transgression and culture. By its very nature, cultural criminology should be open to porousness and fluidity. We see no need to raise protective barriers around disciplinary sub-fields such as 'cultural' and 'critical' criminology and, instead, we are inspired by other disciplines in which culturally based analyses have the 'critical' issues of gender, social class, ethnicity, nationality and sexuality at their heart. The final section of this introduction outlines the topics of each of the chapters of *Transgressive Imaginations*.

The chapters

The key sections and chapters introduced in the summary given here seek to contribute to the field of cultural criminology through analysis of transgression, imaginations, crime and deviance. We also hope that they inspire discussion about the doing, the framing and the usefulness of cultural analysis in working towards a radical democratic imaginary.

Chapter 1 has introduced the key themes and concepts of the book, our frame of reference and analysis. Chapter 2, via a discussion of the adolescent male school shooter, explores how the transgressions of young people symbolise the fears and anxieties of late modern societies. It examines how the school shooter became a folk devil in 1990s America and beyond, and considers representations of school shootings that demystify the folk devil portrayal by confronting the issue of fear. Chapter 3 utilises concepts from feminist criminology and feminist media studies in order to analyse representations of the female avenger. It explores whether the female avenger can be understood as a symbol of feminism, and the relevance she has for criminologists. Chapter 4 continues the focus on gendered transgression through an historically informed analysis of stigmatising representations of sex workers, as well as discussing ethnographic research that challenges this stigmatisation. Chapter 5 takes a psychosocial approach to understanding the experiences of those labelled 'mad' and explores the potential that the psychosocial perspective holds for criminologists. Chapter 6 focuses on the cultural construction of the serial killer, which has always traversed the boundary between fact and fiction. It outlines four main scholarly interpretations of this construction and considers, through analysis of examples, possible ways in which serial killing can be represented ethically.

Chapters 7 and 8 address two specific groups of abject/Othered people, asylum seekers labelled as the folk devils of the twenty-first century; and the most marginalised denizens of inner city 'skid row', the homeless and the poor. Committed to fostering an interpretive role that includes creating spaces for the marginalised/subaltern groups to speak for themselves (O'Neill and Harindranath, 2006), these last two chapters also stress the importance of dialogue and debate on these crucial issues, of opening and keeping open critical criminological spaces for resisting and challenging exclusionary discourses, and the vital inclusion of marginalised and criminalised groups in research discussion and debate. The critical, analytic role of cultural criminology is therefore counter-hegemonic; it contributes to public criminological scholarship and, we believe, a radical democratic imaginary on these important issues.

Do portrayals of violent female avengers have anything to offer to feminist criminologists? Can we find ethical representations of serial killers? Why did sex workers become an outcast group? What and how can we learn from the residents of Vancouver's skid row? These are some of the questions that we address in the pages that follow.

2
Children as Victims and Villains: The School Shooter

Childhood carries a heavy symbolic load. Children embody society's fears about its present and are also emblems of its hopes and dreads regarding the future (Jenks, 2007). When they either commit – or are the victims of – crime, this symbolic freight becomes even heavier. Their transgression or victimisation appears to highlight not just the failure of adult control, but also an underlying sickness in the wider culture. The experiences and behaviour of children and young people are therefore frequently interpreted as 'a window into society's collective future' (Brown, 2008, p. 204). This chapter explores the cultural construction of the 'school shooter' as a late twentieth-century representation of the young person as folk devil, and considers whether this remains a useful concept for cultural criminologists. In doing so, it focuses on an especially contentious and symbolically ambiguous stage of childhood, that of adolescence. As individuals no longer readily identifiable as children but not yet accepted as adults, adolescents occupy a liminal space 'betwixt and between' childhood and adulthood (Kroger, 2004).

The chapter begins by exploring childhood and adolescence as states which are legally and culturally constructed and relates this to criminality and developments in youth justice. It moves on to discuss the news media construction of school shooters in the United States as contemporary folk devils, who symbolise a range of social ills and provoke intense fear. It then analyses three cultural representations of school shootings which subvert and/or complicate our understandings of the school shooter: Ronson's (2006) article 'Bad Tidings', Van Sant's (2003) film *Elephant* and Shriver's (2010) novel *We Need to Talk About Kevin*.

20

As socially and culturally constructed states, childhood and adolescence are historically specific and their development is intertwined with social, political and economic changes. Hendrick (1997) argues that by the end of the nineteenth century in Britain, 'childhood' was a term which was both universally employed and was understood to determine a particular identity. Key legislative and policy measures, such as the recognition of juvenile delinquency as a specific and separate category from adult criminality, the introduction of compulsory schooling, and restrictions on child labour, helped to carve out childhood as a legally distinct status from adulthood. Similar measures were established in the United States during the Progressive Era (Scott, 2002). However, the distinctiveness of childhood is complicated by the fact that it is 'a category with no clear boundaries' (Scott, 2002, p. 119). The length of adolescence – the transitional stage between childhood and adulthood – is affected by social changes such as the extension of the school-leaving age and, more recently, the expansion of higher education, participation in which often requires parental support. Scott (2002) argues that in the United States, the transitional stage of adolescence is frequently invisible in law, with adolescents legally treated as either children or adults. If childhood is socially and culturally defined in relation to adulthood (Jenks, 2007), then the 'in-between' status of adolescence muddies the waters. The liminality of adolescence has the power to make young people symbolic of fear and uncertainty. Pike (2009, p. 648) contends that by the late twentieth century, 'adolescents had become pivotal figures in a cultural war over meaning'.

Young people and the folk-devil representation

Scholars in the United States, and England and Wales have identified a punitive shift occurring in approaches to youth justice at the end of the twentieth century. In England and Wales, this was indicated by the abolition of *doli incapax* for 10- to 13-year-olds, the increased use of custody for under-18s and the use of measures such as Anti-Social Behaviour Orders (ASBOs) to extend control over young people's behaviour (Jamieson, 2005; Muncie and Goldson, 2006; Scraton, 2008).[1] In the United States in the 1990s, many states introduced legislation which eradicated the difference between children and adults for certain offences, meaning that it became possible for under-18s to be tried and punished as adults (Scott, 2002; Brown, 2008). In particular, these measures were constituted as a response to gang crime and the construction of the urban 'super predator': a violent, dangerous, male adolescent. This representation was heavily racialised, constructing youth crime as a problem of minority ethnic young people (Brown, 2008). The punitive elements of approaches to youth justice contribute to, and enshrine in policy, the representation of young people as 'folk devils' (Scraton, 2008; Muncie, 2009).

Folk devils 'represent the evils of society' and threaten its stability (Brown, 2008, p. 204). They are the objects of moral panics and young people are one of the 'familiar clusters' from which folk devils are created (Cohen, 2002, p. viii). As symbols of the future, children and adolescents are subject to cultural fears that they will become folk devils, particularly in the form of the 'juvenile delinquent' (Hay, 1995), or that they will fall prey to folk devils, for example, through becoming the victims of adult sex offenders (Brown, 2008). On both sides of the equation, young people embody fears of social and cultural decay (Hay, 1995; Jenks, 2007; Pike, 2009).

In Britain, the murder of three-year-old James Bulger in 1993 by two ten-year-old boys, Jon Venables and Robert Thompson, became a 'potent symbol for everything that had gone wrong' in contemporary society (Cohen, 2002, p. ix). This murder ruptured perceptions of children as the personification of innocence (Hay, 1995; Jenks, 2007) but also became emblematic of a range of other social ills, such as single motherhood, the state of the 'underclass', and film and television violence (Hay, 1995; Cohen, 2002; Grant, 2004). Hay (1995, p. 198) describes the resultant public dismay as the first 'reflexive' moral panic, in which the folk devil became invisible because he could appear as an innocent child. In previous folk-devil constructions, ten-year-olds figured as the potential victims of adult criminals, not as the threat. Hay (1995) explores how in media constructions of traumatic events such as the Bulger murder, readers are interpellated into the scenario by injecting their own subjectivities into actors in the story through processes of identification, empathy and recognition. In narratives of the Bulger case, readers were invited to project themselves onto the position of James Bulger's mother, and therefore as victim of the crime. However, this projection involves the displacement of '[o]ur repressed anxieties about our own responsibility ... onto those "other" than ourselves as we thus reaffirm our own innocence and status of the victim' (Hay, 1995, pp. 216–7). In this case, these 'others' were the mothers of Jon Venables and Robert Thompson, encoding the moral superiority of the 'disciplinary, privatized, nuclear family unit' over single parent, 'broken' families (p. 206).

The invisibility or 'facelessness' of the late twentieth-century folk devil leads Grant (2004, p. 114) to suggest that we need to move on from the concepts of moral panic and folk devil in order to understand the 'depth of emotion surrounding the Bulger case'. Whereas the mods and rockers of Cohen's (1972) original study were examples of a 'specific and threatening youth culture' and a moral panic that was short-lived (Grant, 2004, p. 115), the prior invisibility of Jon Venables and Robert Thompson symbolised the late twentieth-century experience of crime as a pervasive, 'lurking menace' (ibid.), in which the 'enemy becomes harder to locate' (p. 121). Rather than the folk devil, we are now assailed by the 'faceless killer' (p. 117).

While acknowledging the importance of Grant's (2004) analysis of late twentieth-century fears of violent crime as something which is both menacing and banal, rather than abandoning the 'moral panic' and 'folk devil' concepts, we can consider how they are modifiable to accommodate social and cultural change. In the 1990s, McRobbie and Thornton (1995) argued that social differentiation and audience segmentation entailed plural media reactions to youth cultures. The diversification of media meant that those constituted folk devils could 'fight back'. Youth cultures could also be authenticated and legitimised by media expressions of disapproval, which could be deployed for commercial advantage (as with the 1990s dance-club scene). This media segmentation and proliferation became even more relevant in late 1990s and early twenty-first century context of online digital media, as will be discussed further in relation to school shooters.

School shootings in the media

The 'Columbine Massacre' in Colorado in 1999 became the 'issue-defining incident' in terms of school shootings (Spencer and Muschert, 2009, p. 1373). Two students at Columbine High School, near Littleton in suburban Denver, attempted to blow up their school by planting explosive devices. These did not detonate, so Dylan Klebold, 17, and Eric Harris, 18, instead went on a shooting spree, killing 13 people, including staff and students, before also killing themselves

(Frymer, 2009). There were other school shootings which received high levels of media attention in late 1990s America and there was also a perception that these incidents were on the rise (Springhall, 2008). However, the media reporting of Columbine had a 'turning point quality' that 'quickly captured the public's imagination' (Leavy and Maloney, 2009, p. 273). The news media was on the scene almost immediately following the shootings, turning the tragedy into a spectacle (Frymer, 2009; Spencer and Muschert, 2009). The shootings at Columbine became the largest American news story of 1999, and the seventh most reported event of the 1990s (Muschert, 2009, p. 165).

The incident was highly unusual and represented the most serious loss of life to take place in a school shooting in the United States at that time. Despite its unusualness, Columbine came to typify both media understanding of school shootings and representation of the wider issue of 'juvenile delinquency' (Muschert, 2009). Homicides at American high schools are very rare, accounting for less than 2 per cent of the homicides of school-age young people and of these only a small proportion are the 'rampage' style attacks that would be labelled 'school shootings' (Muschert, 2007, p. 61). As Burns and Crawford (1999) point out, young American people of high school age in the 1990s were at more risk of dying from being struck by lightning than they were from being shot by one of their fellow students. Despite the heavy reporting of Columbine and the perception that school shootings were on the rise, there was no evidence that gun crime was occurring more frequently in schools and young people remained proportionately in far greater danger of facing violence within their own homes (ibid.).

The significance of the Columbine shootings and their media representation lies in the symbolic meaning that they attained. The 'turning point' quality of Columbine was accentuated by a shift in the news media discourse from asking 'how could it happen in a place like this' to stating 'it could happen anywhere' (Cohen, 2002, p. xii). The moral panic that it triggered was focused on the perceived normality and normativity of the suburban, middle-class setting, and on finding the ways in which potential 'evildoers' could be stripped of their invisibility and identified from within the high school population (Burns and Crawford, 1999). This led to an intensification of the use of methods of surveillance and control within American high schools, which was no longer confined to the inner city but spread to suburban and small-town settings. This entailed measures such as hiring security officers to work in schools, installing metal detectors, publishing guidebooks that highlighted the warning signs potential school shooters would exhibit and holding drills to practise evacuation in the event of a shooting incident (Burns and Crawford, 1999; Lewis, 2009).

Another feature of the school shooting moral panic was the scapegoating of certain 'deviant' groups, most notably goths, identifiable by their clothing (particularly trench coats) and their music tastes (particularly the band Marilyn Manson) (Muzzatti, 2004; Pike, 2009; Griffiths, 2010). Dylan Klebold and Eric Harris, it was reported, had been fans of Marilyn Manson and members of a group of high school 'outsiders' called the 'Trench Coat Mafia'. Both of these details were challenged by those who knew them, who pointed out that Dylan and Eric did not like Marilyn Manson and that although they wore trench coats on the day of the shootings, these were not their usual attire. Aitken (2001, pp. 594–5) argues that the post-Columbine panic was similar to that sparked by the murder of James Bulger in Britain in 1993, in that it unleashed fears that 'society was changing for the worst, that childhood had lost its innocence and a whole generation was growing up warped and dysfunctional'.

A key feature of the news media response to Columbine was the search for causal explanations, especially as it now seemed that the site of youth violence could be 'anywhere'. The 'why' question dominated the news reporting, as exemplified by a *US News & World Report* headline that asked simply this (Frymer, 2009, p. 1390). The media focused on the issue of estrangement, highlighting this as central to understanding what had provoked Dylan and Eric to attempt to destroy their entire school. Various explanations for their alienation were proffered, such as being goths, being 'caught up in a seductive virtual world' of violent video games, hating 'jocks', and connected with this last one, their experiences of being bullied at school (Frymer, 2009, p. 1391; Spencer and Muschert, 2009). Estrangement became the dominant explanatory narrative of the Columbine shootings. Spencer and Muschert (2009) argue that the media discourses were at first ambiguous as there was a double casting of Dylan and Eric as both the victims of bullying and as brutal victimisers. This was particularly the case in the coverage of memorial crosses that were erected in a field near Columbine High

School. Initially, there were 15, representing the 13 victims and Dylan and Eric themselves, but the two representing the killers were torn down. Spencer and Muschert explain that this enabled media discussion of the dichotomous and contested construction of the two boys, but that ultimately this was resolved as a story about Dylan and Eric's moral culpability, which closed off the possibility for a more nuanced understanding. Frymer (2009, p. 1393) contends that in turning Columbine into a spectacle, 'the mass media emptied out the social and historical complexity of what was taking place' and instead told a story about 'youth as pathological aliens' (p. 1402).

The story of youth alienation and youth as a symbol of moral decay meant that young people were constructed as a group to be feared, or feared for (Altheide, 2009; Pike, 2009). This played on already existing anxieties about the liminality of adolescence, a stage 'caught between the worlds of childhood freedom and adult responsibility' (Spencer and Muschert, 2009, p. 1373). Pike (2009) conceptualises American fears that young people, who should be society's hope for the future, are in fact emblematic of its moral decline as Protestant 'captivity narratives', which see young people as vulnerable to capture by evil forces. In 1999, when the Columbine shootings occurred, the Internet was little understood by most adults and was predominantly the domain of adolescents. It was perceived as a 'dark space' (Pike, 2009, p. 657), attracting and potentially corrupting American teenagers, which appeared to have happened in the case of Dylan and Eric, who were portrayed as having lived in a 'simulated world' (Frymer, 2009, p. 1401). Althiede (2009, p. 1356) contends that young people are a 'key element' in the contemporary discourse of fear as they symbolise both protection and punishment. As an emblem of wider fears about the transformation of society and the loss of the seemingly stable foundation to social life, the United States experienced 'growing anger at and fear of young people' (Aitken, 2001, p. 595).

This fear can be understood through reference to the changed nature of the folk devil in the late twentieth and early twenty-first centuries. Dylan Klebold and Eric Harris, like other school shooters in the late 1990s, were white, suburban, middle-class and from two-parent families. Unlike the minority ethnic, urban 'super predator', they were not marked as culturally subordinate and could not be immediately differentiated from other white, middle-class teenagers who supposedly embodied normative, 'moral' identities (Aitken,

2001; Pike, 2009). The school shooter was a faceless, invisible folk devil, who did not previously pose an obvious threat. The anxiety that this provoked was succinctly encapsulated by *Time* magazine's front cover on Columbine, which featured photographs of Dylan and Eric above the headline 'The Monsters Next Door' (Springhall, 2008). School shootings, according to Aitken (2001, p. 598), rent the 'myth' of 'society's hallowed places'. The affluent, ethnically homogeneous suburb or small town could no longer be regarded as the idyllic fulfilment of the American dream – (white, middle-class) young people could be violent there too, and it was necessary to be fearful there too (Burns and Crawford, 1999; Frymer, 2009).

The Columbine shootings were culturally traumatic, and constructed as socially significant, because they occurred among the most dominant and privileged group (Springhall, 2008; Leavy and Maloney, 2009). The widespread media reporting ensured that Columbine became part of the American collective memory. Leavy and Maloney (2009) contrast the status of Columbine as a cultural turning point with the Red Lake School shootings, which happened on a Native American reservation in Minnesota in 2005. Sixteen-year-old Jeff Weise shot dead his grandfather (with whom he lived) and his grandfather's girlfriend, before going to his former high school and killing seven people on the campus as well as injuring others. He then shot himself (Lester, 2006). Leavy and Maloney (2009) argue that Red Lake has not made a significant mark on the collective American memory and this can be explained by that fact that, for the American news media, the Red Lake shootings did not happen to 'people like us' (p. 280). Jeff was Native American and lived on a reservation. He did not symbolise the American idyll. The Red Lake shootings remained a predominantly local news story and explanatory discourses emphasised that Jeff was the product of a 'broken' home and that poverty, unemployment and crime were widespread on Red Lake reservation (Lester, 2006; Leavy and Maloney, 2009). The media reporting of Columbine was not explicitly racialised, but the stress placed on the notions of 'people like us' and 'this could happen anywhere' were both an implicit acknowledgement of the whiteness of Dylan and Eric (and Columbine as a community) and of violent crime as racially marked (Aitken, 2001; Leavy and Maloney, 2009).

The invisible folk devil, who is hiding among the dominant social group, can be understood as a symbol produced by new, pervasive styles of governance that shaped late twentieth and early twenty-first century American society. Simon (2007) argues that following the collapse of 'New Deal' style approaches to welfare, the United States has been governed primarily through fear, and especially fear of crime. Government intervention became justified as necessary to wage 'war' on crime and protect citizens from victimisation, rather than to improve people's living situation by enacting welfare measures. Therefore, rhetoric of crime and victimisation spread beyond the criminal justice system to other areas of social policy, such as schooling. The kinds of heightened security measures introduced in schools to prevent violence such as 'rampage' shootings can be understood as symptomatic of this style of governance. Governing through crime has led to punitive measures that disproportionately affect the poor and minorities, but it also shapes the lives of the more affluent. Alongside the demonisation of minority ethnic, urban young men as 'super predators' was the expansion of methods of control in suburban and small town schools to combat the threat within (Lewis, 2009).

The scapegoating of goths, trench-coat wearers and the perceived victims of bullying was an attempt to identify the potential school shooter and to avert the risk he posed. The 'Columbine effect' (Pike, 2009, p. 668) of enhanced security and surveillance in schools was not just a response to school shootings (which constituted a very small risk for American high school students) but was also part of the shift in governance that Simon (2007) delineates. Americans were already familiar with the vocabularies of risk and fear through which the responses were narrated. High school students experienced educational settings that were increasingly militarised in their approaches to control and discipline (Muzzatti, 2004; Lester, 2006), while also experiencing evermore restricted access to public spaces, which were 'relinquished to corporate culture' (Lester, 2006, p. 143). Fear, as Simon (2007) asserts, had become central to American culture and styles of governance before the terrorist attacks on the World Trade Center on September 11, 2001. However, the 'war on terror' provided further justification for government intervention in the form of control and surveillance. Altheide (2009) argues that Columbine was redefined after 9/11, when measures such as lockdowns and the use of security cameras in schools deepened. Terrorism offered a new discursive frame to construct school shootings, which 'fit[ted] into the expanding discourse of fear' (Altheide, 2009, p. 1354).

Before exploring three cultural representations of school shootings which challenge the dominant discourses of risk and fear, it is necessary to discuss some recent issues in relation to the media reporting of school shootings. Following the 'Virginia Tech Massacre' in 2007 and the Northern Illinois University shooting in 2008, attention was focused on shootings carried out by men in their 20s and provoked discussion of 'the extent to which the college student is an independent adult or a dependent child' (Jones, 2009, p. 77). Researchers have explored how school shooters such as Dylan Klebold and Eric Harris arguably draw on scripts of violent masculinity that are encountered in everyday life, which encourage them to see social privilege as their entitlement (see Springhall, 2008; Tonso, 2009), but this was not part of the media construction of Columbine. However, the view of the shooter as trying to achieve mainstream goals of masculinity, from which he had been frustrated, was an aspect of the reporting of the Virginia Tech shootings, carried out by 23-year-old student, Seung-Hui Cho (Jones, 2009). Columbine was reported around the world, and was frequently interpreted as a result of gun-ridden American culture. However, subsequent school shootings in Germany and Finland,[2] which also received international media attention, challenged this perception.

Twenty-first century online media has changed the ways in which audiences hear about, and respond to, school shootings. YouTube means that the CCTV footage of Columbine can be easily viewed at anytime, as can the 'confession videos' that Seung-Hui Cho sent to the American television channel, NBC. The first reports of the 2009 school shooting in Winnenden, Germany, which resulted in 16 deaths, including that of Tim Kretschmer, the shooter, were related via the social networking site, Twitter (Neuner et al., 2009). Online social networking has also provided new opportunities for young people to refute negative representations. Drawing on McRobbie and Thornton's (1995) contention that the folk devil can 'fight back', Griffiths (2010) explores how, via online media, goths in New Zealand, Britain and the United States distanced themselves from Dylan Klebold and Eric Harris, asserting that being a goth was not linked to violence, but rather peace. The rest of the chapter analyses three cultural representations of school shootings, which negotiate the complexity of these incidents and chime with some of the issues raised in the academic literature.

'Bad Tidings'

Ronson's article appeared in the 'Weekend' section of British newspaper *The Guardian*, on 23 December 2006 and is now available from its website. It describes his visit to North Pole, a Christmas-themed town in Alaska, which receives and replies to letters addressed to Santa. The replies are written by 11- and 12-year-olds at the town's Middle School, who perform the role of 'elves'. Ronson explains, 'But there's something else – something bad. Six of last year's Middle School elves, now aged 13, were arrested back in April for being in the final stages of plotting a mass murder, a Columbine-style school shooting.' The article narrates Ronson's quest to 'investigate the plot' and discover 'What turned those elves bad?'

Jon Ronson is a journalist, author and documentary film-maker and 'Bad Tidings' is characteristic of the absurdist style he adopts to explore serious topics such as political extremism (2002) and the use of torture by the American military (2005). This style immediately deflates the potential self-importance of the conventionally journalistic 'why' question in relation to school shootings and also helps to deflect the scapegoating aspects of explanations for these incidents. Early in the article, Ronson asks whether the plot was hatched because North Pole was 'just too Christmassy', a self-consciously ridiculous question but one which implicitly highlights the absurdity of other explanations that have been advanced for school shootings, such as listening to the music of Marilyn Manson. Ronson interviews the owner of a local restaurant, Earl, who tells him that the kids involved in the plot were goths and 'non-Christmassy outcast loners, bullied by jocks'. As discussed earlier, this estrangement narrative became the dominant news media explanation for Columbine. Ronson explains to Earl that 'Goths don't do anything bad in the UK ... They're a gentle and essentially middle-class subculture.'

Ronson explores a number of possible different explanations for why six 12-year-old boys drew up a hit list of fellow pupils and planned to shoot them. Their plot failed, ostensibly because the boy who was supposed to bring the guns to school did not arrive. However, Ronson wonders whether 'it was just a fantasy to them, no more real than the Christmas fantasy is to the adults here', and whether, as a young woman he interviews suggests, the boys were 'all talk – and the town only took them seriously because everyone is terrified of everything these days'. Elements of the plan were clearly unrealistic, such as the boys' intention to disable the school phone system to prevent anyone raising the alert and their intended escape route via train to Anchorage, where they would assume new identities. However, due to their failure to check the timetable, their getaway would have entailed a five and a half hour wait for the train.

Nevertheless, the father of one of the boys explains that his son maintains that they would have gone through with their plan if the guns had arrived. This man, Joe, was a soldier in Iraq, serving in Basra, when he was called home after his son was arrested for conspiracy to commit first-degree murder. As Joe says, his son 'doesn't dress goth', play violent video games or listen to rap music. Ronson suggests the absence of violent influences could be to blame, or 'the town's Christmas theme? The elf business?', to which Joe responds, 'I guess that theory is as good as any.' There is also the possibility that in a town 'hit hard by Iraq', the son of a soldier had been psychically damaged by this war. But ultimately, for Ronson, this too fails as an adequate explanation.

Rather than closing off the complexities and ambiguities of a planned school shooting, 'Bad Tidings' leaves these open by not providing a satisfactory answer to the 'why' question. Standard media narratives are rejected, as is the need to turn the boys involved into folk devils and objects of fear. Their ineffectual plotting reveals them to be recognisable 12-year-old boys. Two threads run throughout the article. One is an exploration of small town conformity, which in the case of North Pole is signalled by a love of Christmas. Admitting to dislike of, or boredom with, Christmas in a town dedicated to it year round is unacceptable. As the local mayor asserts,'if the spirit of Christmas were permeating the entire soul of this community, no child would be feeling that despondent.' In North Pole, dissatisfaction with Christmas is dissatisfaction in general and a rejection of the values of the community. Most members of suburban and small-town communities do not live with the novelty of year-round Christmas, but this figures in 'Bad Tidings' as representative of more widespread pressures to conform and disguise unhappiness in such communities.

The other important thread is the burden placed on childhood as emblematic of innocence, happiness and wonder, and the difficulty that we face in sustaining this. When Ronson travels to North

Pole, it has recently lost a contract with Alaskan Airlines to provide Christmas experiences to tourists, and the mayor is exploring possible strategies to make it more Christmas-themed, such as getting shopkeepers to dress as elves. However, as the location for letters to Santa, the town members are exposed to the pains of childhood, receiving letters that ask for the safe return of fathers serving in Iraq, or simply for parents to stop arguing with one another. Although more shocking, the plot of a group of 12-year-olds to carry out a school shooting in a tourist town similarly strains our perception of childhood as a hallowed, magical time.

Elephant

Gus Van Sant's (2003) film *Elephant* depicts over the course of one day the events of a fictional Columbine-style school shooting in Portland, Oregon. It is fairly closely based on Columbine, portraying two students who plant explosive devices in their high school and roam the corridors while armed, shooting a number of people (staff and students) they encounter. The film is notable for its non-linear narrative, and the languid, dream-like way in which the events unfold, induced in part by the use of long tracking shots (Bradshaw, 2004; Bassett, 2007; Young, 2009). The first two thirds of the film depict an ordinary day at an American high school, with all its anticipated banalities. An alcoholic father attempts to drive his son to school, making him late and therefore getting him into trouble. A teenage girl is reprimanded for refusing to do gym without taking off her sweatshirt, and also begins a job in the school library. Three girls have lunch, talk about boyfriends and their mothers, before making themselves sick in the bathroom. In keeping with the cultural anxiety provoked by Columbine, this unremarkable setting could be 'anywhere' (and consonant with the coded perceptions of 'anywhere' identified by scholars, the school appears to be located in a predominantly white, middle-class area). As Morris (2003) commented in the *Boston Globe*, 'The halls could be the halls you walked.'

The audience already knows that *Elephant* is a film about a school shooting based on Columbine (Edelstein, 2003; Bradshaw, 2004; Bassett, 2007), and both the events it portrays, its structure and its pace offer a representation that is firmly at odds with the news media coverage to which the audience will have been exposed.

Young (2009, p. 15) argues that the depiction of an ordinary day at high school (albeit one which we know will be shattered) reveals how 'violence pervades the space of the everyday so that massacre exists at one extreme end of a continuum that may begin with verbal abuse and social exclusion'. The mundane events of the day, portrayed in real time, also reveal the landscape of the school and open up its internal geography as the space in which young people exist (Kaveney, 2006). There are many tracking shots of students walking down long corridors as they get from one place to another. Lester (2006, p. 144) notes that in *Elephant* adults are largely absent from this landscape, in which young people have been 'abandoned to the sterility, banality, and alienation of a militarized daily regimen'. The film's languid pace emphasises the 'in-betweenness' of adolescence, where high school is experienced as 'a holding cell – a containment facility' before admittance to adulthood (Moore, 2004, p. 46).

The film seems to advance different interpretations for why two teenage boys carry out a school shooting. Kaveney (2006) reads *Elephant* as a simple attempt to pathologise the boys, portraying as it does their penchant for violent computer games and history channel documentaries about Hitler, and Moore (2004) argues that the film dodges discussion of what allows school shootings to take place. However, *Elephant*, as Young (2009, p. 15) argues, offers a 'surfeit' of explanations for the shootings, which illustrate the 'impossibility of determining the cause of violence'. In addition to the computer games and the Hitler documentary, we witness the teasing of the boys at school and the easy availability of guns, which have been ordered from a website and are delivered by van in the fashion of any other consumer goods. These multiple causal factors 'pile up as so much useless information, or so much significant information' (Bassett, 2007, p. 165). No factor is presented as more compelling than another (Mitchell, 2003; Morris, 2003), reducing these possible causes to 'redundant data' (Bassett, 2007, p. 182). As with Ronson's (2006) article, the deliberate failure to answer the 'why' question leaves the possibility for further interpretation open and allows space for complexity. The audience is not provided with the comfort of easily identifiable (and therefore easily solved) determinants of violence. Van Sant has explained that he 'wanted to include the audience's thoughts', rather than 'dictating an answer' (Peary, 2003). This contrasts with television news, which offers explanations that can be quickly understood within 'existing frameworks', whereas *Elephant* provides no such consolation (Bassett, 2007, p. 184).

Far from pathologising Eric and Alex, the two boys who carry out the shooting, *Elephant* portrays their vulnerability and innocence, as well as their violence. In one scene, as they climb into the shower together, one boy asks the other, 'I've never even kissed anybody, have you?' The inference is that knowing it will be their last day on Earth, they have chosen to lose their virginity together. This portrayal of the boys' sexual inexperience and tenderness for each other presents them as more innocent, and concomitantly more 'childlike', than many of their peers, whom we have witnessed discussing their sex lives. This complicates our understanding of the invisible adolescent folk devil lurking among the wider population, as we are confronted with boys who kill violently but are in some senses closer to conventional constructions of childhood innocence.

The film's innovative structure is influenced by interactive digital media in its non-linearity and in staging the same events from different points of view (Bassett, 2007). The tracking shots, which follow characters down the long school corridors recall the way computer games create point of view from the perspective of the character played by the gamer. Van Sant was inspired by the 'interactive imagination' evoked by games such as *Tomb Raider* (Peary, 2003). Viewing *Elephant*, members of the audience must choose their own pathways in order to understand the events portrayed, but they are not led in a particular direction by the narrative. Bassett (2007, p. 182) identifies this choice of pathways as a satire on the 'artificial paradise of consumer culture', where the choice of what to consume is offered as the apotheosis of fulfilled existence.

Young (2009, p. 8) argues for the importance of investigating the implications the 'affects and aesthetics of screen violence' have for the spectator. Interactive media, particularly YouTube, has changed the context in which films are viewed. Individual scenes from *Elephant* can be watched on YouTube alongside a list of suggestions for other videos, which frequently include the CCTV footage from Columbine and amateur recordings of the Virginia Tech shootings. Viewers can leave comments underneath and can also use clips to create their own videos. One such video is 'School shooting et violence' (1oXHaydenoX, 2009), which splices the scene from *Elephant* where Eric and Alex arrive at their school and start shooting people, with footage from Columbine of Dylan Klebold and Eric Harris in the school cafeteria, with other recordings of violence such as bombs being dropped on a warship and the terrorist attack on the World Trade Center. *Elephant*, already a film influenced by interactive digital media, has been recast and reinterpreted and, for YouTube viewers, is likely to be watched alongside non-fictional depictions of school shootings and other violent events. Its affective impact on the spectator has therefore also been reconstituted beyond the cinematic techniques employed by Van Sant.

We Need to Talk About Kevin

Lionel Shriver's (2010) novel takes the form of letters written by Eva Khatchadourian to her husband, Franklin, concerning their son, Kevin. Eva's letters are written between November 2000 and April 2001, during which time Kevin is 17 and incarcerated in a secure juvenile facility, having killed nine people at his high school in suburban New York in April 1999. Eva seeks to deconstruct her relationship with Kevin in order to gain some comprehension of his actions on what she refers to as *Thursday*. She ruminates on why she and Franklin decided to have a baby in the early 1980s, and relates incidents from Kevin's childhood and adolescence leading up to when he committed 'mass murder', as she describes it in her second letter (Shriver, 2010, Letter November 15, 2000).

The epistolary form means that we only have Eva's perspective on her relationship with Kevin and the novel is a detailed reflection on motherhood, from the perspective of a woman who has judged herself (and been judged by others) to have failed at it (Muller, 2008; Jeremiah, 2010). Literary scholars have explored how Shriver challenges the notion of 'authentic' motherhood (Muller, 2008, p. 10) and the belief that women are 'naturally or necessarily able parents', or even that women who are mothers will be 'feminine' (Jeremiah, 2010, p. 169). While unpicking understandings of motherhood is central to the novel, its importance as a cultural representation of school shootings has not been explored. However, the fact that *We Need to Talk About Kevin* deconstructs motherhood through an examination of school shootings in particular is also crucial and requires analysis.

Kevin Katchadourian is a fictional school shooter, but is intertextually positioned in relation to real shootings. It is his fate to have carried out a very carefully planned attack ten days before Columbine and therefore to have been eclipsed by its higher media profile and perceived greater social and cultural significance. Earlier in this chapter, we explored Hay's (1995) contention that the news media coverage of the James Bulger murder in Britain in 1993 interpellated news consumers as victims, enabling them to displace anxieties about their own responsibility onto 'others'. *We Need to Talk About Kevin* performs a reversal of this by only offering Eva's perspective, forcing the reader to identify with her rather than the victims' families, meaning that the repressed anxieties of motherhood are laid bare. In an interview, Shriver stated that 'someone whose child has murdered [rather than is murdered] is a little suspect' (Birnbaum, 2003). Eva, who describes herself as a 'terrible' mother, needs to understand why her son committed mass murder and surveys their relationship in an attempt to find an answer. This is especially urgent because, as we discover at the end of the novel, in addition to killing seven students and two members of staff at his school, Kevin also killed his father, Franklin, and younger sister, Celia, after Eva left for work on *Thursday* morning.

In certain respects, Kevin is a 'typical' American school shooter of the 1990s. He is from an affluent background and lives in a white, upper middle-class town in upstate New York. However, Shriver (2010) dispenses with some prominent school-shooting explanations. The issue of gun availability is completely sidestepped as the (purposefully) novel thing about Kevin's attack is that it was committed with a crossbow, an approach made possible by his archery lessons and possession of expensive equipment. The estrangement narrative that was dominant in the media coverage of Columbine is also irrelevant to Kevin. Although a child who had few friends and remained aloof from his peers, Kevin was not a victim of bullying. In fact, Eva suspects that he was a high school bully, after chaperoning a school dance at which she observed some of the other students avoid him, as if intimidated. She also sees Kevin whisper something in the ear of a girl on the dance floor, which sends her fleeing. As a teenager, he is handsome and Eva notices that he attracts girls' attention. Kevin's victims, as far as Eva is concerned, were selected on the basis of either their talent or enthusiasm. This includes, but is not restricted to, athletic 'jocks' and pretty girls, who would constitute the 'cool' kids. Kevin also targets an academic high achiever and an amateur dramatics fanatic, as well as a teacher who saw potential in him. Eva believes that Kevin could not understand enthusiasm in others, part of his inability to be interested or find enjoyment in almost anything except for archery and spreading computer viruses.

Eva's attempts to pinpoint the roots of Kevin's emotional and spiritual flatness are multi-stranded and provocative, and chime with various popular and academic understandings of the causes of criminality in young people. From birth, Kevin appears to Eva to be preternaturally manipulative and malignant. He refuses her breast milk, which she interprets as a deliberate rejection. Aged four, Kevin ruins Eva's study, which she had decorated with maps she had collected (she has published a successful series of travel guides), by filling his water gun with red ink.[3] To Eva, his actions seem calculated and spiteful and she is convinced he understood how precious they were to her. In adolescence, Eva suspects Kevin of pouring a caustic cleaning product into Celia's eye, resulting in its loss, and of manufacturing sexual harassment accusations against his drama teacher. According to Eva's interpretation, Kevin is intentionally cruel and devoid of tender emotions. Frustratingly for her, he manages to fool others, most notably Franklin who remains convinced Kevin is a 'happy, healthy' boy.

Eva's perception of Kevin's behaviour is simultaneously disturbing and insidiously convincing. Interpellated into her subjective position, the reader must remind himself or herself that Eva's interpretations may be skewed, particularly as they are refracted through the knowledge of the mass murder he commits at 15. As a four-year-old child, it is questionable that Kevin could understand Eva's attachment to her collection of maps and, of course, as a newborn baby he would not have been capable of deliberately rejecting her in order to hurt her feelings. Celia never claims that Kevin poured the cleaner into her eye, and in fact Eva used it shortly before the incident happened, although remains sure that she put it back in the cupboard. The school officials believed Kevin that he was abused by his drama teacher. Viewed through Eva's perception, Kevin is constructed as an abject child who is innately evil and the hidden folk-devil 'monster' of the fears provoked by incidents such as the killing of James Bulger in the UK and Columbine in the US.

From Eva's letters, it is possible to view her as an emotionally and, on at least one occasion, physically abusive mother. When Kevin was six and still wearing diapers, which Eva construed as a wilful attempt to make her life more difficult, she threw him across the room, breaking his arm. Angered by Kevin's destruction of the maps in her study, Eva did not redecorate but left them on the wall as a reminder of her bitterness about something he did aged four. Kevin's relationship with her certainly appears to have been significant to the murders he committed. She was the only member of the family that he spared. Although heavily critical of his father in television interviews, he speaks proudly of Eva and her travel writing business. However, *We Need to Talk About Kevin* defies easy assumptions about the causes of Kevin's behaviour. As Muller (2008, p. 14) argues, 'Eva's construction of herself and Kevin in this narrative finally denies us the "comfort" of the good child turned bad because of bad mothering.' Eva exercises and misuses power in her relationship with Kevin, but so does Kevin. In showing that mothers and children are both powerful in the parent-child relationship, Shriver (2010) reveals adulthood and childhood to be constructed states, over which neither parent nor child has complete control (Jeremiah, 2010).

Eva has become accustomed to being asked why Kevin committed mass murder. At the end of the novel, when Kevin turns 18 and is about to be transferred to an adult prison, Eva finally sees him differently as someone who can be vulnerable and afraid. Her plea 'Look me in the eye and tell me why,' produces only 'I used to think I knew ... Now I'm not so sure' (Shriver, 2010, Letter April 8, 2001). Eva realises that discovering why *Thursday* happened, or whether she is to blame, are not of paramount importance and could never be satisfactorily answered. As she puts it, 'I certainly had no interest in an explanation that reduced the ineffable enormity of what he had done to a pat sociological aphorism about "alienation" out of Time magazine or a cheap psychological construct like "attachment disorder"' (ibid.). She realises that 'out of desperation or even laziness I love my son' and intends to offer him a home when he gets out of prison.

We Need to Talk About Kevin explores the significance of violence to American identity through Eva's relationship with Kevin. She gives him her Armenian surname, Katchadourian, as a preservative marker of an ethnic identity benighted by genocide. As an unusual name, it becomes instead defined by its most infamous bearer, Kevin, designated 'KK' by the media. Jeremiah (2010, p. 177) suggests that Kevin can be seen as symbolic of the 'deadly, glutted empire' of the United States.

This is supported by the temporal setting of Eva's letters, the first of which is written at the time of the disputed election of George W. Bush and the last of which is from 8 April 2001, five months before 9/11.

Demystifying the folk devil

The cultural representations of school shootings discussed in this chapter challenge the mainstream news media-led constructions of these events by subverting their priorities. All three examples work to undo the 'why' question and its answers. Multiple possible causes are presented, which ultimately demonstrate the impossibility of providing what Shriver (2010) describes as a 'pat sociological' explanation. 'Bad Tidings' is distinguished from the other two portrayals, firstly, by being journalism rather than fiction, but also importantly through its use of absurdist humour, which deflates the moral panic surrounding school shootings. Deflating the moral panic also demystifies the folk devil. Ronson highlights something which the academic literature on the scapegoating of goths in relation to school shootings has tended to overlook – that it is ridiculous enough to be funny. Laughing at these stigmatising processes helps to strip them of the power they wield over the young people who have been labelled, and of their power to induce fear in intended audiences. As Boskin (1997) argues, humour can be rebellious and 'possesses transformative qualities' (p. 10), enabling us to deal with confusing situations and to gain perspective. Through its use of humour, the article makes a serious point about the symbolic weight attached to childhood. North Pole, a town based on Christmas which drafts its local 12-year-olds as letter-answering elves, represents our wish for childhood to be happy, magical and uncomplicated, but its real children demonstrate that this is fantasy. Our uncomprehending reactions to childhood criminality are inextricably tied to our longing for childhood to signify innocence (Jenks, 2007).

Elephant resonates more closely with the scholarship on school shootings and social control, as it minutely depicts the everyday world of high school, which 'contains' adolescents 'betwixt and between' childhood and adulthood. The daily experiences of its teenage characters are shaped by the mundane routinisation and discipline that attending high school imposes, but also by the pervasive threat of violence and exclusion. The surfeit of possible causal explanations do not further our understanding but have a deadening effect by presenting any one cause potentially as convincing or unconvincing as any other. The overflow of pathways of interpretation mirrors the symbolic overload of images and representations that attach to childhood (Jenks, 2007). In *Elephant*, this is exacerbated by the liminality of adolescence. As an in-between stage, we are unsure what it should represent and adolescents are shown as occupying a concomitantly uncertain social position. The nightmare scenario it presents plays on audience fears of the invisible folk devil, but also complicates this representation by assigning innocence, one of childhood's most culturally prized attributes, to these very folk devils. Again, once the folk devil is seen to possess a quality they should not, such as innocence, or as in the aforementioned example, being comical, we are forced to view them differently. They become more complex and more difficult to employ as totems of fear and danger.

Through interpellating the reader into the position of the mother of a school shooter, *We Need to Talk About Kevin* reduces the distance between the reader and the fear-inducing adolescent folk devil. Eva's deconstruction of her relationship with Kevin plays on what to adults (and parents) is the unknowable strangeness of children. Through Eva's eyes, his precocious talent for calculated mayhem as a small child foreshadows his carefully planned mass murder in adolescence. The novel's portrayal of an abject child provocatively confronts cultural fears and anxieties about children as figures of horror, and as potential bearers of social breakdown. That the processes of abjection and horror arise from a mother-son relationship makes them profoundly uncomfortable, because in finding Kevin abject, Eva violates her role as an 'authentic' mother. As with 'Bad Tidings' and *Elephant*, we are forced to confront and question our idealisations of childhood (and also, in this case, motherhood), and our fears of children and young people. Shriver provides us with a hyper folk devil, who is a minatory presence in his mother's life throughout his childhood. By exaggerating this representation through the lens of a mother-son relationship, readers are led to tackle questions of evil, culpability and the possibility for redemption, moving far beyond reassuring stereotypes of distancing 'otherness'. Also signalled in *We Need to Talk About Kevin* is the symbolic flexibility of school shootings, which Shriver encodes not as social and cultural decay but as representative of violence as a constituent element of American identity. This further highlights the issue of culpability, whereby the inheritance of violence is understood as an inescapable part of being American, rather than as an aberration. Mainstream culture denies this legacy by projecting it onto folk devils (and their mothers) but Shriver refuses this transference.

All three portrayals respond to, and seek to undermine, contemporary fears of the invisible folk devil lurking among the 'respectable' population, without offering the comfort of easy explanations for school shootings. In offering us representations that demystify the folk devil, they help to destroy this totem and ask us to reject the manipulation of our subterranean dreads, even if this potentially opens up more difficult issues. Chapter 3 shifts from young men to understandings of transgressive femininity, and deconstructs popular cultural representations of the female avenger.

3
Violent Female Avengers in Popular Culture

The criminal woman occupies an anomalous cultural position. Not only does she transgress society's legal codes, she also transgresses its norms of gender as the active flouting of rule and convention that criminality entails is perceived as at odds with feminine passivity. This conception of the female criminal as 'doubly deviant', a term coined by Heidensohn (1996), is now well established within criminology. Heidensohn explains that the effect of double deviance is to stigmatise women in the criminal justice system and to leave them open to harsh punishment. The significance of her thesis is in highlighting how feminist criminologists need to pay attention not only to the formal social controls that can be imposed on women by the criminal justice system, but also the informal social controls regulated by constructions of normative gender. These informal social controls are of course more widely experienced as they extend into other areas of social life such as the workplace, leisure activities and interpersonal relationships.

The concept of double deviance is especially apposite in relation to violent women. Violence is culturally understood to be the province of masculinity, whereas femininity is associated with nurturance and the maintenance of order and stability. For women to enact violent behaviour traverses the male/female gender binary, making violent women culturally troubling figures. Research into cases of violent women, particularly women who kill, has highlighted how they have been constructed emblematic of 'dangerous womanhood' in both criminal justice settings and media reports (Ballinger, 2000; Morrissey, 2003). The representation of violent women can demonstrate particularly clearly how femininity is regulated according to certain discourses such as maternity, domesticity, sexuality, pathology and respectability (Nicolson, 1995; Ballinger, 2000; Frigon, 2006). Together, these discourses help to set the limits of 'appropriate' femininity, which conditions legal and cultural judgements of 'deviant' women.

Violent women bring the edges of femininity into sharp relief and this is what makes them dangerous. Legal and cultural responses to violent women frequently develop along two lines. One is to excoriate the woman completely, making her abject from femininity and therefore monstrous. Birch (1993) argues that this was the reaction to Myra Hindley, a British woman who along with her boyfriend, Ian Brady, participated in the murders of five young people in Manchester in the 1960s. She remained subject to 'unhealthy and retributive fascination' and a target for the tabloid press in particular until her death in 2002 (Jenks, 2003, p. 183). Portrayals emphasised her monstrosity and her 'evil' nature. The murders involved sexual sadism, making Myra Hindley a cumulatively transgressive figure, who not only perpetrated violence but especially shocking violence (ibid.).

In order to be rescued from abjection, violent women must be recuperated into femininity. This is where the more recognisably feminine aspects of a woman's identity are stressed in order to neutralise her threat to the social order. This often involves making the woman's actions appear to be explainable, but also beyond her control. Similar cultural processes of recuperation can be seen in relation to female sex workers, as we explore in Chapter 4, where they are either represented as morally deviant outcasts, or as unfortunate victims in need of rescue. Ballinger (2007) notes how women in capital cases of women who had killed their male partners in twentieth-century England and Wales were more likely to be granted a reprieve if they could be represented as helpless victims. Reflecting on the deployment of similar strategies in cases of women convicted of murdering their abusive partners in the 1990s, Nicolson (1995) explores how constructions which emphasise women's passivity and lack of agency serve to reinforce sexist stereotypes of femininity. In her analysis of press reports on violence, Naylor (2001) highlights the need to make women's use of violence explainable as a recurrent theme. If ready explanations could not be found, women's violence appeared as particularly troubling because it unsettled notions of the feminine.

Recuperation becomes especially important in the rare cases where women participate in murders involving the torture or sexual abuse of the victims, as this is perceived as a serious violation of the normatively feminine attributes of gentleness and nurturance. Such individuals, like Myra Hindley, may not be viewed as women at all but as incomprehensible myth-like figures (Naylor, 1995). Having crossed the boundaries of gender, they must be relocated within femininity to save them from 'monsterization' (Morrissey, 2003). In Canada in the 1990s, Karla Homolka participated in the sexual abuse, torture and murder of three young women, including her own sister, with her husband, Paul Bernardo. Karla was represented both as an abject, evil woman and also as an abused wife who was therefore another of Paul's victims (Morrissey, 2003; Grant, 2004). According to the 'battered woman' portrayal, she had been made helpless by Paul and was an unwilling participant. Morrissey (2003) argues that the construction of a victimised subjectivity for Karla (in which her testimony in court played a vital role) enabled her recuperation back into femininity. As a woman subordinate to her husband, she became recognisably female.

Feminist scholars are concerned with abjection and recuperation in social, legal and cultural responses to violent women as they play a role in maintaining divisions between masculinity and femininity, and in constituting the acceptable boundaries of femininity, which contributes to the wider regulation of gender (Nicolson, 1995; Ballinger, 2000; Seal, 2010). Both strategies are therefore conservative and potentially reinforce restrictive, stereotypical versions of femininity. Feminists have identified a link between reactions to female criminality and attitudes towards feminism, which also threatens to destroy the established boundaries of gender. Jones (1996, p. 14), in her study of women who kill throughout American history, notes how heightened attention to women's lawbreaking follows 'thunderously on every wave of feminism'. Chesney-Lind (2006) examines the significance of 'backlash' discourses to understandings of female offending, particularly to the supposed 'epidemic' of girls' violence in the United States. She argues that the demonisation of women and girls viewed as aggressive is indicative of conservative reactions to the perceived gains made by second-wave feminism.

As the foregoing has demonstrated, feminist discourses on the portrayal of violent women have developed. However, violent women remain potentially troubling figures for feminism. Much feminist research and activism has been devoted to opposing male violence, rendering the participation of women in 'masculine' type violent behaviour possibly difficult for feminists to comprehend (Morrissey, 2003; Seal, 2010). The use of violence is often considered incompatible with feminism, which prizes the development of human relationships based on empathy, respect and equality (Holmlund, 1993). Feminists are often reluctant to endorse women's violence and are frequently sceptical that it can be a route to greater equality – for example, many would argue that the greater incorporation of women into the military implicates these women in the reproduction of patriarchal and colonialist modes of violence (Enloe, 2007). 'Feminism' does not, of course, speak with a unified voice and the term encompasses a multiplicity of political positions related to gender and sexuality that may contain areas of strong disagreement with one another, including around the use of violence. Women's use of violence to defend themselves or others against imminent attack is generally acceptable to feminists and others. Enacting revenge against violent men is more controversial and raises questions about the acceptability of the use of violence and, particularly pertinent for feminist criminologists, debates on the best means of achieving justice.

Pearson (2007, p. 257) examines reactions to Aileen Wuornos, who was described as 'feminism's first serial killer', as she could be interpreted as taking vengeance against violent and sexually exploitative men. Aileen was executed in Florida in 2002 for the murders of six men whom she shot dead (she also confessed to the killing of one other), whom she encountered while soliciting on Florida's interstate highway. She initially claimed that each of them either raped her or attempted to do so and that she shot them in self-defence. She argued that her death sentence sent the message that 'male dominance is okay, and woe to the woman who takes action against a violent man' (Holmes and Holmes, 1998, p. 220). However, she later retracted the self-defence explanation and stated that she deserved the death penalty (Miller, 2004). Aileen's case raises a number of themes important to feminism, such as the links between sex work and violence against women, the restricted choices available to economically marginalised women and the role of images of female deviance in leading to harsh punishment. On a symbolic level, Aileen's reversal of the client-sex worker relationship, in which the client is more likely to be the violent one, shows a woman fighting back against a gender order that subordinates women and makes them vulnerable to mistreatment. Hers was not a 'clean case', however, where the woman is clearly a victim defending herself against imminent attack. As such, she has also been a troubling figure for feminism (Pearson, 2007).

The questions that violent women, particularly female avengers, pose for understandings of femininity and feminism can be considered through analysis of fictional portrayals. The next section explores the debates within feminist film and media studies on female revenge narratives in popular culture.

The development of the violent woman in popular culture

The rise in depictions of female avengers, particularly in Hollywood films, has been an aspect of the vast increase in portrayals of women as action heroes since the late 1980s onwards. These were not the first cinematic representations of women with a capacity for violence; there was the 'femme fatale' of 1940s film noir (Frigon, 2006) and Schubart (2007) identifies Pam Grier as playing the first female action hero roles in low-budget exploitation films in the 1970s. However, the late 1980s and early 1990s witnessed the flowering of the aggressive female hero, willing to fight and use weapons, such as Ripley in the *Alien* franchise, Sarah Connor in *Terminator 2* (1991) and Thelma and Louise in the film of the same title (Tasker, 1993). These films placed women at the centre of the action narrative and, particularly with the Ripley and Sarah Connor characters, depicted women with what Tasker (1993) describes as 'musculinity', a form of masculinity signalled by a physically fit and muscle-bound body that was no longer exclusively embodied by men. In addition to the action heroine, a rash of films starred 'Deadly Dolls' (Holmlund, 1993) or 'Super Bitch Killer Beauties' (Frigon, 2006); strong, attractive but calculating female villains (frequently murderesses) – for example, *Basic Instinct* (1992), *The Hand that Rocks the Cradle* (1992) and *The Last Seduction* (1994). From the mid-1990s, television series such as *Buffy the Vampire Slayer* (1997–2003) and *Xena: Warrior Princess* (1995–2001) showed women in warrior-style roles previously reserved for men (Early and Kennedy, 2003). Neroni (2005) argues that the violent woman has become a staple of American films (which are, of course, exported around the world).

As the violent woman has become more established in popular cultural representations, conventions have shifted. Holmlund (1993) notes that the female action heroes of the 1980s and early 1990s may have been muscular but rarely got dirty, something which cannot be said of the Bride's blood-drenched quest to avenge her rape and theft of her daughter in *Kill Bill* (2003, 2004). In the later 1990s and into the twenty-first century, action heroes and warrior women did not necessarily possess 'musculinity', but could in fact be 'girlie' in appearance as in the *Charlie's Angels* films (2000, 2003) (Read, 2004) or Sarah Michelle Geller's performance as Buffy. Schubart (2007) highlights a significant change in the move away from the need for female heroes to suffer major setbacks or misfortunes as part of their quest – to be 'brought low' as if in punishment for their attempts to exercise freedom. She cites *Kill Bill* as an example of a film that does not require its heroine to be disciplined in this way. Young (2010), through a visual analysis, highlights the way the film gives the Bride's memory of her rape 'the force of law' by depicting it from her interior gaze. 'Proof' of her experience of sexual violence is therefore not contingent upon corroboration from an external point of view. She contrasts this with *The Accused* (1992), in which the rape of the main character, Sarah Tobias, is mediated by a male lawyer in the courtroom scenes and a flashback memory from the viewpoint of a male bystander in the bar where Sarah was raped.

Feminist interpretations of popular culture's violent women

These new, violent females have generated intense interest and debate among feminist scholars of film and media studies, as well as among non-academic critics. These debates have centred on how feminists should interpret these characters and whether these representations can be understood as feminist or anti-feminist. Part of this interest derives from the fact that the female action hero of the late twentieth century emerged as a response to feminism, which had criticised the portrayal of women as passive objects (Tasker, 1993). Popular understandings of the 'liberated' woman made tougher images possible and women no longer had to be represented solely through codes of femininity (Inness, 2004). These new constructions offered the possibility of enjoyment for feminist audiences, who could now see strong, active women portrayed in mainstream films and television programmes. They disrupted the masculine/feminine gender binary, which created the potential to subvert conventional representations of femininity (King and McCaughey, 2001). However, violent women 'present quagmires for feminists' (King and McCaughey, 2001, p. 5), not least because, as discussed in the section on feminist criminology, violence is frequently conceptualised as anti-feminist (Holmlund, 1993).

One of the strongest feminist critiques of portrayals of violent women in popular culture is that far from depicting liberation they in fact tend to reproduce misogynist fears. Creed (1993) argues that female characters in American horror films symbolise monstrous castrators, mobilising deep-seated male fears of women's malign power. These fears, which could also be understood as masochistic fantasies, are related to pornographic representations and borrow from this genre. Herbst (2004) analyses the animated physical form of the Lara Croft character in the *Tomb Raider* computer games. She notes how the character's unfeasibly tiny waist and extremely narrow hips suggest that two potentially 'horrifying' aspects of the female body, menstruation and pregnancy, are impossible for her. In this way, Lara's depiction represents male fear of the all-engulfing, monstrous mother.

A related feminist criticism of fictionalised violent women is that they are endowed with masculine characteristics and are therefore not actually portrayals of women. According to this criticism, muscle-bound female action heroes such as Ripley and Sarah Connor evoke male identifications, rather than female ones. They are 'phallic women' who both look and act masculine. In particular, female characters' use of guns renders them symbolically male, as in films that are also read as feminist, such as *Thelma and Louise* (1991) and *Blue Steel* (1989) (Tasker, 1993). Clover (1992) argues that the rape avenger narrative transforms a female victim into a masculine avenger and, as such, is not feminist. She also contends that the horror film's 'final girl', the virginal and often dowdy female character who makes it to the end without being killed, is actually masculine and symbolises masochistic fantasies of castration.

When violent women are not masculinised, they are excessively sexualised, with their physical features representing male, heterosexual desires (Herbst, 2004). Holmlund (1993) and Frigon (2006) employ the terms 'deadly dolls' and 'killer beauties' to emphasise the propensity for Hollywood films to portray female violence as sexually titillating, with the actresses chosen to portray them being usually 'white, lithe and lovely' (Holmlund, 1993, p. 128). These representations are not empowering but reproduce depictions of women as sex objects for masculine gratification (Holmlund, 1993), and are representative of other stereotypes, such as normative femininity connoting a white, middle-class, heterosexual standard (Inness, 2004). There has been a move away from compulsory heterosexuality in the recent representation of women in popular culture, but heroines are still usually white and middle class (Early and Kennedy, 2003). The need for female action heroes to be conventionally attractive risks undermining their toughness by reassuring the audience that gender boundaries remain intact. Inness (2004) argues that female heroes are often 'pseudo-tough'; they know how to fight and use weapons, but the narrative recuperates them back into femininity by ending with heterosexual union or the performance of motherhood.

Feminist discomfort with fictional portrayals of violent women arises from the concern that these representations often serve to uphold, rather than subvert, the dominant social order (King and McCaughey, 2001). This happens when violent female characters must be recuperated into femininity, but also when, through masculinised constructions, they reinforce approval of the use of violence to underline patriarchal dominance. In the *Alien* films, Ripley employs military style violence to defend what has been read as a colonialist regime symbolising American hegemonic power. Lara Croft, according to Herbst (2004), is a militarised killing machine, almost redolent of fascism. The Bride in *Kill Bill* does not stand in for military power; her quest is one of personal revenge. However, Coulthard (2007) argues that this individualised portrayal represents capitalist markers of power as any notion of collective political action or female solidarity is disavowed. Ultimately, this endorses the status quo.

These critiques demonstrate how representations of violent women in popular culture create feminist dilemmas in terms of how to read these portrayals. On the one hand, the activeness and vitality of female heroes can be attractive to feminist viewers; on the other such portrayals may seem to undermine feminist aims. However, the value of analysing popular culture lies in uncovering these very ambiguities and ambivalences (Read, 2000). Tasker (1993, p. 166) cautions against dismissing popular cultural forms such as action films as 'dumb movies for dumb people' because to do so erases audiences' own 'meaning making activities', which provide a variety of readings that can go beyond the reproduction of dominant values. For Read (2000), popular culture must be understood as one of the primary realms in which representations of both femininity and feminism are lived and experienced. As King and McCaughey (2001, p. 16) argue, '[t]here must be more to analysis than condemnation, the perpetual unmasking of violent women as frauds whose "resistance" to some reified patriarchy must always be undercut by recuperation into a "dominant" order.'

Female heroes are often ambiguous figures, who can be subject to both progressive and reactionary readings (Early and Kennedy, 2003; Schubart, 2007). Portrayals may be rooted in stereotypes, while simultaneously challenging them, for example, through use of parody (Inness, 2004; Read, 2004). Read (2000) examines how in the rape-avenger narrative, the gap between the victim's transformation into avenger enables the representation of different versions of femininity, and different versions of feminism. Feminist audiences may be ambivalent about these representations and find in them both pleasure and discomfort (Schubart, 2007). However, it is not necessary to judge whether representations of violent women in popular culture are 'truly' feminist or not (Read, 2000; Schubart, 2007) – instead, analysing these portrayals can help us to assess how far they present us with a means of thinking through constructions of femininity and feminism, which are pertinent to feminist criminology. The rest of the chapter analyses three examples of fictional female avengers: *Lost, Hard Candy* and *The Girl with the Dragon Tattoo*.

Lost – Kate Austen

The first female avenger for our consideration is the Kate Austen character from television series *Lost*, which aired in 2004–10 and is based on a plane that crashes en route from Sydney to Los Angeles. The survivors find themselves marooned on a mysterious island that has its own special powers and unexplained phenomena. The series comprise several interlocking narratives based on a variety of characters, which jump backwards and forwards in time. Kate is one of the main female characters and is portrayed as active and adventurous, frequently setting off on expeditions and displaying a willingness to fight to protect herself and others. She is not the only female character in *Lost* to be represented in this way, but Kate is particularly interesting for feminist criminologists as it is revealed in the first series that she murdered her violent stepfather. Early flashbacks show Kate handcuffed and accompanied on the flight by US Marshals.

Although it is established in series one that Kate's stepfather was abusive towards her mother and that she killed him after he threatened her with sexual violence, the moral ambiguity of her character is an ongoing theme. Some of Kate's behaviour on the island suggests a fundamental decency that is conventionally feminine: she listens to the problems of other characters, offers sympathy and assists another character, Claire, when she gives birth. At other times, as already mentioned, she displays heroic qualities, engaging in physical fights and using guns when she or her friends encounter danger. Ambiguity is introduced via the unfolding flashback narratives. After killing her stepfather, she fled and adopted a new identity, settling down to marry of all people, a police officer. However, Kate abandons this relatively safe and secure existence and goes back on the run, hooking up with a new, bank robber boyfriend, becoming a bank robber herself. Her criminality therefore extends beyond the more understandable and explainable transgression of blowing up her repugnant stepfather.

Analysis of the Kate Austen character can be made within a framework of post-feminism. The post-feminist context is one which acknowledges and responds to feminism, but usually a selectively defined feminism that either ignores, or displays ambivalence about, its political aspects (Early and Kennedy, 2003; Tasker and Negra, 2007). In popular culture, it is characterised by multiple representations of femininity that offer the possibility for flexible audience identifications (Tasker and Negra, 2007). Post-feminism is different from the notion of 'backlash' as it is not a disavowal of feminism, but an incorporation.

Kate's travails and dilemmas present the audience with an opportunity to contemplate her choices. When she decides to leave her police officer husband, it is partly because she can no longer stand deceiving a man who has been kind and supportive towards her. However, it is also because she finds cosy domesticity stifling. Kate's flight from the relationship is precipitated by a pregnancy scare; she realises that she does not want marriage and motherhood. She explains to her husband that sitting at home waiting for him on 'taco night' is not for her. *Lost* dramatises a post-feminist dilemma – whether to sacrifice a life of potential action and excitement for domesticity. In doing so, it shows the attractions of a long-term relationship, such as comfort and emotional warmth, but also Kate's need to reject this.

By series four, when some of the characters manage to leave the island, her character has undergone development. Kate takes Aaron, the baby of the Claire character, with her to Los Angeles as she believes Claire has been killed. In this series, the split narrative between characters still on the island and those who have returned to the 'real' world shows that Kate has embraced motherhood. She has an unsuccessful relationship with Jack, one of the lead males, which ends because of his inability to recover from trauma or to live with the deception that everyone else from the flight is dead that the returning characters must maintain. By contrast, Kate is emotionally strong and looks after Aaron as a single mother – this time, she is ready for motherhood.

It is significant for feminist criminologists that despite being a criminal woman, Kate is never portrayed as deviant through the standard discourses such as sexuality, pathology or domesticity. A pathological discourse is completely absent; in contrast with some of the other male and female characters in *Lost*, Kate is very mentally stable. Although shown to be a sexual woman, there is no suggestion that this should imply deviance. Kate's ongoing divided loyalties between Jack and the Sawyer character serve to dramatise another post-feminist dilemma – which man should she choose? The two characters mirror different aspects of her own personality. In the end, she professes her love for Jack, the more emotional and ethical of the two men. Despite an ability to use a gun, Kate is revealed to be a good mother, who can perform domesticity successfully if she chooses to.

As a post-feminist character, there are feminist objections that could be made to Kate's portrayal. As played by Evangeline Lilly, she conforms to the requirement for female heroes to be young, white and attractive. Her talent for motherhood could be read as the recuperation of a criminal woman back into femininity, with some of the character's moral ambiguity resolved through demonstrating good motherhood and the conventionally approved female qualities of nurturance and care. According to this reading, the character's subversive potential is undermined by reclaiming her into appropriate femininity. Instead of an adventurer or a warrior, Kate becomes a (good) mother. Similarly, the eventual breaking of the love triangle between Kate, Jack and Sawyer by Kate's declaration of love for Jack could be interpreted as an acceptance that ultimately heterosexual monogamy must prevail as an ideal. Kate is disallowed a sexuality which is too brazen or unruly; it must be contained within a relationship with one man, and must not trouble the boundaries of heteronormative morality.

While this type of feminist reading is possible, the narratives and character portrayals in *Lost* can be understood as more complex and multiple than this. Although it is certainly the case that Kate is played by a beautiful actor and as such is presented as an object of desire for the audience, so are the male leads Jack, as portrayed by Matthew Fox, and Sawyer, as performed by Josh Holloway, a model. Kate is *both* a female warrior and a good mother and is therefore a potentially subversive figure as these characteristics are presented as compatible. She remains an appealing and sympathetic character across the six series and although there are situations where she may be in the 'heroine' position of needing to be rescued, there are others where she is the rescuer. This blurring of gender boundaries is represented by other characters in *Lost* that cross traditional gender lines. Jack Shephard is a trained spinal surgeon and as a leader on the island, he displays nurturance and sometimes intense emotionality. His medical training means that he takes care of others when they need it and he exhibits arguably 'maternal' qualities.

The portrayal of Kate is post-feminist in that political issues relevant to feminism are not addressed; for example, there is no exploration of the wider contexts of gender and socio-economic inequality as they relate to violence against women in the storyline about her stepfather in series one. However, the Kate-based narratives develop a theme of female solidarity, which is most clearly exemplified in her loyalty to Claire, the biological mother of Aaron. Series six establishes that Kate has returned to the island to find Claire, not for heterosexual union with either Jack or Sawyer. This turns out to be no easy task as Claire has been emotionally and psychologically damaged by the loss of her son and by a strange, malign force on the island, and Kate has become the focus for her rage. Nevertheless, Kate perseveres and makes sure that Claire is not left behind again when some of the characters finally find a plane that allows them to escape the island. This forms the basis of her motivations and makes possible a reading that does not entail heterosexual resolution.

Hard Candy – Hayley Stark

Lost has a main character who can be understood as both a female avenger and a hero, but, as a blend of sci-fi and fantasy, it is not primarily focused on crime and criminality; Kate's storylines are simply one aspect of its multi-narrative structure. The next two examples have female avengers at their centre and are explicitly about crime. *Hard Candy* (2005) is a low-budget film that generated a certain amount of controversy and debate upon its release. It is based on two characters, 14-year-old Hayley Stark and 32-year-old photographer, Jeff Kohlver, who have arranged to meet in a Los Angeles coffee shop following online correspondence under the monikers 'Thonggrrrl14' and 'Lensman'.

The audience is primed to fear for Hayley's safety, having already witnessed the inappropriately flirtatious tone Jeff uses in his Internet chat. Hayley accompanies him back to his fashionable and highly desirable apartment, where she actively flirts with him before mixing them each a cocktail. As Jeff drinks his, he becomes woozy before passing out and awakens to find himself tied up and naked from the waist down. Hayley's manner is frighteningly transformed, as she informs him 'Playtime's over' while sharpening a scalpel with which she threatens to punish him for his paedophilia. The rest of the film dramatises her torture of Jeff, during which she is at all times in control. Rather than blood and gore, it relies mainly on dialogue and the threats that Hayley makes. Having tricked Jeff, she has placed him completely in her power. *Hard Candy* is purposefully opaque in terms of the overall messages that it has to give and leaves space for the audience to make their own readings. We shall examine some possible readings and also consider which themes are of particular interest to feminist criminology.

The film's role reversal conceit unsettles notions of victimhood and vulnerability. The opening scenes establish Jeff as a predator; he 'grooms' young girls through Internet chat rooms before inviting them back to his apartment. His manipulativeness is underlined by the way he checks out teen popular culture references online so that he can fake knowledge of them. The audience knows this narrative of the predatory paedophile who can find his way into young girls' rooms via the Internet, tricking them into an abusive sexual relationship. *Hard Candy* completely destabilises this by revealing Hayley to be several steps ahead and the one who has trapped Jeff. Critics noted that Hayley's red hoodie calls to mind Little Red Riding Hood and we expect her to need rescuing from the Big Bad Wolf (Kermode, 2006; Nelson, 2006). The film's promotional poster features a shot of Hayley, as played by Ellen Page, from the back with her red hood up. Having seen the film, the visual reference point recalls *Don't Look Now* (1973), in which Donald Sutherland's character pursues what he mistakenly believes is an imperilled child in a red jacket through the streets of Venice before she turns round and is revealed instead as the killer.

The role reversal device is the film's dramatic lynchpin and works well as a means of destabilising the audience's expectations. It is less clear what it actually says about victimhood. Simply exchanging the victim for the aggressor does not tell us much about the power dynamics involved in sexual abuse, or why this is something that should concern us. *Hard Candy* warns us not to take vulnerability as a given, but as that warning is couched in a narrative of torture and the threat of castration, it is not one that can be heeded particularly seriously. Without a scalpel, some rope, a stun gun, barbiturates and a finely tuned plan, Hayley would be vulnerable to Jeff. More interesting is its representation of girlhood. Feminists have noted how in American and British popular culture, a 'girl' is usually white and middle class (Gonick, 2006; Ringrose, 2006). Hayley conforms to these expectations, but rather than being a bitchy 'mean girl', whose destructive scheming is confined to a high school setting and can be fairly easily laughed off, she commands attention in a deeply disturbing scene in which she tricks Jeff into thinking that she has castrated him. *Hard Candy* takes a knowing, ironic approach to the castration subtext of horror films, as suggested by feminist scholars Clover (1992) and Creed (1993), by making it an explicit theme.

Hard Candy is a revenge fantasy and the key to unlocking different readings is to consider whose fantasies it represents. One is arguably feminist, whereby an exploitative and abusive male gets his comeuppance from a young girl. Instead of being placed in the position of the hunted, women can fantasise overcoming the helplessness of fearing or experiencing sexual abuse by seeing the perpetrator reduced to a quivering victim. Jeff is revealed to be thoroughly reprehensible when Hayley searches his apartment and discovers a photograph of a local girl, Donna Mauer, who is missing. She eventually forces him to confess that he was present when Donna was murdered, although he claims only to have watched while another man, Aaron, killed her. It is then that we discover Hayley has already caught up with Aaron, who said the same thing about Jeff. There is the possibility for experiencing a grim satisfaction that these men have been outsmarted and punished by someone from the very group they victimised. Hayley induces Jeff to kill himself or be exposed as a paedophile and murderer, and has rigged a noose for the purpose. Jeff tries to escape and to pursue Hayley but she is not to be beaten. In the end, he hangs himself by jumping off the roof of his building, after which Hayley dons her red hoodie and sets off home through the woods, driving home the Little Red Riding Hood in reverse trope.

Feminist scholars have noted that revenge fantasies produce ambiguous heroines, who can provoke ambivalence in feminist audiences in particular (Read, 2000; Schubart, 2007). Hayley has all the best lines in the film and is always in control, but her steely precision and precocious intelligence render her a somewhat unattractive character. She has no warmth (as the film's title implies), and as nearly all the action takes place in Jeff's apartment, we have no other context in which to place her. On the one hand, this means there is no cosy recuperation of Hayley – we do not see her as a daughter, friend or schoolgirl. On the other, it means that we could read her as an evil sadist, and given the castration theme, find a misogynistic streak in the narrative. Dargis (2006), reviewing *Hard Candy* for *The New York Times*, argued 'this avenging angel is really the demon daughter of Valerie Solanas and Lorena Bobbitt, and consequently as reprehensible as her prey'.

The film is built around the punishment of Jeff, a thoroughly bad man, as meted out by a vigilante teenager. In this sense, it is a punitive fantasy where paedophilia earns castration (or at least the threat of it) and execution. One way of reading the film is that in dramatising the audience's bloodlust for punishment through pain, it holds up a mirror to show how ugly, and ultimately undesirable, this is. However, in choosing to reveal Jeff as a truly dangerous figure of parental nightmares, it makes this reading less likely than one which applauds his suffering. Justice is meted out crudely, without oversight, and in contradiction with the criticisms of retributive punishment that many criminologists would make. Rather, it seems to endorse the need for harsh punishment.

Finally, we can read *Hard Candy* through analysing the causes that it identifies for Jeff's bad behaviour. At least two interpretations can be made. The first potentially speaks to feminist concerns about the commodification of female sexuality and the sexual objectification of young girls in particular. Jeff works as a photographer for the advertising industry and as such symbolises the means through which this commodification and objectification take place. The walls of his apartment are adorned with sexualised photographs of teenage girls. These are not proscribed images, but the kind that would be used to advertise products, illustrating the potentially thin dividing line between 'acceptable' and pornographic representations. More broadly, the film could be interpreted as indicting twenty-first century consumerism, which replaces morality with the desire for products and easy, instant gratification. Jeff's expensive looking apartment shows us that he is successful in his glamorous, creative career. By making him reprehensible, our desires for consumption are exposed as reprehensible.

This reprehensibility is, however, a double-edged sword. *Hard Candy*'s distaste for consumerism and its purveyors might chime with certain feminist concerns (see Gonick, 2006), but it also has a right-wing flavour. Jeff is urban, hip and works in the creative industries. At one point, by way of attempting to prove he is not all bad, he pleads with Hayley that he has also carried out work for environmental organisations. On the surface, Jeff appears to be a 'liberal' but any pretence to values or morality on his part is revealed as a sham. In satirising the preoccupations of the modern, techno-savvy, urban elite in this way, *Hard Candy* warns of a moral void, potentially offering a conservative reading that bemoans the loss of family values and community ties.

The Girl with the Dragon Tattoo – Lisbeth Salander

Larsson's Millennium Trilogy is three crime thrillers set in Sweden, which are all huge bestsellers in several countries. Their principal characters are Lisbeth Salander, an androgynous young woman in her 20s who is an expert computer hacker and Mikael Blomqvist, an investigative journalist who works for a monthly current affairs magazine, *Millennium*. Both of them live in Stockholm, although most of the action in the first book, *The Girl with the Dragon Tattoo* (2008), takes place in the fictional village of Hedestad, on a remote island in northern Sweden. Unlike the two previous examples, Larsson addresses big themes related to Swedish society, politics and the role of the state, making them a potentially satisfying read for criminologists. He also purposefully addresses feminist issues, although readers are divided as to how successfully he does this.

Larsson has clearly set out to create a female action hero who does not reproduce stereotypes of femininity as a male fantasy figure. Lisbeth is pierced, tattooed and extremely skinny. She favours old black leather jackets and rides a motorbike. Her androgyny is signalled not only by her physical description, but also by her talents and passions. Under the pseudonym 'Wasp', she is one of Sweden's pre-eminent computer hackers, which enables her to be the best researcher at Milton Security, the private security firm for which she works. She is also a skilful chess player, able to solve extremely complex mathematical equations and reads scholarly articles on the latest research in genetics for fun, despite having received patchy formal schooling and no higher education. She is largely asocial and we learn that those who have got to know her suspect she has Asperger's Syndrome. Lisbeth's prodigious analytical intelligence coupled with a restricted emotional repertoire presents us with a character who possesses what would more usually be understood as masculine traits and in doing so crosses the gender binary. Her natural brilliance and eccentricity recall a crime-fiction tradition of the maverick detective that stretches back to its nineteenth-century progenitors, C. Auguste Dupin, Monsieur Lecoq and Sherlock Holmes, with the difference being that Lisbeth is a young woman.

The Girl with the Dragon Tattoo establishes Lisbeth as a female avenger via two set pieces. Her background is developed in the subsequent two books (and forms an important element of the plots of both), but in the first we learn that she spent most of her teenage years institutionalised or with foster families. She has been declared incompetent, which means that she must have a state-appointed guardian to manage her financial affairs and keep oversight of her movements. Her guardian up until the age of 25, Holger Palmgren, is a decent man with Lisbeth's best interests at heart. He has persevered to establish a positive relationship with her, and is regularly beaten by her at chess. He helped Lisbeth to get her job at Milton Security and does not exert control over her finances. Disastrously, he suffers a bad stroke and goes into a coma. Lisbeth is given a new guardian, the cruel and sexually exploitative Advokat Nils Bjurman. He submits her to a horrifically violent rape at his apartment, and clearly intends to continue abusing her. As someone who has been judged incapable of managing her own affairs, Lisbeth has few official avenues of redress. Bjurman will simply attribute her complaints to the delusions of a disturbed and mentally handicapped young woman.

He has not, however, bargained for Lisbeth Salander. Unbeknownst to him, she has installed a camera in his apartment and recorded the rape. The next time she visits, Lisbeth is armed with a Taser that she uses to incapacitate Bjurman. After tying him up and gagging him, she tattoos his chest with the statement 'I am a sadist, pervert, rapist pig' and rapes him with a dildo. She also forces him to watch the recording of his attack on her and informs him that if he wishes to avoid exposure, he must give her freedom of movement, control of her own finances, and must submit monthly reports on her progress that she has written herself. Of interest to criminologists is the context that Larsson provides for Nils Bjurman's sexual violence. His state-mandated position as Lisbeth's guardian means that he believes he can easily exploit her. Their relationship is very asymmetrical in terms of power relations, with Bjurman enjoying professional authority as a lawyer and official backing from the courts, whereas Lisbeth has been pathologised by male doctors and made, on the face of it, socially powerless. She overcomes this through her toughness, intelligence and thirst for revenge. Larsson explicitly presents rape as imbricated in multiple relations of power, such as gender, class and age, and criticises methods of state control that invite such abuses.

The second incidence of Lisbeth's heroism is the rescue of Mikael Blomqvist from the clutches of a serial killer, Martin Vanger, which goes beyond the rape-revenge narrative to establish her as an avenging hero. Lisbeth and Mikael team up to investigate the disappearance in the 1960s of the favourite niece of a wealthy industrialist, Henrik Vanger. The action takes place away from Stockholm in a small town called Hedestad in the remote north. In researching the vanishing of 16-year-old Harriet Vanger, they probe the Nazi sympathies of members of the Vanger dynasty and possible connections with a string of apparently anti-Semitic murders. Mikael is captured by Martin, who like his late father, Gottfried, is a serial killer. Lisbeth rescues Mikael from Martin's basement, where he is about to be hanged. Armed with a golf club, she attacks Martin who is quickly subdued by finding himself on the receiving end of violence and flees while Lisbeth unties Mikael in order to prevent him from asphyxiating. Martin is killed in a car accident trying to escape. Her heroism reverses the usual action narrative, where the female victim needs to the rescued by the male hero. Mikael is made completely helpless by Martin and would have died without Lisbeth's physical intervention, and also without her sleuthing abilities as she realises that Martin is a serial killer after doing some research in the family archives. Like Advokat Bjurman, Martin Vanger is exposed as weak and cowardly, and when he is no longer in control of the situation he simply runs away. This portrayal of a serial killer stripped of his power is radically different from the more usual depictions, which present male serial killers as potent, vital figures (see Chapter 6's discussion of *The Killer Inside Me* for an expanded discussion of this).

The basement where he intended to murder Mikael is covered with the photographs of the immigrant women he has tortured and murdered there over the years. As with Nils Bjurman's rape of Lisbeth, Martin's violence against women is placed in a wider context of unequal power relations. Martin's victims are socially marginal women whom is he able to kill partly because no one realises that they are missing. He is protected by his status as the president of a successful corporation and his wealth, which enables him to hide his activities in a specially designed basement. Martin's crimes symbolise the exploitation of the marginalised by the powerful in Western, capitalist societies.

Larsson explores the transmission and reproduction of misogynistic attitudes. Martin was initiated into rape and murder by his father, Gottfried, beginning with participation in the sexual abuse of his sister, Harriet, who, it transpires, drowned Gottfried in a boating lake before leaving Sweden for Australia. The importance of the exploration of misogyny as a theme is highlighted by the book's Swedish title, 'Men Who Hate Women', and the statistics on violence against women in Sweden that are provided at the beginning of each section. Larsson was a campaigning journalist and opposition to violence against women was one of the social causes he supported (Smith, 2008). He consulted with Swedish feminist, Karen Leander, about violence against women and she provided him with the statistics.[1] Lisbeth has been read as 'a revenge fantasy come to life' (Smith, 2008), but Larsson has also been criticised for offering potentially titillating, detailed depictions of violence against women, such Lisbeth's rape, which seem to undercut the book's claim to be a critique of misogyny (Newman, 2009). Some feminists may find this, and the details given about Gottfried and Martin Vanger's serial killings, unpalatable to the point where any feminist message the book may wish to have is obscured. However, especially when the trilogy is taken as whole, these descriptions are relatively few, and it could be argued that it would be equally problematic if Larsson had chosen to sanitise the themes of rape and serial killing. The Millennium trilogy examines contemporary Sweden in the light of its recent past and highlights themes such as the legacy of far-right politics, the effects of anti-immigration policies, the subversion of democracy by the secret services and the misuse of welfare measures by those who work for the state. In doing so, it challenges the notion that Sweden is a fair and hospitable society for all and Larsson's depictions of the violence that takes place beneath its safe, clean surface is part of this.

The trilogy is a work of popular fiction and the characters that populate it are drawn with a broad brush. This approach also applies to its moral landscape and feminist politics, which are fairly straightforward. Good male characters such as Mikael Blomkqvist are attracted to (and attractive to) women who are more powerful than they are; bad male characters are out and out misogynists with no redeeming features. Larsson does not present the reader with trickier propositions, such as men who may enjoy viewing exploitative pornography or paying for sex but who are also capable of having successful relationships with women, or the participation of women in the mistreatment of other women. In this sense, it does not capture the complexities of the issues of sexual exploitation and violence against women.

In considering the debates generated by *The Girl with the Dragon Tattoo*, we can return to Read (2000) and Schubart's (2007) recommendation that it is not necessary to resolve whether a representation is 'truly' feminist or not. Rather, the portrayals of female avengers such as Lisbeth Salander provide an opportunity to think through the issues that are raised about femininity and feminism. Feminists will disagree about the nature and effectiveness of these representations, but they open up a space for the discussion to take place.

Fictional Female Avengers and Feminist Criminology

The three female avengers analysed in this chapter quite clearly connect with feminist debates about representations of violent women in popular culture. They can all be read as challenging the boundaries of gender through portraying active female characters who employ physical force to avenge themselves or others. The representation of Kate Austen in *Lost* is of a recognisably feminine woman, who also possesses warrior-like qualities and is portrayed as non-deviant despite her criminal past. *Hard Candy* unsettles the notion of girl-hood as connoting vulnerability and light-hearted superficiality through the depiction of the tough and clinically well-organised Hayley Stark. Lisbeth Salander similarly defies expectations of victim-hood and has the kind of mercurial genius and outsider independ-ence rarely granted to female heroes. To interpret the characters as simply recuperated in the case of Kate, or masculinised in the cases of Hayley and Lisbeth, is to overlook the ways in which they can be understood to rewrite aspects of femininity. It is useful for feminist criminologists to consider how femininities can be remade in ways that avoid or perhaps transform derogatory stereotypes, as this is part of the work of opposing such representations. The 'masculine' woman, for example, has been a recurrent negative construction of the criminal woman in both criminological and popular discourses (Seal, 2010). Fictional characters who are both heroic and cross the boundaries of gender help to challenge the perception that female masculinity is deviant or pathological.

In addition to thinking through femininity, these portrayals also enable us to reflect on aspects of feminism. All three characters are, of course, 'unrealistic' in the sense that their behaviour and experi-ences do not mirror those that would be typical of real women. They are instead fantasy figures, and the questions they raise for feminists derive from which fantasies they appear to represent. This has been discussed in relation to all three representations and multiple read-ings are possible. If, as Schubart (2007) argues, the audiences of female action heroes find themselves caught between pleasure and guilt, we can consider how *Hard Candy* and *The Girl with the Dragon Tattoo* in particular offer the pleasure of women avenging male violence but induce guilt through endorsing punitive fantasies, which are contrary to feminist aims to reduce violence. A salient question that the female avenger raises is how to constitute female agency and heroism with-out depicting female violence – if, indeed, we find violence always objectionable. This question resonates with the real-life case of Aileen Wuornos discussed earlier in this chapter. To an extent, Aileen can appear heroic and justified in her use of violence against men who threatened and attacked her. However, she gave different, conflicting explanations for shooting her victims and this position cannot be adopted unambiguously. There are also wider consequences to bear in mind, such as the impact the men's deaths had on their families. In sharp contrast with a revenge fantasy figure, Aileen Wuornos did not triumph but faced the most extreme penalty possible in the form of execution, a stark reminder of the further issues related to harsh punishment and human rights that feminist criminologists must also tackle. Chapter 4 continues the focus on femininity and examines representations of sex work.

4
Transgressing Sex Work: Ethnography, Film and Fiction

> Prostitutes are as inevitable in a metropolis as sewers, cesspits and rubbish tips; the civil authority should treat the one as it does the other – its duty is to supervise them, to reduce the dangers inherent in them as far as possible, and to this end to hide them and relegate them to the darkest corners; in short, render their presence as inconspicuous as possible.
>
> Alexandre Parent-Duchâtelet, speaking about Prostitution in the city of Paris in 1836, cited in John (1994, pp. 44–8)

> It is safe to say that most sex workers are not in the industry for the sex. Specifically it is *fast* money that pulls people into the industry and often keeps them there even where there are other alternatives.
>
> Willman cited in Ditmore, Levy and Willman (2010, p. 143)

The first quotation by Alexandre Parent-Duchâtelet in 1836 illuminates the fact that prostitution is accepted by bourgeois society (selling sex is not illegal) but the prostitute, the whore is not accepted, she is 'other' perceived as immoral, a danger, a threat to 'normal' femininity and, as a consequence suffers social exclusion, marginalisation and 'whore stigma'. On the other hand, the second quotation illustrates that there are deeply embedded economic and sociopolitical dynamics involved in explaining and understanding prostitution.

Like the 'criminal women' discussed in Chapter 3, sex workers occupy an anomalous cultural position, and selling sex is much more complex than either a question of morality/immorality or economics. In this chapter analysis is undertaken of certain cultural representations of sex workers. Representations of women who sell sex are discussed in relation to historical and contemporary discourses and analyses of prostitution that define the 'prostitute body' as a deviant body *and* a site of transgression. In the final section of the chapter, drawing upon a performance text created at the borders of ethnography and performance art, we expose the construction of sexual identities and sexual politics within patriarchal capitalism, the tension between the prostitute as a figure of abjection and desire, and transgression as both a symbolic practice that allows people access to taboo desires (Stallybrass and White, 1986) and the counterhegemonic possibilities of transgression.

Representations of sex workers in filmic texts are never simple mimetic re-presentations, but are mediated by a range of factors, including the reworking of the figure of the prostitute in the imagination of the writer/director/audience. What we know from the available literature is that the portrayal of women and men who sell sex as deviant criminals is instantiated in law through various street and sexual offence legislation as well mass media images and representations, fictive and filmic texts (O'Neill, 1997, 2001; Sanders, O'Neill and Pitcher, 2009). The regulation of the sale and purchase of sex takes place predominantly through the enforcement of laws which focus mainly on women who sell sex both on and off street. Historical analysis evidences that in the combination of legal and sociocultural factors a particular ideology of prostitution is reproduced.

Historical context: Transgression and the making of an outcast group

The history of prostitution is framed by attempts to repress and make morally reprehensible the women involved in prostitution while aestheticising the desires and fantasies symbolically associated with the whore, the prostitute, the fallen woman (Corbin, 1990; Stallybrass and White, 1986). This history is also tied to the history and social organisation of sexuality, cathexis and the social organisation of desire; gender relations; masculinity and property relations, capitalist exchange relations which increasingly commodify everything, even love (see Bertilsson, 1986; Connell, 1987, 1995; Theweleit, 1987, 1989; Giddens, 1992). Flaubert in a letter to Louise Collette writes:

> It may be a perverse taste, but I love prostitution, for it, independently of what is beneath. I've never been able to see one of those women in décolleté pass by under the gaslights, in the rain, without feeling palpitations, just as monks' robes with their knotted girdles arouse my spirit in some ascetic and deep corner. There is, in this idea of prostitution, a point of intersection so complex – lust, bitterness, the void of human relations, the frenzy of muscles and the sound of gold – that looking deeply into it makes you dizzy; and you learn so many things! And you are so sad! And you dream so well of love! Ah, writers of elegies, it is not on the ruins that you should go to lean your elbows but on the breasts of these gay women!
>
> Gustave Flaubert from letter to Louise Colet (1853)
> cited in John (1994, pp. 64–5)

Historical research highlights relationships between women selling sex, the state, working-class/underclass communities, and the regulation of public space and moral order. Historians working in this area have identified the Victorian era in particular, as a time in which we find evidence of what Walkowitz (1977) calls 'the making of an outcast group'. For example, the 1824 Vagrancy Act introduced into statutory law the term 'common prostitute'. The 1839 Metropolitan Police Act made loitering an offence in London, and was extended to towns/cities outside of London in the 1847 Town Police Clauses Act. The Contagious Diseases Acts of 1846, 1866 and 1869 introduced the compulsory medical examination of prostitute women in 11 naval ports and garrison towns (1846); extended police powers and introduced (following the French system) registration and fortnightly inspection (1866); and, in 1869, extended the number of towns where the Act was in force. This legislature enshrined in law the category 'prostitute' – what she does (sells sex) becomes who she is. Her identity is fixed as 'prostitute' through registration, cautioning, imprisonment in pseudo-prisons and lock hospitals. She is also made an 'outcast' from the working-class communities she lived and worked in, set apart as the 'Other', labelled a 'common prostitute'. Poor women sold sex in Victorian England to survive, and many sold sex in addition to their 'day' jobs, for which they earned a pittance. The economic basis for entry into sex work is thus based upon social inequalities, patriarchy as well as the organisation of sexual and labour relations. Walkowitz (1977, p. 77) states:

> For most 'public' women prostitution represented only a temporary stage in their life that they would pass through. The age concentration of registered women in their early twenties strongly supports the likelihood that they had prior work experience outside the home as well as having engaged in non-commercial sexual activity. In addition registered women appear to have stayed in prostitution for two or three years, leaving in their mid twenties at a critical point in their lives – when most working class women were settling into some domestic situation with a man, whether it be formal law or common-law marriage. The timing here is very important. For as long as prostitution represented a temporary stage in a woman's career, and as long as she could leave it at her discretion, she was not irrevocable scarred or limited in her future choices.

However, according to Walkowitz (1977, p. 72), the registration of women as common prostitutes facilitated 'official intervention into their lives' and offered the police

> [a]n easy opportunity for general surveillance of the poor neighbourhoods in which they resided ... Their temporary move into prostitution reflected the fluid social identity among the casual labouring poor who so violated Victorian society's sense of order and place.

The development of a deviancy model emerged in Victorian time tied to the identification of women selling sex with symbols of immorality and disease and the enactment of laws (e.g. the Contagious Diseases Acts in England) that prevented women's access to public spaces where they might sell or exchange sex for money. Thus, the identity of the prostitute was naturalised and reified around the notion of the deviant individual woman transgressing moral order, patriarchal order and the law. The problem of prostitution was then dealt with by regulating the women involved through a combination of legal and medical discourses that regulated and controlled women's sexuality and bodies, with particular regard to the sexual health of their bodies, and women's access to public spaces.

In *Women For Hire: Prostitution and Sexuality in France after 1850*, Corbin (1990) identifies how the inter-related discourses of municipal authorities, hygienists, the police and judiciary combined to organise the regulation of prostitution around three major issues. These were the need to protect public morality, the need to protect male prosperity and finally the need to protect the nation's health. The prostitute was perceived as an active agent for the transmission of disease. For Corbin, these three major issues are rooted in five key images of the prostitute:

The prostitute as the *putain* 'whose body smells bad' (p. 210).
The prostitute as the safety valve which 'enables the social body to excrete the excess of seminal fluid that causes her stench and rots her' (p. 211).
The prostitute as decaying and symbolically associated with the corpse, with death.
The prostitute as diseased symbolically associated with syphilis.
Finally, the prostitute as submissive female body 'bound to the instinctive physical needs of upper class males' (p. 213).

For Corbin, these five key images reinforce the ambiguous status of the female body – the lower class, submissive body of the prostitute 'at once menace and remedy, agent of putrification and drain ... at the beck and call of the bourgeois body' (pp. 212–13). Drawing upon Foucault, Corbin goes on to illustrate how these discourses led to a series of principles which structured the regulation of prostitution: the principle of tolerance, the principle of containment and the principle of surveillance. Contain and conceal, but keep under continual surveillance. 'The first task of regulation is to bring the prostitute out of the foul darkness and remove her from the clandestine swarming of vice, in order to drive her back into an enclosed space, under the purifying light of power' (p. 215). With the rise of utilitarianism the image of the brothel, 'a seminal drain' (p. 215) closely supervised by the police, develops out of the image of the brothel symbolic of debauchery, perversion, disease and decay.

The legal regulation of sex work in the UK was built up in a piecemeal way through three major periods of regulatory reform: the Victorian era and the Contagious Diseases Acts; the 1950s with the Wolfenden Committee and the Street Offences act; and the flurry of legislative activity and policy guidance of the current period (1990s to 2011) that focus upon rehabilitating and responsibilising the sex worker as 'other' (O'Neill, 2010a; Scoular and Sanders, 2010). This regulation of sex work instantiates in law, discourses and representation the abject status of the sex worker, who is defined as a morally deviant Other, who may also be a victim, of her own making or of another: a man, brothel owner or trafficker; and ultimately who needs to be responsibilised (Scoular and O'Neill, 2007). What remains relatively hidden across these three periods of law reform is the poverty experienced by women and their families, the growing market and availability for sex work at a local and global level, and the fact that social justice for sex workers is therefore circumscribed.

Hence any attempt to understand prostitution in current times must be very clear about the various ways that selling sex is constructed and maintained as a social problem and regulated via discourses of deviance, transgression, control and social order, out of which emerge interventions in law, welfare, policies and guidance. Clearly, 'deviant identities become the basis of law reform rather than the social factors that construct those identities in the first place' Phoenix (2009, p. 160). The transgression associated with prostitution is well documented in cultural texts, in art and literature (Kishtainy, 1982; O'Neill, 2001).

Transgression and liminality: Sex and the city

Walter Benjamin writes about the fascination with the prostitute in art and literature of the nineteenth and twentieth centuries for she is both salesperson and commodity in one, an organic body (a subject) and a commodity (an object). He writes that in the act of prostitution, there is an unconscious knowledge of man, an empathy with commodities for the commodification of women's bodies is premised upon capitalist exchange relations and the female body is a metaphor for the commodity body. The prostitute is also 'a 'threshold-dweller' (Weigel, 1996, p. 92) working in the liminal zones of the city. Benjamin suggests that the fascination with the threshold dwellers, with prostitutes, is related to the intersection of sex, money, transgression and loss of self, captured in the taboo desires projected onto the bodies of women selling sex. In the public imagination the prostitute as abject-body symbolises dirt, decay, corruption, *but* she is also an instrument of pleasure, of thrill, frisson and (illicit) desire. And, given Flaubert's quotation mentioned earlier, it is around the figure and body of the prostitute 'that the gaze and touch, the desires and contaminations, of the bourgeois male were articulated' (Stallybrass and White, 1986, p. 137). These contradictory discourses have led to the ongoing regulation of prostitution and the bodies of prostitutes (Corbin, 1990) particularly in certain areas of towns and cities.

Contemporary 'red-light areas' emerged from spatial organisation that excludes 'disorderly' 'polluting' prostitutes and prostitution from 'orderly' 'purified' sites of sexual morality. Spaces where selling sex takes place, whether on or off street, are usually the poorest neighbourhoods in towns and cities (Hubbard, 1999). In a chapter called 'The Sewer, the Gaze and the Contaminating Touch', Stallybrass and White (1986) document the ways in which social reformers such as Chadwick, Mayhew and Engels surveyed the poor, in their abjection, while also 'producing new forms of regulation and prohibition governing their own bodies' (p. 126). In the works of social reformers, the poor were associated with filth, slums, sewage and disease, they 'were interpreted as transgressing the boundaries of the 'civilized' body and the boundaries which separated the human from the animal' (ibid., p. 132).

> [T]he Irishman allows the pig to share his own living quarters. This new, abnormal method of rearing livestock in the large towns is entirely of Irish origin ... the Irishman lives and sleeps with the pig, the children play with the pig, ride on its back, and roll about in the filth with it.
>
> Engels (1971, p. 106) quoted in Stallybrass and White (1986, p. 132)

Such associations with filth and disease were especially linked to the prostitute in the work of reformers. Through 'the discourse of prostitution they encoded their own fascinated preoccupation with the carnival of the night, a landscape of darkness, drunkenness, noise and obscenity' (ibid., p. 137). And, 'the "prostitute" was just the privileged category in a metonymic chain of contagion which led back to the culture of the working classes' (ibid., p. 138). Thresholds, slums, sewers, alleyways, passages merged with the prostitute as threshold dweller, lower class, polluted, contaminated. Baudelaire focuses much attention on the prostitute, 'there is, indeed, no exalted pleasure which cannot be related to prostitution' (Benjamin, 1983, p. 21) yet at the same time he writes about 'contaminated' women and wrote obsessively about 'Hygiene Projects' (Stallybrass and White, 1986, p. 136).

Moving beyond this notion of transgression as abjection, the concept is theorised along two further lines in the work of Stallybrass and White (1986). First, transgression as a ritual or symbolic practice allows people temporary access to their taboo desires, a 'delirious expenditure of the symbolic capital accrued (through the regulation of the body and the decathexis of habitus) in the successful struggle of bourgeois hegemony' (Stallybrass and White, 1986, p. 201) as evidenced in the references previously to Benjamin, Flaubert and Baudelaire. Second, there is a radical potential to transgression that involves countering, criticising, disrupting and denaturalising the existing social order (Eagleton, 1981). Analysis has shown that such transgression is usually incorporated into the dominant hegemony through a process of commodification of the transgressive activity and labelling the transgressive group as deviant.

Analysis of prostitution in the nineteenth century exposes the foundations on which the bourgeois system of class, patriarchy, power and privilege was based (Self, 2003). Given the absolute poverty of many of the labouring classes, selling sex for women who could not survive on their wages as shop girl, domestic or seamstress is indeed a rational and pragmatic act. Instead they are labelled, as filth, dirt, made abject and their activity is commodified and identified as immoral, symbolic of their transgression of the norms, rules and laws of 'civilised' society. In doing historical excavation of this work (the images, representations, historical documents), we can produce through critical analysis 'knowledges of resistance' (Walters, 2003, p. 166) that can inform our research and public policy on prostitution in current times.

Transgression as resistance

Historical research shows that there were examples of resistance to incorporation. Confined in certain spaces/places/locations, some sex workers resisted the exclusionary geographies of prostitution (see O'Neill, 2004, p. 224). In Portsmouth, confined in 'lock hospitals' due to the Contagious Diseases Acts, women 'rioted and smashed windows ... were given to "insane frenzy", singing, dancing, swearing or destroying the blankets and rugs given them to sleep in' (Walkowitz, 1980, p. 220).

Current-day examples of resistance have included the use of advertising cards in telephone boxes; the creative use of CCTV cameras and techniques of surveillance to make the gaze of surveillance and situational crime prevention work in their favour to support women's safety on the streets (O'Neill, 2004). Women resist attempts at control and surveillance through the use of time and space, working later or earlier shifts (to avoid police cautioning) and making use of back alleys, pubs, cafes and off-street premises for the sale of sex. Unionisation, demanding employment rights as sex-trade workers and resisting labelling and othering are important examples of resistance. The GMB union serves to reinforce the basic premise that 'prostitutes' are 'sex workers' and reform should address the identity of sex workers within the context of European and International Labour law.

However, despite such resistance, in the next section we show, through analysis of filmic and fictive texts that the status and representation of the prostitute is maintained by and large through a set of self-sustaining discourses and images which are part of the representation of women and men more generally in late modernity/postmodernity. Examining cultural texts such as film and literature, there is a dominant focus upon the prostitute as body object or the Trauerspeil (tragedy) of the 'Prostitute Body' aligned with the regulation of predominantly female bodies throughout recorded history. More recently, given the work of third-wave feminists, there is also an emphasis upon performance and performativity of the 'prostitute' that is linked to globalisation, neo-liberal capitalism and the global sex industry as a postmodern leisure phenomenon.

It is argued later here that by combining ethnographic research with analysis of cultural texts such as films that both re-present and imagine women, we can get closer to analysis that explores the radical potential of transgression: (a) as a ritual or symbolic practice that allows people temporary access to their taboo desires and (b) as transgression that criticises and disrupts.

Cultural methodologies

Prostitution and film: Transgression as symbolic practice

The importance of combining analysis of cultural texts (film, literature, poetry, photography) with ethnographic life stories/biographical accounts is to recover and retell lived experiences and the multiple representations of women, so that we might better understand the many issues involved. What we must always remember is that the biographical and autobiographical involves a re-telling of 'experience', not of a pre-given reality, but rather our life stories are the discursive effect of processes that we call upon to construct and reconstruct what we call 'reality' (Brah, 1996, p. 11). Presdee (2004, p. 44) argues for taking a biographical approach to transgression, to 're-insert the subject into the discourses of crime. Crime itself is constructed deep in the cracks that make up everyday life.' The role of the cultural criminologist is to 'excavate not celebrate' (p. 45), by enabling people to tell their stories 'without hindrance' (p. 44), examining their emotional world and forms of resistance. Combining analysis of cultural texts such as fiction and film with historical and biographical research can tell us so much more about the realities and complexities of women's lives and the social and historical contexts through which they lived their lives.

For example, in 'Saloon Girls: Death and desire in the American West', O'Neill (1998) analysed three different examples of the genre of the Western – *Rio Bravo* (1959), *The Wild Bunch* (1969) and *Unforgiven* (1992) – alongside historical analysis of the letters and diaries from women who had sold sex, census and other records, in order to explore the representations of women and work and the saloon as a workplace. O'Neill writes that an understanding of fictive texts alongside detailed historical work can lend itself to possibilities for immersing oneself in the social and psychic processes that these frontiers people would have experienced, inhabited, produced and reproduced. The isolation and the loneliness; the development of social organisations such as laws, schools, workplaces; the interactions with others, the transcendent and transgressive possibilities; the process of Western colonialism developing amidst the construction and reproduction of communities and societies are all documented through diaries, journals, letters, newspaper items and census documents (see O'Neill, 1998, pp. 117–30). Combining ethnography, critical theory and feminist analysis, she suggests that exploring fictive texts as 'feeling forms' alongside historiography can help us to better understand the multiple experiences, realities, 'truths' of women's lived experiences and lived relations.

As a 'feeling form', film can represent dominant cultural attitudes, values and feelings towards 'prostitutes' and can be read to not only see how the meanings that underpin the signs function (Hirschman and Stern, 1994) but also to uncover transgressive possibilities, for pleasure as well as sites of resistance. In O'Neill's (1998) analysis, the social organisation of prostitution in the West, the saloon as a workplace and prostitution as a cultural practice throw up similarities as well as differences with the lives and workplaces of sex workers today.

Saloon girls

In all three films, women are represented as 'outlaws' – transgressors of the norms of femininity and morality, representative of a dangerous sexuality, suffused with frisson. In *Rio Bravo* the saloon as workplace is evident in three major scenes in the film, it is an in-between space but also a space of entertainment and caregiving. In *The Wild Bunch* it is a space far away from civilisation, literally on the borders of a violent and hedonistic world where anything goes. In *Unforgiven* it is a place where men find respite, and the sex is prioritised over caregiving or entertainment. Violence, actual or potential is ever present.

What is clear is that the negation of the norm represented by the women identified as 'prostitutes' – 'Feathers' in *Rio Bravo* (Angie Dickenson) and Teresa (Sonia Amelio) in *The Wild Bunch* – has to be resolved to maintain the norm associated with law and order. 'Feathers' undergoes a symbolic death of her old lawless life and order is restored through her relationship with Sherriff John T. (John Wayne). This shift happens in a scene where she is getting ready to entertain putting on her corset, stockings and boots. He forbids her to go outside the room dressed like this, and she replies, 'I waited so long for you to say that. I thought you were never gonna say it. ... Tell me something why – why don't you want me to wear them?' He replies, 'Because I don't want anyone but me to see you.'

In *The Wild Bunch* the lyrical Western is replaced by brutal realism. The 'Wild Bunch' are outlaws chased by an ex-outlaw, who has been

Figure 4.1 John Wayne and Angie Dickinson on the set of the movie 'Rio Bravo' in 1959 in Tucson, Arizona
Photo by Michael Ochs Archives/Getty Images.

commissioned to find them by the owner of the railroad. In this film, the whore, Teresa, has to die, she is a good girl turned bad, but there is no hope of redemption (rehabilitation) through love of a good man. She is shot by her childhood sweetheart, one of the 'outlaws', for her 'whoring'. This trope of the death of bad girls or their trans-formation into a 'good' woman is particularly strong in fictive texts of the nineteenth and indeed twentieth centuries and still it lingers on, despite the gains of feminism and gendered politics.

Bronfen (1992) writes eloquently about this using a number of examples. She argues that Prosper Merimee's novella, *Carmen*, pro-vides 'one of the most persistent myths responding to archaic desires and fears about women marked as "other"' because Carmen 'embod-ies a fascinating sensuality and passion which is disruptive of mascu-line order, reason and control' (Bronfen, 1992, p. 187). Such women must be either sacrificed, and so cultural norms are reconfirmed; or transformed into 'good girls' which also serves the purpose of reconfirming cultural norms. Either way, through the death of such a woman or her transformation into 'good', 'pure', 'submissive' woman, social order is re-established which was momentarily lost and existing norms are preserved (Bronfen, 1992).

In these two films, saloon girls fulfil the gendered stereotype. And, as Bronfen writes, 'the stereotype of the other is used to control the ambivalent and to create boundaries. Stereotypes are a way of dealing with the instabilities arising from the division between self and non self by preserving an illusion of control and order' (Bronfen, 1992, p. 182). As the end stop in discourses on good and honest women, the very category prostitute is based upon symbolic and legal representations of Otherness. As Pheterson (1989, p. 8) states, 'don't be bad like those women or you too will be punished ... You'll never be as good as "those women" unless you're bad, and then you're no good. Meanwhile, "those women" are legally stripped of human status.'

Yet, in *Unforgiven*, this stereotypical image of the prostitute is in part transgressed. The women are there to 'hump every man in town' but at the same time they resist the stereotype of being used and abused like commodities – they state that they are 'not horses'. They provide care, sex and emotional labour to men who were also on the margins of frontier society and what is very clear from historical analysis is that saloon girls, prostitutes, were very important to the development of frontier society, to social order and social control.

To an extent, in *Unforgiven* it is the women who triumph following Delilah's knife attack by a client leaving her with a 'cut up face'. The 'saloon girls' avenge Delilah's injuries and neither she nor they have to die for cultural norms to be resumed. Delilah had laughed at the client's 'little pecker' the ultimate sin in the Western, where men's 'peckers' are usually symbolised by the guns they wear and use. Sherriff John T. in *Rio Bravo* carries a rifle as well as guns, and in the final scene of *The Wild Bunch* the outlaws raze the village to the ground with a machine gun, creating absolute carnage.

Other filmic representations of prostitutes offer similar narratives that allow people temporary access to their taboo desires and reinforce the transgressive nature of the 'prostitute'. Hirschman and Stern (1994) examine cultural attitudes toward the commoditisation of women as prostitutes in three Hollywood films *The Blue Angel* (1930), *Pretty Baby* (1978) and *Pretty Woman* (1990). For the authors, films are vehicles of popular culture carrying and communicating consumption ideology.

Film has great impact as an agent for consumer behaviour as well as 'encoding and enforcing society's views of "woman's place"' (p. 576). By revealing the images and representations of the prostitute in film accessing the sedimented truths of the social world in fictive texts, we can reveal examples and the contradictions of female oppression through the specific experiences of the 'prostitute'. However, in order to generate a more thorough cultural analysis of these texts, we also need to explore the 'prostitute' as subject-object. We can do this by listening to women working as prostitutes, by understanding that for many women prostitution is a 'resistance' as well as a 'response' to their experiences within patriarchal capitalism, marked by unemployment, poverty and difficult, destructive relationships with some men, and/or their families.

O'Neill and Campbell (2001) were commissioned by Walsall South Health Action Zone to undertake a participatory action research on prostitution in Walsall. In the Walsall study they found that a pivotal issue for the sex workers they spoke to was how susceptible they were to violence from clients as well as passers-by, and how few *rights* they had as a 'common prostitute'.

> They think you've got no rights. In the papers it will say 'a prostitute' has been murdered. Does it matter that she's a prostitute, she's dead? She is a woman too.
>
> O'Neill, M. and Campbell (2001, p. 83)

Using participatory arts methods facilitated by artist Kate Green, some of the women who participated re-presented their lives and experiences using digital photography. The image given next transgresses the stereotype of the sex worker as 'victim' and highlights resilience and resourcefulness in her work as well as the sharing of her 'tips' through the artwork. This and other images were exhibited at the Walsall Art Gallery as part of the dissemination of the project. (For more information see www.safetysoapbox.co.uk.)

Triangulating information gained from exploring historical and fictive texts with the life-story narratives of women working as prostitutes can enable us to get a much clearer understanding of transgression that criticises, resists and disrupts. In the following section the outcome of collaboration across ethnographic research and visual and performing arts is documented that, it is argued, captures the critical and disruptive transgression associated with selling sex.

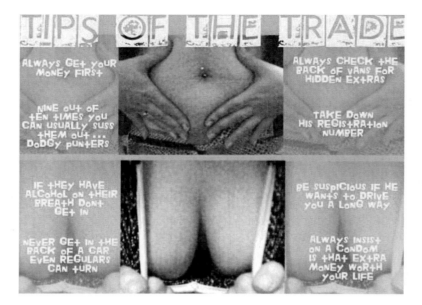

Figure 4.2   Tips of the Trade
Photo: Kate Green.

Prostitution, transgression and resistance: Not all the time... but mostly...

A series of artworks, a nine-minute video and two phases of movement-based performance were developed as part of an interdisciplinary collaboration between O'Neill and Giddens between 1997 and 2001 called 'Not all the time... but mostly...' as part of O'Neill's larger project on exploring the connections between art practice and social research. Ethnographic interviews with sex workers, heavily anonymised, were re-presented in the visual and performance texts. Life stories transcripts embedded in the performances showed the multiple roles that each woman fulfilled: the management of self and self-identify as commodity and seller, wife, partner, daughter, mother, sister; issues of economic need; resistance and transgression. The performance (and video) aimed to embody the ethnographic text. O'Neill and Giddens (2001) felt that by representing women's lives in art form, especially the visual immediacy of live art, could help audiences to see and understand aspects of women's lives that could not be conveyed by words alone and indeed such representations might enable a richer understanding of the complexities of women's lived experiences and the role and meaning of transgression and resistance in their lives.

Multiple meanings were generated through the combination of women's narratives, sound and movement through space, linking immersion in the story of a life, with the fragmentation and indeed blurring of the performative and prostitute body through the performance text. The performance text highlights their situatedness between the real and the fictive involved in doing/acting/performing prostitution, being a client's 'fantasy woman' and the very real dangers and risks involved.

Judith Butler's (1990) performative theory of gender enables us to move beyond binaries of good/bad women and grasp the multiple dimensions of gender identities and the 'management' of gendered relations. For Butler, the gendered body is performed, and acts, gestures and enactments that purport to perform an 'essence of identity' are in fact not an 'essence' at all but 'manufactured and sustained through corporeal signs and other discursive means' (Butler, 1990,

Figure 4.3 Tools of the Trade
Photo: Kate Green

p. 336). The 'essence' of identity, for Butler, is manufactured through public and social discourses which help to maintain and sustain the 'regulation of sexuality within the obligatory frame of reproductive heterosexuality' (ibid., p. 337).

Drawing upon Butler, one could argue that the actual performance of doing sex work highlights the distinction between the gender being performed (stereotypical heterosexual sexualized woman/whore) and the social organisation of desire rooted in hegemonic heterosexuality and fantasies revolving around women or woman in the patriarchal imagination.

In Giddens' performance the sign 'prostitute' is transgressed. The ritualised practice of the prostitute as performer undercuts a simple reading of the prostitute as reinforcing patriarchy or heterosexual hegemonic practices marked by desire and fetishism.

In his reading of the performance, Rolland Munroe states that the sign 'prostitute' hides our own fetishising of exchange. For example, in the performance, the exchange relationship articulated between prostitute and client is evident in the way the young woman talks about coming to a point where she stops seeing people for who they are and starts seeing them as potential clients. Munro states that this highlights the chiasm in which we live. In fact, we 'are all at it ... seeing others as friends one moment and crossing them into a prospective client, a regular, the next'. He defines some of the crossings we make: 'the attractive person at a party (might buy us dinner) or the colleague who is our friend (could advance our career)'. This fragmenting of others and then 'enrolling the bits into our interests – has us in strict denial: immediately we are refracting our commodifications back into friends/good blokes/lovers – forms that carry the acceptable face of society'. Indeed 'chameleon like we cross over and back using the ferryman of class, gender and personality to forget our own fetishizing of exchange' (Munroe, 1999).

In the process of interpretation we become aware of the ideology of exchange being played out before us as instrumental reason – the reduction of our social world to 'thing-like' equivalences. 'Little by little, this drive for ... "equivalence" which is a feature of instrumental reason comes to pervade all aspects of human life' (Battersby, 1998, p. 128). This also includes the tendency to treat persons as equivalents which helps to separate the 'good' women from those 'bad' women involved in selling or buying sex. Munroe reminds us that the prostitute in contrast sees what she/we are up to. The prostitute turns the artefacts of exchange (high heels, zips, slit skirts) back from fetish to function, and in one part of the narrative she throws out of her house the friend who sits on her sofa and denies what has paid for it.

[M]y boyfriend's friend sat watching the telly and said look at them dirty prostitutes ... and I said just remember I am a prostitute and this is my settee paid for by prostitution and my TV and my carpet and everybody looked at me horrified.

O'Neill (2001, p. 93)

Munroe tells us that we may deny her as we will, but

it is the prostitute who sees life as it comes. Yes! Yes! And it is the same figure who – as the unacceptable face of exchange – helps us deny our own everyday commodification of each other.

Munro (1999)

The combination of interpretive ethnography and performance art in *Not all the time... but mostly...* transports us 'bodily into the everyday world of prostitutes' (Munroe, 1999).

In summary, the 'prostitute' is marked out as 'other', as separate from ordinary women, a body-object of fascination and desire, an 'aestheticized' body. Our gendered bodies are heavily symbolised in the social construction of everyday life. Embodiment is a cultural process whereby the body 'becomes a site of culturally ascribed and disputed meanings, experiences, and feelings' (Stanley and Wise, 1993, p. 196). Jessica Benjamin (1993) stresses that feminist theory should address structures of domination by exploring the relationships between the powerful and powerless, not by imagining a feminine realm 'corrupted by the culture of phallic symbolisation and paternal idealisation' (p. 223) but rather through mutual recognition – intersubjective feminist theory.

For Irigaray, the 'phenomenological account of the lived body and the lived world needs to be complemented by the awareness that there is an interaction between the lived experience, the imaginary, and the discursive and social construction of both' (Irigaray, 1993, p. 52). Moreover, we urgently need models that 'allow us to register both difference and sameness' (p. 127). Intersubjective mutual recognition is crucial to research that works with women as subject-objects. It is pivotal in order to build bridges across the feminist binary divide that stresses on the one hand that selling sex is about violence and harm to women and on the other that selling sex is labour/work and women should not be criminalised and stigmatised but protected under labour law.

Exploring the transgressive aspects of sex work as resistance to capitalism, poverty, normative sexual identities and patriarchy, we go some way to dismantling binaries and thinking dialectically. There are no easy solutions. Women working as prostitutes are very clear about the ways in which they work to support and flatter the male imaginary. 'Being a sex worker is first and foremost an act, and this audience is paying. Changing after the show makes a personal distinction between work and not-work, and is a strategy to avoid labelling and stigma' (Murray, 1995, p. 68). As O'Sullivan states in Murray (1995, p. 69), we need to get beyond the 'tired old stereotypes of sex worker as sad (junkie/victim), bad (immoral nympho slut) or mad (acting out unresolved childhood abuse), but unfortunately this is not so'.

Certainly, for many theorists the imaginary is central to utopian political thinking and so we need to transgress and revolutionise our image worlds. The possibilities for our sign worlds of sexuality are both creative and destructive. Opening up new and more democratic ways of 'being' and 'becoming' are dependent upon imagination, imaginaries and hope for the future. The links between the self-sustaining discourses and images which are part of the re-presentation of women and men more generally and the social organisation of desire are deeply rooted in our psychic worlds. The corporeal morphology of the body informs the symbolic and the social at many levels. Whitford tells us that to live one's own morphology as 'woman', to be for oneself in the current social order and social spaces, is to 'forge' a 'tenuous identity against or in the margins of the symbolic' (Whitford, 1991, p. 153). Moreover we need to account for both feeling/sensuous knowing (mimesis) and reason (constructive rationality) in challenging and changing sexual and social inequalities, and discourses of abjection and liminality with sex workers, underpinned by research that works *with women*, utilising participatory, performative and visual methods, not on or for. Chapter 5 continues our focus on liminality through an exploration of 'madness' as transgression.

5
Madness and Liminality: Psychosocial and Fictive Images

Madness has historically 'proved to be the grand transgressor'.

Jenks (2003, p. 135)

In this chapter, psychosocial analyses (Gadd and Jefferson, 2007) are used to explore representations of madness and liminality. We focus our attention upon filmic representations to generate new knowledge and understanding of the poetics and possibilities of transgressive imaginings of madness in the context of mediated constructions of deviance, care and control. This chapter examines a film by Janice Haaken (clinical psychologist, professor of psychology, feminist and film-maker) *Guilty Except for Insanity*[1] to explore psychosocial constructions of deviance, care and control in the lives of some of the inmates of Oregon State Hospital for the criminally insane in Portland who pleaded 'not guilty by reason of insanity'. We subsequently make an argument for the transgressive, transformative potential of film-making and psychosocial criminology by drawing upon the work of Scheff (2010) and Lorenzer (2002).

Oregon State Hospital was famously the place where *One Flew Over the Cuckoo's Nest* (1975), a film directed by Milos Forman, was made. Haaken's film uses clips from Forman's film alongside interviews with patients, families, staff members and her own observations to tell the stories of five of the current inmates in Oregon State Hospital as well as the criminal justice and mental health processes, and the decisions and perspectives of various staff members that led to these individuals being treated in the mental health system rather than the criminal justice system. The preview for the film tells us that

> the stories tell a larger tale of broken lives and raggedy safety nets, and the craziness of an American system where you have to commit a crime to get psychiatric help. The film movingly portrays the deeply human dilemmas behind public images of the criminally insane, and probes the consequences of the American medical management of madness.
>
> Haaken (2010)

Psychosocial criminology

As Jenks (2003) points out, madness is recognised as a motive for transgression but is also 'mitigation for having transgressed' and ultimately must be 'contained and governed' (p. 136). Crossley's (2004) sociological research in this area draws on Foucault (2006) and highlights the ways that the mental health system, a vast and complex infrastructure, is underpinned by 'a monopoly of expertise, authority and rights of treatment' (Crossley, 2004, p. 163) that is reinforced and embodied by some of the most explicitly coercive practices observable in democratic societies (e.g. compulsory detention without trial and compulsory treatment with mind-altering drugs and ECT). Much of the power of psychiatry is a symbolic power of definition and judgement, and its violence is the symbolic violence of stigmatisation and disqualification (ibid.).

Psychoanalytic approaches to crime and punishment are gaining ground in criminology but until recently have not been part of the mainstream despite the fact that there is both a long history and diversity of psychosocial perspectives on deviance. Indeed Brown states that 'despite the influence of psychoanalysis on the twentieth-century history of criminology each paradigm within criminology has its reasons to dismiss psychoanalytic ideas' (2003, p. 421). This is because, as Brown (2003) documents, on the one hand, historically, the psychoanalytic lens in criminology has tended towards 'correctionalism and conservatism', or is described as 'unscientific' and 'associated with a retreat from politics' primarily due to a dominant focus on intra-psychic worlds and hence individualism.

On the other hand, the development of a psychodynamic approach within criminology that takes analysis beyond the intra-psychic towards the interpersonal and hence the social is very useful and pertinent to understanding crime, deviance and criminal justice processes and practices. Hence,

> [p]sychodynamic ideas can assist us to examine the processes of criminalization, to examine violent institutions and the pervasiveness of retribution and punitiveness. Such an approach extends beyond the realm of family and intimate relations, beyond individual biographies and beyond the Sociology of the emotions. Moreover, it opens up for exploration the relationship between criminality, social taboos on weakness and fear and the nature of security offered (or not) by the institutions of late modern societies.
>
> Brown (2003, p. 434)

Within the context of the recent postmodern/late modern turns in criminological and social theory[2] the psychosocial turn (Frogatt and Hollway, 2010; Hollway and Jefferson, 2000) rightly takes its place within contemporary analysis of crime, deviance and social justice. Moreover, it could be argued that psychosocial approaches do in fact integrate the recent turns to culture, biography and emotion, ushering in a renewed period in understanding and problematising crime, criminality and crime control. Hollway (2008, p. 2) provides a useful distinction between psychoanalytic and psychosocial approaches:

> The reason for calling this research psycho-social, rather than just Psychoanalytic, is to emphasise that the social and societal parts of analysis should be inextricable from the psychoanalytic. Whereas the relational turn has often emphasised just that – relationality (among people in both the external and internal worlds), psychosocial research attempts also to situate this explicitly in the societal settings involved.

Gadd and Jefferson offer a similar definition arguing that, to date, criminology offers 'inadequate conceptualizations of the subject' (2007, p. 1) and there is a vital need for a 'more adequately theorized psycho-social subject' (ibid.) in order to better understand the causes of crime but also related issues such as victimisation and punishment. It is important to Gadd and Jefferson to 'hang on to both the psychic and the social, without collapsing the one into the other' (ibid., p. 4).

Taking up Gadd and Jefferson, and Brown's challenges, this chapter critically examines Haaken's film, her methodology, the processes of criminalisation and the constructions of deviance, care and control in the individual lives she documents, the account of the criminal justice processes that are given, and the care and control offered by Oregon State Hospital.

Guilty Except for Insanity: A film by Janice Haaken

In a public screening of the film at Durham University, UK, in 2010, Haaken described the film as raising awareness of the fact that the guilty except for insanity plea as a defence in criminal cases is associated with a long history of public controversy. The film focuses upon the inmates and the staff at Oregon State Hospital in Portland, USA; the processes at work in pleading guilty except for insanity; the lived experiences of five of the inmates and for some, their transition into families and communities. Here Haaken, tells us that the majority of patients are there because they have pleaded 'guilty except for reason of insanity'.

In Haaken's (2008) work there is 'a close affinity between psychoanalysis and radical politics', in that both are concerned 'with subtexts and knowledge at the margins of what is most readily noticed'. Indeed, 'any radical project of social change requires means of re-interpreting the world and of generating working understandings of anxieties and defences associated with social change. Radicals, like good therapists, must be able to locate sites of conflict, consider the timing and framing of interpretations, and convey a sense of hope and possibility for change.' (Haaken, 2008, p. xx). Haaken's filmic work and research is deeply psychosocial, documenting and analysing subjectivity within the context of historical and social forces. Her documentary film *Guilty Except for Insanity* (2010) is a good example of cultural analysis in action that combines social theory and psychoanalysis that is deeply rooted in Haaken's ethnographic experiences and analytic understanding as clinician, academic and activist.

Haaken's film, on general release in 2012, tells the stories of five people who entered Oregon State Hospital having pleaded guilty except for insanity following deviant or criminal acts that led to their arrest. It explores their processing by the criminal justice system;

their evaluation and treatment by the mental health system; and the subsequent control of their bodies, behavior and existence in a total institution – Oregon State Hospital for the criminally insane. While the secure hospital is managing the risks associated with the borders and boundaries of the system as well as the behaviour of the patients and side effects of the multiple psychiatric drugs, the patients are managing grief, loss, their status as partial citizens, abjection, the effects of the drugs, as well as living together in a total institution. The institution is governed by the State under the management of mental health professionals at varying levels and the intersections with criminal justice.

The film tells a story of the tension between the criminal justice system and the mental health system, the processes and structures involved in the journeys of the five individuals who worked with Haaken and her team. It also engages the psychiatric staff and the criminal justice agencies, including the police and attorneys, who, in talking with Haaken, make sense of their roles and decisions in the tensions between criminal justice and mental health care. What becomes obvious is that the lack of community mental health care means that some people only gain the mental health support they need by committing a crime. One of the inmates is a young man called Nick. Nick is described by his Father as having been a popular, sporty boy who was happy until he went to high school. Then, everything changed when he experienced the onset of bipolar disease. Nick himself tells how early one morning he was driving his car, with his foot all the way to the floor and he hit a bend and crashed. In the process he could have hurt himself or others. He was lucky, he survived, but was arrested and charged. He was very scared of going to prison. His Dad tells us that the only way they could get him help was to take him to the state hospital, but the only way they could get him there was if he committed a crime.

Haaken's film engages in a deeply human way with each of the people involved and gives the viewer access into the system, the institution and the hopes and meaning-making practices of the five people assigned the status of patient, as well as the mental health professionals who shared their stories. Before looking more closely at the film and the role of deviance, care and control in the lives of the five people who took part, it is important to understand what it means to plead guilty except for insanity.

The Insanity Defence: The *McNaughton* rule – not knowing right from wrong

The Insanity Defence requires lack of awareness of what a person is doing and so cannot form intent to do wrong. The first legal case for insanity took place in England in 1843 in the *McNaughton* case. Daniel McNaughton shot and killed Edward Drummond (secretary to the Prime Minister Sir Robert Peel) in an attempt to kill Peel. In court his lawyers argued that he was insane and did not understand what he was doing. The court acquitted McNaughton 'by reason of insanity', and he was placed in a mental institution for the rest of his life. However, the case caused a public uproar, and Queen Victoria ordered the court to develop a stricter test for insanity. Later that year the House of Lords issued the McNaughton Rule and this became the standard form of insanity defence. The 'McNaughton Rule' was a standard to be applied by the jury, after hearing medical testimony from prosecution and defence experts. The rule created a presumption of sanity, unless the defence proved 'at the time of committing the act, the accused was labouring under such a defect of reason, from disease of the mind, as not to know the nature and quality of the act he was doing or, if he did know it, that he did not know what he was doing was wrong'. The US adopted this defence also and the Insanity Defence Reform Act 1984 that followed the assassination attempt on President Reagan requires the defendant suffer from *severe* mental defect, and places the burden on the defendant to prove it. There are currently three states Montana, Idaho and Utah that do not allow the insanity defence at all.

Recently in the UK, the insanity defence plea came under scrutiny when Germaine Greer argued that the jury in the case of John Hogan (who threw himself off a hotel balcony with his children in 2008, following his wife's decision to end their relationship) was wrong to accept a guilty except for insanity verdict. Here sexual politics – the tensions between gender-based crime and the inequalities in the treatment of men and women who kill their partners – are central to Greer's (2008) argument. In a rejoinder a few days after Greer's article, Kinton (2008) argued that the concept of the insanity defence must be upheld: 'There are common, if extreme, depressive states that have psychotic and delusional characteristics, from which people can recover, and which can and do form the basis of a legal insanity defence, in this country and across the world.' The Internet discussion threads responding to the latter article were extremely critical of the success of the insanity defence in this case, reinforcing the criminal, abject and stigmatised aspects of Hogan's crime and story and the contested nature of understandings of sanity and insanity. These complex issues are raised in Haaken's film.

The tensions between criminal justice and mental health care

In Haaken's film the interviews with psychiatrists and forensic psychiatrists are compelling and illuminate the complexities involved in deciding whether or not someone is guilty except for insanity (GEI). What becomes clear is by pleading GEI the person is stating that she/he is guilty. At the first point of arrest, depending upon what the arresting office decides, a person could either be processed by the criminal justice system and sent to prison, or sent for an evaluation (known in Oregon as a 370 evaluation) at the state mental hospital. This important first step could make the difference between prison and a secure mental health institution. After having had the plea for GEI accepted on the basis of the evaluation, the person is given the maximum sentence and will only be released having moved successfully through the various transition phases under the careful scrutiny and monitoring of the Psychiatric Review Board. The latter are described in Haaken's film as extremely conservative in relation to deciding to release people into the community.

Moreover, the *Diagnostic and Statistical Manual of Mental Disorders* (DSM), the criteria for the classification of mental disorders, published by the American Psychiatric Association (which totals over 900 pages) includes five axes or dimensions relating to various conditions. Axis One includes mostly bipolar and psychotic conditions, which are more likely to support a guilty except for insanity plea than Axis Two disorders, which are largely personality disorders. The DSM reflects an approach to mental illness that categorises people into two major camps when it comes to categorising intent. According to one of the clinical psychiatrists Haaken interviewed, personality disorders are more likely to be processed by the criminal justice system as this category is thought to be somehow more intentional than Axis One disorders. One could argue that personality disorders make people more abject because they do not easily or clearly fit into binary understandings of sanity/insanity. For Haaken, the prisons are the bottom layer of the state security net for mental health sufferers (see also Wacquant, 2009).

Biographical narratives and film-making

The stories of the inmates at Oregon State Hospital are tragic and deeply moving. Haaken's film enables the viewer to engage with lives damaged by tragedy, mental health problems and, for some, harmful social or familial relationships. One young man, David begins his narrative by saying: 'I am in the mental health system and not the criminal justice system because of a tragic accident and pleading guilty except for insanity.' We learn that David was a graduate in chemistry. He developed depression at university and describes 'a dark gloomy cloud descending on me, the undertow sucked me under and I was drowning'. His relationship with his Father was troubled and he blames his Father for his problems. During an argument, his Father threatened him and David lost control, he was feeling disturbed, deeply disturbed and fearful and he shot his Father. He then describes the stress and loss in the aftermath, the loss of his Father, his life, his employment and his family with whom there was no longer any contact.

Tino's story is similarly tragic. He was working in construction and was sheeting a roof and describes feeling irritated and harassed by his co-workers, he fell through the roof and was told that he pulled out a claw hammer and hit the guy he was working with. Although he was arrested there and then he has no memory of the incident; he had fallen through two floors. He only remembers calling his brother to say he was being arrested for assault. Tino was sent for evaluation at Oregon State Hospital and was there initially for one year because he was considered psychotic based on 'an interest in numbers and codes'. He was treated with Haldol. Tino said he wanted to keep his mind busy and so writing things down helped him, he did not consider himself psychotic. He was then sent to prison for one year as his then psychiatrist deemed that because he could define certain concepts he was seen as competent (an Axis Two personality disorder) and so competent to go back to court and jail. He was returned to the hospital and at the time of film-making was refusing psychiatric medications and asking to be treated psycho-therapeutically. Given the regimes under which the treatment and medication of inmates takes place, this was a brave stand. His psychiatrist asked whether they place him (i.e. give him treatment) or wait until he takes the medication. Because of this choice, he would more than likely never be released and would only get as far as transition to the independent cottage in the hospital grounds.

Tamara was being stalked by her son's father and describes this turning into a really bad situation. He took the car apart so she couldn't drive it, went through the grocery list telling her why she should not buy things. She talks about everything falling apart, her anxiety for her son, who was hard to manage at this time and her anxiety about violence. She states that in the end it was she who was violent – she shot her son.

What Haaken's film shows so well are that mental illness and the hospital serve as a repository of fear and abjection. Such liminal places help to secure the borders of society and define what is normal. In the public imagination, Oregon State Hospital, forever connected to *One Flew Over the Cuckoo's Nest*, is a place where risk and harm are managed and contained but also where resistance to institutionalisation was highlighted.

Some of the participants talk about feeling uptight on the ward and that these feelings make them feel unsafe and so hypervigilant. Tino states that this feeling reminds him of home, feeling unsafe, being on constant alert. Tino's vulnerability, his ethnicity as Latino, his gentle nature and fear of bullying mark him out as Other in the outside world and in the hospital. On the other hand, the hospital is also a place of safety (as well as fear and anxiety), and can serve as a holding environment. When Tino is placed in a cottage in the hospital grounds, the pleasure in his eyes is clear. He talks to Haaken about waking up and looking out of the window to see what the weather is like, remembering what it is like to wake up and go for a walk and stand in the weather, and imagines being on his back porch drinking coffee – although he states, 'I can't do that here.'

The razor wire, bars, locked doors, use of restraint and sound of the heavy doors banging shut add to the experience of the hospital environment. As one psychiatrist says, this is a micro-society with it lots of boundaries. When you throw together a lot of challenging people can bring out the best and the worst in them. This is reflected in the use of restraint and the experiences of restraint. For Tamara, being restrained was one of the worst things she had ever gone through. For another young woman, Brandy, it was comforting – she prefers restraint to being put in a side room in solitary and describes the body armour she is wearing, a tight lycra suit, imposed to stop her self-harming. She describes feeling protected by the suit: 'like someone is holding you and you feel you get this great big hug'. She goes on to say that for 'people who did not have a motherly or even a fatherly person in their life who would hug you, this is very helpful'. Brandy is due for release in 2024 and is nervous about leaving the hospital for a group home; she describes institutionalisation as a wonderful thing. 'Going to look at a place in the real world away from the razor wire is difficult. Hopefully I will go with open arms and things will be cool.'

The tension between deviance, care and control is complex and clearly if community mental health services were available to David, Tino, Tamara, Brandy and Nick they might not be in Oregon State Hospital.

The role of film in psychosocial analysis and cultural criminology

Watching Haaken's film at a special screening at Durham University encouraged us to reflect upon the change causing potential of art and filmic texts and the way that film has the capacity to engage our senses, pierce us in the sense that Barthes speaks of in using the concept 'punctum'. They can bring us in touch with lived experience in ways that move us, make us think in more deeply engaged ways that may also motivate us to act, speak out and mobilise for change. *Guilty Except for Insanity* is a remarkable and inspiring film and certainly focuses attention on the transformative role and capacity of art – in this case film – and the importance of biographical narratives and the usefulness of participatory approaches.

Based upon social action research, interdisciplinary analysis and digital video, the film raises awareness about the loss of community mental health services and the management of risk through the mental health system, in this case secure hospitals. It is also counter-hegemonic, in that it offers representational challenges. People are given spaces to speak where they otherwise would not have them. They have situational authority in the film, the film-maker is an absent presence and this offers humanising challenges to dominant hegemonic stereotypes of madness, badness and criminality that are usually demonstrated through abjection, liminality and Otherness.

In reflecting on the film and psychosocial analysis, there are connections between Haaken's work and the work of Tom Scheff (2010) and Alfred Lorenzer (1981), which taken together underscore the need for a psychosocial criminology. All three are eminent examples of psychosocial approaches rooted in psychoanalysis, but with a clear analytic understanding of the interpersonal, cultural, biographical, historical and social dimensions of their analysis.

Scheff's (2010) focus on labelling, normalising and attunement are particularly pertinent in relation to the personal biographies of the five participants in Haaken's film and the participatory ways that she conducted the film-making – working with people, and using music made by the inmates as the soundtrack to the film. The work of Lorenzer is highly relevant to the turn to emotion, culture and the psychosocial in criminology. Like Scheff, Lorenzer understands people as embodied, individual, relational and social, and although these exist in tension, they are for him 'mutually constitutive – that is to say, they are made and remade in ongoing dialectical relations' (cited in Bereswill, Morgenroth and Redman, 2010, p. 222).

Lorenzer's work is little known to English speaking criminologists and much of it is untranslated, but a recent special issue of *Psychoanalysis, Culture & Society* (2010) brings his work and contemporary analyses of it to Anglophone academic communities. Lorenzer, who died in 2002, was a Marxist, psychoanalyst and cultural theorist connected to the Frankfurt School. He is described by Redman, Bereswill and Morgenroth (2010, p. 213) as placing psychoanalysis on a materialist footing and is a significant intellectual figure in post-World War II Germany. He defined his psychoanalytically informed approach to cultural research as the 'depth-hermeneutic method'. This method did not just import psychoanalytic technique into non-clinical settings but rather in the depth-hermeneutic method he developed tools for cultural and social research, such as 'scenic understanding, a process by which researchers reflect on their affective and embodied experience of their data ... Lorenzer himself applied his psychoanalytically informed ... method to the analysis of literary texts' (ibid., p. 217). The claim that cultural (and other) texts work on or provoke the reader – and that attending to this process is an important aspect of a researcher's task – is central to Lorenzer's thesis. In fact, it is at the heart of the depth-hermeneutic method itself (Bereswill, Morgenroth and Redman, 2010, p. 223). In the next section we focus on Scheff and Lorenzer and the usefulness of their work for cultural criminological analysis of madness and liminality and the tensions between deviance, care and control.

Tom Scheff: Labelling, normalising and attunement

Thomas Scheff pioneered analysis of our emotional-relational worlds, specifically the labelling theory of mental illness and how this relates to restorative justice, violence, shame and humiliation. In a recent paper Scheff (2010) returns to his earlier work on labelling theory that

> sought to challenge the medical model of what is called mental illness with a social model. In this model symptoms of mental illness are recast as violations of residual rules: social norms so taken for granted that they go without saying. Most social rules, perhaps, are largely invisible.
>
> p. 1

Scheff develops his work on normalising as the opposite of labelling, suggesting that being more aware of the transformative and destructive possibilities of both might not only help people to be better therapists and teachers, leading to changes in medical, psychotherapeutic institutions but might also 'help both individuals and societies grow and prosper' (Scheff 2010, p. 7).

A key effect of labelling, Scheff states, is implied by Goffman's concept of facework – 'the saving or losing face. When one is labelled, one loses face and gains embarrassment, shame or humiliation. There is a social-emotional element in all human contact' (ibid., p. 2). To explain, Scheff draws on Robert Fuller's (2003) work on somebody and nobody feelings: 'We feel like a somebody when we are accepted, and like a nobody when we are not' (Scheff, 2010, p. 2). The social-emotional process is complex as both flagrant and subtle rejections exacerbate the nobody feelings, and feeling accepted and connected can be hard to achieve in social life. Scheff talks about the state of being accepted, or connected, using terms such as 'attunement' and 'shared or mutual awareness'. He uses a filmic example, *Lars and the Real Girl*, to elaborate on the concept of normalizing as the opposite of labelling.

Lars and the Real Girl

Scheff describes the film as 'teaching a powerful lesson: how a community might manage mental illness without the social side-effects' (2010, p. 3). We quote Scheff at length here:

> The crucial moments occur early in the film. Because Lars has been treating a life-size doll as a real person, his brother, Gus, and sister-in-law, Karin, bring him to their family doctor. Early in the session, the Doctor asks:
>
> > Has Lars been functional, does he go to work, wash, dress himself?
> > Gus: So far.
> > Doctor: Has he had any violent episodes?
> > Karin: Oh no, no never. He's a sweetheart – he never even raises his voice.
>
> This dialogue establishes the limits the film sets to normalizing: able to take care of self, unlikely to harm self or others. However, there are many other limits that must be set in order to avoid enabling. For example, does he take drugs?
>
> Gus: Okay, we got to fix him. Can you fix him?
> Doctor Dagmar: I don't know, Gus. I don't believe he's psychotic or schizophrenic. I don't think this is caused by genes or faulty wiring in the brain.
> (Preliminary normalizing statement, rejecting diagnosis)
> Gus: So then what the hell is going on then?
> Doctor: He appears to have a delusion.
> Gus: A delusion? What the hell is he doing with a delusion for Christ's sake?
> (Gus's manner implies that Lars's behaviour is abnormal)
> Doctor: You know, this isn't necessarily a bad thing. What we call mental illness isn't always just an illness. It can be a communication, it can be a way to work something out.
> (This is the doctor's central normalizing statement: Lars is not abnormal, he is just communicating)
> Gus: Fantastic, when will it be over?
> Doctor: When he doesn't need it anymore.

In this fable, Lars has been scripted to find an extraordinarily unconventional doctor ... A vast difference of outlook separates the great majority of labelling physicians from the few normalizing ones ... A much more likely response to Lars in real life would have been for the doctor to say:

'OK. Let's start him on an anti-psychotic medication, since we don't want his symptoms to get worse.' If Karin had said, 'But what about side effects? Aren't they sometimes more dangerous than the illness?' The doctor: 'Karin, I'm sure you realize that he could become much more ill, or even violent.'

For drama and comedy, the film enlists the whole community to help Lars. But in real life, perhaps fewer people would be needed; even one person might be enough. Jay Neugeboren (1999) investigated many cases in which there was great improvement or complete recovery from what had been diagnosed as 'serious mental illness.' The common thread he found was that at least one person treated the afflicted one with respect, sticking by him or her through thick or thin.

Scheff (2010, pp. 2–3)

Normalising is thus for Scheff an important corrective to the labelling theory of mental illness, embedded in a deep understanding of the emotional-relational worlds of people for whom connection or attunement are hard to achieve. Using Stern's concept of *attunement* Scheff (2007) refers to the cognitive, connectivity between people and argues that emotions and social bonds might play an important if disguised role in political mobilisation. For Scheff the emotional-relational world is important 'since it constitutes the moment-by-moment texture of our lives' and 'it is intimately linked to the larger world; it both causes and is caused by that world' (2007, p. 2). In *Lars and the Real Girl*, Lars works through the unconscious emotions, including grief, that underpin his delusion with the help of his family and community who treat him and the doll as normal, helping to foster connection, communication and attunement.

In Haaken's film we gain access to the emotional-relational worlds of the five individuals who shared their biographies, their stories. How different might their lives have been if they had had access to the kind of care, support and treatment offered by clinicians such as Scheff or indeed Doctor Dagmar? The reality is that Tino, Brandy and David clearly did not enjoy the familial support and holding that family and the community offer so unconditionally in *Lars and the Real Girl*. Brandy sees restraint and the wearing of body armour as akin to a hug. Tino relates the tension and hostility he experienced on the ward with being at home. For David the relationship with his father led to his depression and to him committing murder. What we know is that with murder there is a low rate of re-offending, the trauma involved in the act and the criminal justice consequences ensure this is the case. For Tamara the destructive relationship with her jealous and abusive husband led to her falling apart and everything falling apart. The madness and liminality represented in *Guilty Except for Insanity*, and the secure mental hospital institution, changes shape under the individuals' engagement with Haaken the filmmaker and researcher. We become attuned to the people who tell their stories; we are able to engage in an embodied sense with their emotional-relational worlds. And, in the process of making the film, what is absolutely clear is that the participants are treated with dignity, respect and recognition, and the film becomes a holding space. The film directly highlights the need for focusing attention on community mental health care, for creating spaces for the subjugated knowledge and voices of recipients of mental health and those who need mental healthcare, and for building community mental health around psychosocial understandings and practice.

Reflecting back on the historical limitations of psychoanalysis for criminology Brown (2003) suggested that there was too much of a focus upon the individual and correctionalism at the expense of the wider psychosocial issues; yet for Haaken (2008, 2010), Scheff (2010) and also Lorenzer (2002), it is important to reflect upon the social aspects, not just for the individual, but for social life more generally. Via critical psychosocial analysis, one is more likely to reflect upon transformative or utopian possibilities for social life. Hence, for Lorenzer, the differences between clinical and cultural psychoanalytic research are as follows:

> If the function of clinical work is to identify what an individual patient finds difficult or troubling to symbolise, and to make a therapeutic response to this difficulty, the function of social research is to identify the specifically social factors present in

failures of symbolisation and to reflect on the consequences of these failures for social life. For Lorenzer, an important aspect of this socially orientated task lay in uncovering that which resists the unsatisfactory character of existing social arrangements. In particular, he was concerned to identify the utopian potential present in scenic material that is excluded from symbolisation: the conceptions of life [Lebensentwurf] that indicate the possibility of a better world.

p. 28, quoted in Bereswill, Morgenroth and
Redman (2010, p. 224)

Psychosocial and fictive transgressions

At one level Lorenzer's work, alongside Scheff's and Haaken's, has a number of implications for our understanding of the state of community mental health care and the tensions between deviance, care and control in both the criminal justice system and the mental health system in Western societies. First, the narration/story that unfolds is likely to contain a latent meaning. Second, this latent meaning is likely to provoke us as readers – to play on our subjective experience of the story and focusing upon this we may gain further insight. Third, some aspect of this latent meaning is collective in nature, perhaps relating to that which is excluded from representation in the wider culture.

For ourselves, the latent meaning resides in the alienated lives lived by Tino, Brandy, Tamara and David in particular. Reflection on the latent meaning provokes reflection upon the issue and importance of relationships of mattering, of being connected, of being held and supported, in the way that the community offers Lars in Scheff's analysis. The collective process and the importance of collectivities for our societies, for living livable lives is vital, as well as for balancing trust and risk, crime and sanctions. A focus on connecting, attunement and the role of restorative justice offers an important corrective to the cold checks and balances of the globalised, neo-liberal systems of twenty-first century Western societies, which create what Wacquant (2009) terms 'prisons of poverty'. A psychosocial criminological perspective enables us to shift attention from a psychoanalytic focus on the individual intra-psychic realm to one that addresses the collective social, cultural dimension of our lives together, our being in common, and helps us to explore the place of psychosocial matters in our personal and collective lives. Using a psychosocial and cultural analysis to challenge the reproduction of sexual and social inequalities may also enable us to imagine a radically democratic future, based upon principles of connection, attunement and mattering – and in the process to uncover and address that which is excluded from representation and wider social life. The next chapter analyses a cultural representation of extreme 'badness' – the figure of the serial killer.

6
Serial Killers and the Ethics of Representation

In the late twentieth century, the figure of the serial killer became culturally ubiquitous and 'a flashpoint in contemporary society' (Seltzer, 1998, p. 2). He (serial killers are usually male) was depicted across a profusion of films, television programmes and novels (Jarvis, 2007) and narratives based on serial killing developed into a genre of their own (Simpson, 2000). The news media enthusiastically seized on such cases, through which they articulated stories of good battling evil and cautionary tales about the nature of modern society (Fleming, 2007). Serial killers became celebrities at the centre of an industry, exemplified by the market for 'murderabilia' – artefacts that belonged to famous serial killers, such as bricks from Jeffrey Dahmer's apartment and locks of Charles Manson's hair (Schmid, 2005; Haggerty, 2009). According to Seltzer (1998), this fascination is indicative of changing relations between self and society in the mid to late twentieth century. He argues '[t]he spectacular public representation of violated bodies, across a burgeoning range of official, academic, and media accounts, in fiction and in film, has come to function as a way of imagining the relations of private bodies and private persons to public spaces' (Seltzer, 1998, p. 21). This chapter examines the development of the serial killer as a 'cultural flashpoint' and the blurring of fact and fiction that this has entailed. It identifies four main interpretations of the serial killer's cultural importance and then analyses three recent portrayals in film and television that attempt to subvert dominant representations. Finally, the chapter assesses how far these recent portrayals offer new ways of representing serial killing.

Defining the serial killer

There is no single definition of the serial killer, but one that frequently appears in the criminological literature is the killing of four or more victims 'by one or a few individuals attempting to satisfy personal desires, such as power, profit, revenge, sex, loyalty, or control' (Fox and Levin, 1998, pp. 407–8). Serial murder 'spans a period of days, weeks, months, or even years', distinguishing it from mass or spree killings, which have no 'cooling off' period (ibid., p. 410). Robert Ressler, a former FBI investigator, claims to have coined the term 'serial killer' in 1976, inspired by the 'serials' he watched at the cinema as a child, although Jenkins (2002) suggests that conceptualising incidents of crime and violence as occurring 'serially' dates from criminological writing in the 1960s. The definition from Fox and Levin (1998) is applicable to different types of serial murders that could have a range of motivations, but in the popular imagination, 'serial killer' tends to evoke 'savage men hunting down defenseless [sic] women' (Jenkins, 2002, p. 3). The serial killer is a predator motivated by unstoppable sexual desire and is frequently a 'ripper' who mutilates his victims (Jenkins, 1994, 2002; Tithecott, 1997). Jenkins (2002) explores how the notion of the 'sexual predator' became so successful in the United States that in the 1990s, various states passed punitive laws designed to control him, transforming into technical language a term that had largely appeared in fictional narratives previously. There have been many serial killers who do not fit this mould. Harold Shipman, a British doctor who killed over 200 of his elderly patients, is one of the most prolific known cases of a serial murderer, but he did not 'hunt' his victims, or sexually assault them (Wilson, 2007). Those labelled 'serial killers' are not always male, as the cases of Myra Hindley and Aileen Wuornos demonstrate. However, the male sexual predator or 'ripper' is the culturally archetypal serial killer and is the central focus of this chapter. The cultural representation of violent women is discussed in Chapter 3.

Many 'iconic' serial killers predate the mid-1970s coining of the term. The prototype of the sexual predator who hunts down and mutilates his female victims is Jack the Ripper, the unknown perpetrator of the murders of at least five women in 1880s London (Caputi, 1987; Seltzer, 1998). At this time, 'expert' notions of sexual pathology were developing, which provided a frame through which these killings could be understood (Walkowitz, 1982; Cameron and Frazer, 1987). In the 1940s and 50s, the sexually perverted, 'compulsive' killer was a sexual psychopath, prey to 'overwhelming urge[s]' (Karpman, 1954, p. 490 cited in Jenkins, 2002, p. 7). Mid-twentieth century murderers such as John George Haigh, Neville Heath and Ed Gein were constructed in this way, both in legal and media discourses.[1] As Haggerty (2009, p. 169) points out, 'serial killing can appear a-historical and a-cultural', but it is crucial to recognise that it arises from a wider social context. The serial killer is culturally and historically specific (Schmid, 2005) and his emergence as a cultural type is interlinked with the development of modernity, defined by Haggerty (2009, p. 171) as 'entailing a series of distinctive changes in the nature of science, commerce (the rise of capitalism), urbanism, the mass media and personal identity'.

The dependence of the serial killer on modernity can be illustrated by returning to the prototypical example of Jack the Ripper to illustrate the centrality of Haggerty's (2009) themes of urbanism, mass media, scientific expertise and personal identity. This anonymous killer was able to disappear into the urban cityscape of late Victorian London, just one stranger among many (Haggerty, 2009). A burgeoning mass media, in the form of a national press and an increasingly literate population, meant that news of the killings and speculation as to the motivations of their perpetrator, made the imagined 'Jack' famous. As discussed, mental health and sexuality (and the inter-relationship between the two) became increasingly the subject of scientific, expert understandings, leading to changes in the way identity was understood. Jack the Ripper is the prototype of the twentieth-century serial killer because of these recognisably modern features.

More than most crimes, where serial killing is concerned, 'no easy distinction between the 'fact' (reality) or 'fiction' (representation) ... can be drawn' (Simpson, 2000, p. xiv). Fictional representations are often based on real-life cases. Norman Bates from *Psycho* (1960), Leatherface from *The Texas Chainsaw Massacre* (1974 and 2003) and Buffalo Bill from *The Silence of the Lambs* (1991) are all at least partly based on Ed Gein (Grixti, 1995). In 1957, in Plainfield, Wisconsin, it emerged that in addition to killing at least three people, Gein, a local man, had plundered graves for body parts from which he had made masks of skin and furniture from bones. Tithecott (1997) examines the interplay between the film version of *The Silence of the Lambs* and media representations in the case of Jeffrey Dahmer. In 1991, Dahmer, who lived in Milwaukee, Wisconsin, was discovered to have severed heads and other body parts, along with pictures of mutilated corpses, in his apartment. He had practised cannibalism, famously a peccadillo of *The Silence of the Lambs'* Hannibal Lecter. The film of Thomas Harris'1988 novel was released in 1991 and was hugely successful, acting as a reference point for media stories on the Dahmer case, which broke in August of the same year.

In addition to fictional representations interacting with the portrayal of 'real-life' serial killers, they have also influenced the tracking and investigation of such killers. Jenkins (1994) explores how Thomas Harris based the character of FBI agent, Jack Crawford, on a composite of actual FBI detectives, Robert Ressler, John Douglas and Roy Hazelwood who were based at the United States Justice Department's Behavioural Sciences Unit in Quantico, Virginia. This Unit was established in the early 1970s and pioneered the use of profiling and other 'scientific' techniques in attempting to solve cases of serial murder (Jenkins, 1994). According to Douglas, Harris was inspired by sitting in on courses at Quantico, but he also admits that the BSU's antecedents 'go back to crime fiction more than crime fact' (Douglas, 1995, p. 32 quoted in Seltzer, 1998, p. 16). As Jenkins (2002, p. 15) observes, '[i]deas and images travel freely' between criminal justice and fiction 'in a highly postmodern way'. This blurring of fact and fiction means that both actual and fictional cases have contributed to interpretations of the characteristics, and cultural importance, of serial killers.

Characteristics of the serial killer

Contrasting characteristics and functions of the serial killer have been developed in fictional, media and academic portrayals. There are four main analyses of this figure that are important in enhancing our understanding of his cultural representation. These are: the serial killer as an evil genius, as the 'mass in person', as a transgressive outsider, and as an upholder of the social order.

Evil genius

This is one of the most potent and recurrent images of the serial killer, according to which he is powerful, vital, sexual and highly intelligent. The 'evil genius' representation of the serial killer is almost celebratory, and identifies him with masculine virility (Tithecott, 1997). Caputi (1987, p. 30) argues that this awe for the serial killer, which began with Jack the Ripper, transforms him into a mythical figure and 'mysterious force of nature', obfuscating serial killing as gynocide and the product of a patriarchal society. Fictional portrayals 'dramatize the rules of sexual power, imbue their participants with renewed faith or renewed terror, and celebrate that most fundamental patriarchal practice – female sacrifice' (Caputi, 1987, p. 92). The image of the serial killer as powerful and essential supports male domination and feminine subordination.

The apotheosis of the serial killer as evil genius is Harris' Hannibal Lecter (Grixti, 1995). Lecter is a 'genius, vampire and dark angel' (Picart and Greek, 2007, p. 248), a brilliant psychiatrist who also has impeccable taste in wine, food, travel, art and opera. Tithecott (1997) compares the portrayal of the heterosexual Hannibal Lecter in *The Silence of the Lambs* with that of its other serial killer character, Buffalo Bill. Unlike the powerful and impressive Lecter, Buffalo Bill is an effeminate, pathological 'homosexual' who likes to apply make-up and wear women's clothes. Tithecott (1997) observes that although Jeffrey Dahmer's cannibalism recalled Lecter, as a gay man his media portrayal was closer to Buffalo Bill. In *Time* magazine, Prud'homme (1991) made the difference between Dahmer and Lecter clear: 'Unlike Hannibal ("the Cannibal") Lecter, the brilliant mass-murdering psychiatrist in *The Silence of the Lambs*, the creature who apparently turned Apartment 213 into a private slaughterhouse is an unassuming 31-year-old ne'er-do-well named Jeffrey L. Dahmer.' Dahmer, 'unassuming' and a 'ne'er-do-well', cannot be compared with Lecter, the vital genius.

Tithecott (1997) links reactions such as these with homophobic conceptions of gay men as the perverted occupants of an uncivilised, subcultural 'netherworld' that exists in opposition to 'respectable' society. Jeffrey Dahmer departed from the archetype of the serial killer as predator of women, but also from the 'myth' of the serial murderer as the embodiment of male power. Picart and Greek (2007) note that the evil genius trope is only successful when the killer in question is white, middle class, heterosexual and male. Aileen Wuornos, who was lower class, lesbian and female, was perceived as a 'lumbering Frankenstein' rather than a genius (ibid., p. 253). Chapter 3 explores her case in more detail.

Mass in person

Contrary to the serial killer as possessing the remarkable qualities of an evil genius, he is instead 'abnormally normal' or 'extraordinarily ordinary' (Seltzer, 1998). Like American serial killer John Wayne Gacy,[2] he can appear to those who know him as a conventional neighbour and member of the local community. He is the 'mass in person', a cipher whose killing represents in microcosm the routinised patterns, repetitions and counting behaviours of industrial and post-industrial modern societies (ibid.). Dennis Nilsen, convicted in 1983 of murdering six men and attempting to murder two others, was an outwardly unexceptional civil servant living and working in London. Nilsen described himself as the 'monochrome man' (Seltzer, 1998, p. 10), which was underlined by his archetypally ordinary job as a cog in the bureaucratic machinery of the modern state. The film *Se7en* (1995) provides an example of the serial killer as cipher in the form of John Doe, whose very name signals his character's blankness and lack of any discernible motivation in carrying out a moral crusade to kill victims according to whether they have committed one of the seven deadly sins. Both Doe's actions, and the human failings of his victims, merely serve to highlight the moral destitution of the large, unidentified American city in which he lives.

The repetitious nature of serial killing and the fact that such killers often display predilections for particular types of victim or ways of killing them, sometimes even retaining keepsakes or body parts as 'trophies', have led scholars to identify parallels between serial killing and capitalistic consumerism (Grixti, 1995; Lefebvre, 2005; Jarvis, 2007). The serial murderer's powerful desire for acquisition mirrors that of the 'normal' consumer on a shopping spree (Jarvis, 2007). Lefebvre (2005, p. 51) argues that 'serial killers turn their victims into serial objects, no different in that regard from the object-types produced on the assembly line and consumed in large surface retail stores – that is, objects of *serial consumption*' (italics in original). Therefore, not only is the serial killer himself an anonymous figure, he also removes the humanity and subjectivity of his victims, turning them into disposable things instead of people. This is symbolised especially clearly by serial killers who cannibalise their victims because '[r]ead allegorically, they show us what happens to human bodies as they are incessantly fed to us in advertising, in fashion, in images of all sorts, and also in medicine' (Lefebvre, 2005, pp. 51–2).

This link between serial killing and consumerism is made in Brett Easton Ellis' satire on corporate 1980s America, *American Psycho* (1991). Patrick Bateman, the psycho in question, works in 'mergers and acquisitions' (or 'murders and executions' as he refers to it) and fits seamlessly into his surroundings as a high-earning, highly educated, upper middle-class, white American male. Bateman is both a voracious consumer and a voracious killer. He describes in meticulous detail progressively violent murders alongside banalities such as his skin moisturisation routine, favourite pop stars and the optimum way to cook a pizza. It is crucial that Bateman is ordinary in his milieu as Ellis excoriates rapacious capitalism by confronting us with Bateman's cruelty and savagery (Jarvis, 2007).

Transgressive outsider

The serial killer as transgressive outsider also develops themes of anonymity in mass society, but instead of interpreting serial killers as exemplars of routinised modernity, their actions become a means of transgressing and transcending everyday life. Rather than being continuous with the modern self, the serial killer is a novelty (King, 2006). To return to the example of *American Psycho*, King (2006, p. 116) argues it is only in the 'moments of intense bodily transgression' that Bateman experiences when killing that he can express his identity and escape 'the mass [which] threatens [him] with boredom and anonymity'. The surface normality of many serial killers intensifies the transgressive nature of their acts. Ted Bundy, who confessed to murdering more than 30 American women in the mid-1970s, 'was particularly disorienting to many because he looked so decent and ... he seemed to epitomize many of the most cherished American notions of wholesomeness' (Grixti, 1995, p. 89). The serial killer represents the evil that can lurk behind normality (Simpson, 2000). Although he has the appearance of a human, his actions are demonic, making him a human/monster hybrid after the fashion of vampires and werewolves. Not knowing which among us might be the serial killer means that he becomes a focus for 'free-floating social anxiety' (Simpson, 2000, p. 6).

This anxiety can be engineered and exploited to serve ideological and bureaucratic ends. Jenkins (1994) delineates how the FBI propagated and utilised the serial killer threat in the 1980s to expand and gain greater resources, while the Republican 'new right' highlighted serial killers as an example of post-1960s' cultural degradation. The construction of serial killers as latter-day monsters reassures us

> about the rightness of the current state of civilized society, since the monsters repeatedly emerge as the exceptions that make the rule, the chinks and cracks in the social fabric that ... are actually made to remind us of the structural soundness of the fabric itself.
>
> Grixti (1995, p. 95)

Therefore, serial killer panic often serves conservative ends. However, there is a cultural ambivalence because the serial killer's ability to slough off the bonds of civilisation is also exciting. He represents an 'elemental existence where one may be free' but also poses the threat of becoming one of his victims (Simpson, 2000, p. 5). For Simpson (2000), he satisfies the audience's desires for both the culturally forbidden and the socially conservative.

Upholder of social order

Rather than transgressing society's boundaries, serial killers can be interpreted as helping to keep them in place. Their victims are disproportionately drawn from marginalised and culturally devalued social groups, meaning that serial killing can be perceived as reinforcing the dominant social order (Haggerty, 2009). As touched upon in the section on the serial killer as evil genius, radical feminist critiques of serial killing, which identify it as belonging to a continuum of male violence against women in patriarchal society, make this argument. Serial killing helps to uphold the dominant order of male supremacy and is not an aberration but rather an extreme form of the social control of women through fear and terror (Cameron and Frazer, 1987; Caputi, 1987). This is supported by the fact that not only does the violence itself exhibit extreme misogyny, but serial killers sometimes view themselves as having a divine mission to rid the streets of perceived immoral and undesirable women. Jouve (1986) examines how Peter Sutcliffe, a British serial killer also known as the 'Yorkshire Ripper', described himself as 'cleaning up the streets' and claimed to have been told by God to kill prostitutes. This contempt for his victims extended beyond Sutcliffe to the police, who only began to take the case seriously when he killed 'innocent' women, in other words, women who did not work as prostitutes.

The cultural devaluation of the victims of serial killers extends beyond issues of gender inequality (although according to Egger (2002), women who work as prostitutes account for the largest portion of victims killed by serial killers). Egger (2002, p. 80) explains how

the victims of serial killers, viewed when alive as part of a devalued stratum of humanity, become 'less-dead' (since for many they were 'less-alive' before their death and now become the 'never-were'), and their demise is experienced as the elimination of sores or blemishes cleansed by those who dare to wash away these undesirable elements.

Typically, the 'less-dead' comprise 'prostitutes, homosexuals, street people, runaways, or the elderly' (Egger, 2002, p. 81). They are disproportionately vulnerable to serial killers because of their marginalised social position. Gary Ridgway, the 'Green River Killer', murdered over 70 women in Washington State in the 1980s and 90s. Most of them either worked as prostitutes or were runaways, making it relatively easy for Ridgway to pick them up, but also less likely that their disappearance would be investigated or even noticed. Wilson (2007) argues that Harold Shipman was able to kill so many victims (more than 200) because it was not only less suspicious for elderly people to die, they were also people viewed as having low social worth.

That the victims of serial killers are frequently economically inactive (older and homeless people) or employed illegitimately (sex workers) means that serial murder can be understood as a form of 'capitalist recreation', where economic categories perceived as enemies are destroyed (Newitz, 1997 cited in Simpson, 2000). Haggerty (2009, p. 179) draws on Agamben (1995) to analyse how 'cultural frameworks of denigration' mark certain groups of people as social pariahs and undeserving of the law's protection. Those positioned as liminal, such as female sex workers, are seen as lesser human beings (see Chapter 4 for a more developed discussion). Serial murderers '[t]hrough a distorted mirror ... reflect back, and act upon, modernity's distinctive valuations' (Haggerty, 2009, p. 180).

These four interpretations demonstrate that the figure of the serial killer is heavily symbolic and also polysemic, capable of representing contradictory or opposing forces, such as order/disorder, transgression/upholding boundaries (Simpson, 2000). Jenkins (1994) argues that the serial killer in the 1980s was totemic for different, seemingly irreconcilable social and political causes, ranging from the conservative 'new right' to radical feminism. This ability for images of the serial killer to carry different meanings and symbols will inform the analysis in this chapter of three recent fictional representations. The first example, *The Killer Inside Me* (2010), is a film shown through the eyes of a psychopathic murderer. The analysis explores how far it adheres to or departs from familiar representations of the serial killer. The second and third examples, television drama *Five*

Daughters (2010) and the film *Jindabyne* (2006) have been chosen because they decentre the figure of serial killer, rewriting the conventions of his cultural representation.

The Killer Inside Me

This film is an adaptation of Jim Thompson's 1952 pulp fiction thriller, which Seltzer (1998, p. 159) describes as 'a remarkable prototype novel of compulsive killing'. As such, the film is based on a depiction that precedes Hannibal Lecter and the 1980s' cult of the serial killer, and reaches back to the era of the 'sexual psychopath'. Seltzer (1998) analyses Thompson's novel as an example of the 'popular psychology' of the serial killer. Its protagonist, Lou Ford, a small-town deputy sheriff, is the killer as 'mass in person'. His name recalls the Model T car, the mid-twentieth-century emblem of American industrialised society and mass production; he inhabits the anonymous sounding 'Central City', a 'hyper-typical American place' (Seltzer, 1998, p. 160). Lou is a clichéd character who narrates his own story in clichés. Although a psychopath, his pathology is the sickness of his times. He conforms to 'a normal madness' of the mass society (ibid., p. 162), where the 'inside' of the self becomes public, leaving only a void.

The 2010 film is faithful to its source matter, retaining Lou Ford's first person narration and telling the story entirely from his perspective. The setting is shifted forward slightly to 1958 and it adopts the pulp and noir genres of the novel. Lou Ford is an outwardly respectable and upstanding member of the Texas town in which he lives. As deputy sheriff, he both upholds and symbolises order. Lou has the smooth manners of a Southern gentleman and adheres perfectly to the expected conventions of day-to-day social interaction. However, the viewer discovers the killer inside Lou when he brutally murders Joyce, the town's prostitute with whom he is having an affair. He later kills a local boy, Johnnie, and his own fiancée, Amy. Lou is incarcerated in an institution when it is revealed that Joyce, although badly beaten, survived his attack on her. By the end of the film, it becomes clear that Lou, who has narrated the story post-mortem, has provided us with a version of the events filtered through his dark fantasies, which is as such unreliable.

The Killer Inside Me offers a number of possible readings, although ultimately it fails to subvert either the audience's expectations of a film about a compulsive killer, or the cinematic conventions related to the representation of extreme violence. Thompson's novel raised questions about identity and mass society, which were contemporary. The twenty-first century film is a period piece, offering us a vision of the 1950s refracted through the lens of the subsequent 50 years, so it is worth asking what the rendering of the historical setting tells us about the present. As a Southern deputy sheriff from a well-respected family, Lou should exemplify decency. The fact that he is sadistic, cruel and emotionally void suggests that the society which produced him is similarly flawed, with its values lying on the surface only. This satirises the hallowed place the 1950s occupy in the socially conservative rhetoric of the early twenty-first century, where they are mythologised as a lost, more morally upright era, preceding the cultural debauchery of the 1960s. The film's small-town setting shifts the focus from the city as the locus of evil and is a counterpoint to portrayals such as *Se7en* and *American Psycho*, which implicate the city in the creation of the serial killer. *The Killer Inside Me* challenges their unspoken assumption that smaller, more close-knit communities are the antidotes to compulsive or motive-less violence. An additional layer of meaning is added by the Texan location, as it is the state where George Bush developed his political career as governor and whose presidency following the War in Iraq came to symbolise pointless excessive violence.

As a neo-noir, the film depicts violence in a different register from the horror or splatter genres that are often the setting for serial killer narratives. Extreme violence has become a staple of Hollywood films, but unlike 'torture porn' movies such as the *Hostel* or *Saw* franchises, *The Killer Inside Me* is not based on ever more creative and gory ways of making the victims suffer.[3] Rather, Lou's violence is sickeningly straightforward. He repeatedly punches Joyce in the face, her disfigurement taking place before the audience's eyes. He brutally stamps on Amy until she is heard to gasp for her last breaths. The violence is not that of a cartoon or computer game.

These depictions of violent attacks on women generated controversy, particularly as Lou's murder of Johnnie is not shown on screen and this led to the criticism that the film is misogynistic. When *The Killer Inside Me* premiered at the Sundance Film Festival, a female audience member challenged the film's selection in the question and answer session, stating, 'I don't understand how Sundance could book this movie? How dare you? How dare you Sundance?' (*Indiewire*, 2010). Director Winterbottom's response was that the violence is supposed to be shocking, which is an integral aspect of film noir. However, he stated that the violence is intended to be 'shocking and brutal', rather than a portrayal 'where the audience gets off on it' (ibid.). Reviewing *The Killer Inside Me* for *The Guardian*, Bradshaw (2010) argued that 'Winterbottom has consciously taken to extremes a situation that other types of drama would evasively sentimentalise' and is 'confronting the audience with the reality of sexual violence and abusive power relations between the sexes that cinema so often glamorises'. Winterbottom, and favourable reviewers, also noted that the film is from the perspective of a madman; Lou is not supposed to be a hero (Matheou, 2010; Travers, 2010).

The problem with *The Killer Inside Me* is that it succumbs to what Walkowitz (1982) describes as 'the myth of male violence'. Lou is not a pleasant or admirable character, but he is wily, intelligent and physically in control of his victims. Both Joyce and Amy appear to adore him despite his sadistic treatment of them and, if anything, this is portrayed as something they enjoy. The film is of course from Lou's perspective and he is an unreliable narrator who is also a misogynist. To Lou, Joyce and Amy are interchangeable women without humanity. As depicted on the screen, this is highly problematic as neither Joyce nor Amy is provided with a character – there is no inducement for the audience to care about these ciphers. Reviewers noted the serious tone of the film and Romney (2010) criticised its lack of irony in *The Independent*, arguing that this prevented the story from being told with sufficient complexity. This lack of irony means that Lou's virility and masculine power are never subverted or shown to be in question. Although he is captured, he is never cowed. Here, the film and novel differ, as Thompson includes episodes which let the reader know that Lou is sometimes the object of derision from his fellow townspeople, who are amused by his inability to stop talking in clichés. The film ultimately relies too heavily on the serial killer as 'evil genius' portrayal and does not take the opportunity to subvert Lou's powerful image of himself. This drains the effectiveness of its intent to be a critique of screen violence.

The Killer Inside Me may set out to counter glamorised depictions, but as a visually sumptuous neo-noir, it is very stylised and does not lay bare the choreographed nature of movie violence in the way that, for example, *Man Bites Dog* (1992) does so successfully through use of a mock documentary approach. In that film, a documentary crew sets out to follow the exploits of a serial killer, gradually losing its distance from his acts of violence and becoming participants themselves. The violence looks neither attractive nor balletic and highlights for the audience the artificiality of what is usually portrayed on screen, while also showing how audiences are routinely implicated in the enjoyment of acts of sickening violence. Writing in *The Independent*, Romney (2010) questioned the effect of seeing an actor famed for her beauty such as Jessica Alba, who plays Joyce, violently disfigured. He cautioned that this offers 'a sinister taboo thrill' to the audience and will 'become a YouTube favourite with people who enjoy that sort of thing' (ibid.).

Five Daughters

Five Daughters is a three-part television drama that aired in the United Kingdom on BBC 1 in April 2010. It is based on the lives of the women who were the victims in the 'Ipswich Murders' which occurred in December 2006. Five women were killed by Steve Wright, a local taxi driver, over a three-week period. Wright was a regular client of sex workers in Ipswich and he was able to exploit his familiarity to the women in order to target victims. *Five Daughters'* originality lies in its focus on the stories of these women, rather than on Wright or the police's attempts to catch him. Although the police investigation is dramatised, the series is not about the 'hunt' for the killer as in the standard police procedural (Frost, 2010). Wright is virtually absent from the episodes, appearing in the final one shortly before he is arrested. Serial killer narratives are usually characterised by the anonymity and interchangeability of their victims (King, 2006), something which *Five Daughters* turns on its head. In doing so, it subverts the representation of 'victim' as passive cipher.

The series was made with the co-operation and participation of three of the women's families. The writer, Stephen Butchard, found that the families were 'distressed that these people they knew and loved had ended up with the label of prostitute' and aimed to correct this by gaining a sense of their personal biography (Masters, 2010). The drama concentrates on the women's relationships with their families, friends and partners, and portrays their struggles with drug addiction and their ambitions for a life beyond street sex work. In doing so, it reverses the dehumanisation enacted by the serial killer's violence, and by media reports that simply described the women as 'five prostitutes' as if that were all that needed to be known about them. As women embedded in social and emotional relationships, the characters in *Five Daughters* appear ordinary and recognisable, rather than liminal, polluting 'whores'. Egger (2002, p. 81) argues that

> [o]nly when the 'less-dead' are perceived as above the status of prostitutes, homosexuals, street people, runaways, or the elderly does our own vulnerability become a stark reality. Until that time, the killer's aberrant behaviours are imbued with a kind of rationality or logic born of our class consciousness.

Divesting the women who were killed in Ipswich of the label 'prostitute' and instead portraying them as 'somebody's sister, somebody's daughter, somebody's mother' (*Five Daughters*, 2010, Episode 2) challenges this rationality. A review in *The Independent* noted that *Five Daughters* employed 'the established rhetoric for a crime like this in television drama', but departed from this when it restored 'all the moments when these women were something other than just the next victim' (Sutcliffe, 2010). The formal aspects of the series are conventional, but its subversion of the serial killer narrative is not.

In addition to the young women and their friends and families, the drama portrays the work of a local drug-outreach project and also Janet Humphrey, a community police officer who wants to help women move on from sex work and addiction. In doing so, it adopts a welfarist perspective on sex work, which emphasises the need to help women take their places as 'respectable' members of society. As discussed in Chapter 4, a focus on rehabilitation can result in 'responsibilisation', where female sex workers are constructed as individually responsible for their transformation to respectable citizen, while insufficient attention is paid to issues such as poverty and the growing market for sex work (Scoular and O'Neill, 2007). This arguably makes the acceptance of those with transgressive identities as people of worth contingent upon their intention to cast off their deviant selves, which threatens to hamper the drama's message. However, it should be noted that *Five Daughters* avoids a judgemental portrayal of women involved in sex work.

The series challenges the 'myth of male violence' by largely disregarding Steve Wright, the serial killer. The audience is encouraged to see the five women he killed as being of far greater interest and importance. He is certainly not represented as an evil genius, but neither is he made symbolic of present-day selfhood or turned into a monster. In telling a story about serial murder that does not have the serial killer or his violent attacks at its centre, *Five Daughters* offers fertile new ground for the cultural representation of painful 'real-life' cases. The more usual genres for the serial killer narrative, such as horror and film noir, rely on tension and shock. *Five Daughters* eloquently shows the destructive effects of extreme violence by depicting the grief of those who loved or cared about the victims and the tragedy of the loss of these five women. Unlike *The Killer Inside Me*, it emotionally involves the audience by telling a story about relationships, rather than the mechanics of violence.

Jindabyne

Like *Five Daughters*, *Jindabyne* (2006) displaces the serial killer from the centre of the narrative. The film is an adaptation of Raymond Carver's short story 'So Much Water So Close to Home' (2009), which is narrated by Claire, the wife of a man who, when on a fishing trip with friends, finds the body of a murdered girl. Instead of reporting it immediately, the group of men decide to continue with their weekend of fishing and drinking before doing so. Carver's story explores Claire's inability to understand what she perceives as her husband, Stewart's, callousness, and its subsequent effect on their relationship. *Jindabyne* transposes the story to a small town in a mountainous region of New South Wales. Near to its beginning, a white man in a truck drives alongside a young aboriginal woman in a car. He shouts at her and asks her to stop, before swinging the truck in front of her to block off the road. It is the body of this young woman, Susan, that Stewart and his friends find floating in the river. Reluctant to curtail their once-a-year fishing trip in the wilderness, they tie her to the riverbank by her ankles and report it to the police on their way back home.

This casual, uncaring attitude to the desecrated body of an aboriginal woman from a group of white men causes a scandal and damages relations between aboriginal and white groups in the town.

Claire is particularly horrified by the men's decision to bind Susan's ankles with twine, something which further damaged her already broken body. The controversy that happens in the aftermath of the discovery of Susan and the men's return home is generated by their perception of her as the 'less-dead' (Egger, 2002). Susan is different from the white men on the fishing trip. As an indigenous woman, she is historically and legally less of a person. The incident opens up fissures in the local community and in the main characters' relationships with one another.

Lambert and Simpson (2008, p. 81) argue that *Jindabyne* is the product of 'a culture living within the ongoing effects of the past'. The murder of Susan and the indifference shown by the men who discover her body bring ongoing issues of dominance, racism and colonisation from Australia's past to the surface. Susan's floating body is metaphorical of this resurfacing, she 'bears the semiotic weight of colonial atrocity and non-indigenous environmental development' (ibid., p. 84). Although *Jindabyne* evokes Australian history and culture, Ray Lawrence, the director, has stated that '*Jindabyne* offers a view of the way the world is now in Britain and America, the attitude to foreigners or indigenous people, the view of anyone that is different' (Fairweather, 2007, p. 49). It explores the ongoing significance of cultural frameworks of denigration in Western, postcolonial societies and the way in which the serial murderer's 'distorted mirror' reflects back 'modernity's distinctive valuations' (Haggerty, 2009, p. 180).

Like *Five Daughters*, *Jindabyne* concentrates on issues related to victimisation rather than the characteristics of the serial killer, but it places these within a wider cultural and socio-historical framework. *Five Daughters* undertakes the important work of re-humanising the women who became the victims of a serial killer and expressly challenging the denigrated label of 'prostitute'. However, it focuses closely on drug addiction and the need to treat it as central to understanding the vulnerability of the women to the violence of the serial killer. This is an important issue to understand but the series does not consider wider social injustices. *Jindabyne* more fully addresses themes of complicity and responsibility, and is an account of 'what it means to live with history and in connection with Others' (Probyn-Rapsey, 2007, p. 65). The men's plea that they have done nothing wrong because they did not kill Susan rings hollow because they are complicit in the greater silence surrounding Australia's legacy of colonial violence (ibid.). Their failure of compassion is interpreted by some in the community as a hate crime. Claire appreciates this issue of complicity particularly keenly and attempts to make amends for her husband's actions, although some of her attempts misfire. Her sense of complicity derives not just from her connection to men from the trip, but also her status as a white woman living in Australia.

Jindabyne does something which is very rare – it subtly evokes the figure of the serial killer. It focuses on personal and communal relationships and is not a crime drama. The pace of the film is languid and there are only two moments that depict the threat of the killer on screen. One is at the beginning, which shows the audience how Susan met her killer; the other is when he uses the same technique of blocking off the road to intimidate Claire. Claire does not know that this is an encounter with Susan's murderer. She remains in her car and he drives on. As in *Five Daughters*, the serial killer is on the drama's periphery rather than at its centre. The police's investigation is not an aspect of the film and the audience only becomes aware that Susan has been classified as the victim of a serial killer from a conversation that takes place among some of the characters at a barbecue. Like the history of colonial violence, the murderer 'hover[s] in the background' (Lambert and Simpson, 2008, p. 83). *Jindabyne* explores the disruption he creates without introducing him as a proper character into the film. Instead, he symbolises the potential violence of the 'ubiquitous white male presence' on the virtually empty country roads (ibid.).[4]

The ethics of representing the serial killer

In different ways, these three recent narratives grapple with the ethics of representing the serial killer in the context of his cultural ubiquity, celebrity status and appearance as a staple of popular entertainment. *The Killer Inside Me* returns to a foundational text of the serial killer genre in order to challenge the audience with questions about screen violence. The violence is brutal, shocking but executed without the need for props or elaborate settings. By removing these elements, it seeks to expose the use of film violence when it is graphically employed for enjoyment and titillation, and also when it is sanitised in order to protect the audience from its real effects. *The Killer Inside Me* attempts, but fails, to offer a more ethical engagement by portraying Lou Ford's violence in a way that is shocking without being entertaining, and that reminds us Lou is both despicable and unbalanced. The film's impact is actually limited by this commitment to appal the audience, firstly because set pieces based on violence against women cannot be guaranteed not to have entertainment value and secondly because it propagates the 'myth of male violence'. Lou may be a psychopath, but he is also a powerful, vital figure and *The Killer Inside Me* does not manage to destabilise the conventions of serial killer entertainment sufficiently to undermine them.

Five Daughters and *Jindabyne* both offer new possibilities for ethical engagement with issues associated with serial killing. Neither is structured around the figure of the serial killer as in both representations he is a minor, peripheral figure. By unseating him as the driving force of the narrative, the serial killer is not portrayed as hero or anti-hero and his importance is diminished. Although both *Five Daughters* and *Jindabyne* explore the devastating effects of the serial killer's actions, they are not in thrall to his mystique. They provide new ways of dramatising the serial killer narrative that concentrate on issues other than the predatory violence of the killer and the police's hunt for him. In both representations, the serial killer is not depicted as exceptional or even interesting – he is someone who causes profound damage to others but is not worthy of the audience's preoccupation. This decentring of the serial killer makes it possible to transcend the 'myth of male violence' and to escape the need to turn murder into entertainment.

Instead, the narratives of *Five Daughters* and *Jindabyne* have a different focus. *Five Daughters* is the story of women who became the victims of a serial killer, but in making them the subject of the drama, it overcomes stereotypes of the victims of such crimes as passive or faceless, and also challenges portrayals that devalue or denigrate them as the 'less-dead'. This is particularly important as *Five Daughters* is a dramatisation of a real case, which occurred just over two years before it was aired. Part of its ethical commitment is to portray its subjects as ordinary women possessing humanity and social value, and to counter negative representations of them as worthless 'prostitutes' that appeared in the news media. The series does this successfully and it also depicts the women's struggles with drug addiction, although it does not link this to wider issues of social and economic inequality.

Jindabyne moves the audience even further from the standard serial killer narrative as it is not a crime film and adopts hardly any of the conventions of the crime story – the killer is marginal, but so is the police's investigation. A serial killer is the original cause of the events that unfold, but not only is he peripheral to the narrative, so is the fact that he is a serial killer. *Jindabyne* is woven from themes of marginalisation, racism, colonial history and guilt. It is ethically engaged with the issue of complicity – the serial killer is responsible for the murder that is at the heart of the film's dilemmas but the white Australian characters are implicated in the history and legacy of the genocide and exploitation of indigenous peoples. In raising this issue, the film is at once about a particular place at a particular time and also concerned with the complicity of the relatively privileged in the mistreatment of those who are culturally denigrated in other Western nations. Along with *Five Daughters*, *Jindabyne* shows how it is possible to ethically address themes related to serial killing in ways that are also creatively enriching. Chapter 7 examines constructions of asylum seekers and refugees as marginalised 'folk devils'.

7
Outlaws, Borders and Folk Devils

Refugees and asylum seekers have become the folk devils of the twenty-first century. This chapter explores research undertaken with people situated in the asylum-migration nexus (refugees, asylum seekers and undocumented people), through participatory and biographical research and selected filmic texts. Key themes addressed in the chapter include the tension between human rights, human dignity and humiliation in the lived experiences of migrants, many of whom exist in the margins of the margins, and the possibilities for a radical democratic imaginary in our cultural criminological work in this area.

Reflecting upon creative consultation workshops conducted with refugees and asylum seekers in the UK, we make a case for the use of participatory and visual methods for generating multi-sensory and dialogic understandings of the lived experiences of asylum seekers, migrants, 'others'. This chapter reinforces the usefulness of cultural criminological methodologies to better understand lived experiences, to feed in to policy and praxis, to challenge and change sexual and social inequalities. It also stresses the inclusion of marginalised and subaltern groups in dialogue and debate in order to resist and challenge exclusionary discourses and contribute to public criminological scholarship.

Asylum and migration: Protecting borders

Recently one of the authors gave a public talk on issues of asylum and migration. Some of the responses by audience members were based upon perspectives and attitudes that perceived asylum seekers as 'illegal' immigrants and as deeply problematic. The definitions of 'illegal' were fluid and the key issues that concerned the questioners revolved around access to resources such as housing and health care as well as the perceived spatial limits of the UK: 'we are a small country and full-up'; 'illegal immigrants take housing and there are thousands of local people on the social housing waiting lists'. Audience members were also concerned about the risks of globalisation and the need for strong controls at the borders of the nation states. The concept of 'open borders' was seen as 'fanciful'. Strong emotions were elicited by the issues raised in the talk despite the fact that asylum applications fell considerably in 2010 with 22,000 applications in the same year that 368,000 people emigrated from the UK. A similar talk in the same location and with some of the same audience three years earlier did not elicit such strong emotions and questions. Inevitably the author surmised that the impact of the recession and current public-sector funding cuts together with the scapegoating of 'immigrants' in the tabloid media had created more potent 'us and them' emotions in the public imagination; and asylum seekers and even international students were the targets of hostility, othering and humiliation.

Yet, what we know from the available research is that forced migration takes place either within or between developing countries; that the cost of enforcing borders is very high in resource terms and an enormous amount of money is spent securing the borders of Western nations (Castles, 2003; Marfleet, 2006; Sales, 2007). Moreover, we know that migration will continue to be a reality of the twenty-first century.

What is very clear is the conflict at the centre of Western nations' responses to the plights of asylum seekers and refugees. On the one hand a commitment to Human Rights and the 1951 Convention exists; the UK government remains signed up to what has become known as the refugee convention. On the other hand powerful rhetoric aimed at protecting the borders of nation states is underpinned by the ideology of sovereignty. Yet, in an era of globalisation, the sovereignty of states is waning given the rise of supranational bodies like the United Nations, the IMF and World Bank alongside powerful multinationals. As a number of migration scholars (Marfleet, 2006; Pickering, 2005) have shown, sovereignty is 'vigorously asserted at the borders of nations'. In the UK, borders are protected by the recently renamed 'UK Borders and Immigration Agency'. This highly charged focus on protecting borders of the nation state masks the realities of globalisation and capitalism and prevents us thinking more broadly about the role of nation states in the *production* of the world's refugees and the fact that the displacement and humiliation of people and subsequent transnational migration is reshaping societies, politics, national and global governance, including discourses on 'rights', and impacting at psychosocial levels on individuals, groups and communities.

The conflict at the centre of governmental responses is indicated by the contrast between legislation that is committed to protecting the rights of refugees and a strong focus upon protecting and policing the borders; indeed Kushner and Knox (1999) suggest that the UK is committed to the concept of asylum, without the possibility of entry. Mechanisms of integration exist alongside surveillance, tagging, containment, detention and, for some, destitution. For those whose country is deemed safe or whose case is not found the option is either voluntary removal, forced removal or going underground and becoming 'illegal'.

Media representation and the mediatisation of the asylum issue provides another source of conflict: the scapegoating of asylum seekers and the tabloid headlines that help to create fear and anxiety about the unwelcome 'others' serve to set agendas that fuel racist discourses and practices. Asylum seekers are nameless and are represented by others; they rarely represent themselves. This void creates space for the withdrawal of humanising practices and the 'othering' of asylum seekers, refugees and migrants and what emerges to fill this space is racism, misrecognition and unbelonging – what Agamben (1995) calls 'bare life'. Tyler (2006, p. 186) argues that 'the figure of the asylum seeker increasingly secures the imaginary borders of Britain today'. Moreover, that

> the identification of a person as an asylum-seeker has become an 'instrument for the refusal of recognition' (Butler, 2002: 11), which in turn shores up a normative fantasy of what it means to be British. Indeed, as it shall be argued, the identification of the figure of the asylum-seeker is increasingly constitutive of public articulations of national and ethnic belonging.
>
> Tyler (2006, p. 189)

Figure 7.1   Photo: The 'othering' of asylum seekers. What's the story? Article 19 and Cardiff School of Journalism

Figures 7.1 and 7.2 are symbolic of the construction of the 'asylum seeker' as deviant is well documented. Indeed, government responses to asylum seekers are framed by law-and-order politics represented by the media, law and the courts.

Yet, in order to be recognised as a refugee under the terms of the 1951 UN Convention on Refugees a person must make a claim for asylum at the port of entry or the UK Borders Agency offices in Croydon or Liverpool as soon as possible on entering the country. Most asylum applications are refused and if the authorities refuse an asylum application, an applicant is able to appeal against the refusal, although some asylum seekers will only be able to appeal once they have left the UK (Refugee Action, 2006).

As Blunkett warns of menace from asylum gangs, shock new figures for the capital...

ONE IN 20 IS A MIGRANT

Figure 7.2 Photo: A culture of disbelief. What's the story? Article 19 and Cardiff School of Journalism

Hence, the social and cultural context that asylum seekers experience is marked by a culture of disbelief, underpinned by law-and-order politics. This is combined with a focus upon strengthening and protecting borders which places responsibility on the asylum seeker for their situation. This impacts upon the experience of seeking safety for people fleeing persecution, human rights violations, violence and war. Their experiences are marked by humiliation, shame, racism and misrecognition.

As Bauman (2004, 2007) and other theorists have documented (Smith, 2006; Marfleet, 2006; O'Neill, 2010a), the processes of modernity and globalisation are underpinned by deep social inequalities that lead people to leave home in search of a better life through choice and/or compulsion, or literally, to flee for their lives. Forced migration is not 'the result of a string of unconnected emergencies, but an integral part of North-South relations' (Castles, 2003, p. 9). Millions are displaced each year as a consequence of development projects, dams and civil unrest. The World Bank suggests that this is in the region of ten million people per year. At the close of 2009, 43.3 million people were forcibly displaced 'the highest number of people uprooted by conflict and persecution since the mid-1990s' (United Nations Human Rights Commission, 2011). However, the number of refugees able to return to their homes had fallen to the lowest level in 20 years.

> High Commissioner Guterres outlined some of the challenges. He said the main challenges were the 'growing resilience of crises,' the shrinking humanitarian space in which refugees can find shelter and humanitarian agencies can work, and the erosion of asylum space.
>
> ibid.

As Bauman states, 'The numbers of homeless and stateless victims of globalisation grow too fast for the planning, location and construction of camps to keep up with them' (2004, p. 37). What is very clear from any examination of the literature on forced migration is the *humiliation* of those who bear the label. The Independent Asylum Commission report identified a 'culture of disbelief ' that pervades so much of the policy and decision making of the last decade, which has made it increasingly difficult for asylum seekers to receive a fair hearing. As stated, for those whose claims are refused, the option is voluntary return, forced return or going underground and 'undocumented'. 'I used to be a respectable teacher back home, owning my own house and a car. But now I am a beggar – I can't believe it' (cited in Jackson and Dube, 2006, p. 11). 'Sometimes I begged for £1 or £2 to buy food but begging made me feel very ashamed. I mainly survived by eating chips and pitta bread' (Hamid cited in Taylor, 2009, p. 12). Something of this humiliation is captured by Bauman (2007) in the concept of 'negative globalisation'.

Negative globalisation

'Negative globalisation' is the selective globalisation of trade, capital, surveillance and information, violence, weapons, crime and terrorism; and is itself a cause of injustice, violence and conflict. Negative globalisation is embedded within five key themes and challenges. First, the passage from solid to liquid modernity (social forms – structures and institutions are no longer solid and 'cannot serve as frames of reference for human actions and long-term life strategies' (Bauman, 2007, p. 1)). Second, the disembedding of the nation state's power and sovereignty in a globalised world and global political arena. Third, the rolling back of state welfare functions, the subsidising or contracting out of functions of the state, the withdrawal of support and insurance against 'individual failure and ill fortune'. Fourth, the weakening or loosening of social structures which lead to long-term thinking, planning and acting inscribed over a long duree. Bauman speaks of 'life fragmented into lateral rather than vertical orientations, we speak of portfolios, no longer careers but series of jobs' (p. 3). Finally, the responsibility for such shifts and changes are placed 'onto the shoulders of individuals – who are now expected to be "free choosers" and to bear in full the consequences of their choices' (pp. 3–4). Bauman argues, 'The risks involved in every choice may be produced by forces which transcend the comprehension and capacity to act of the individual, but it is the individuals' lot and duty to pay their price' (p. 4).

In Bauman's terms this sociopolitical, cultural and economic context (liquid modernity driven by global consumer capitalism) is responsible for the creation of an excess of 'human waste' (literally, the excess consumption that embodies consumer capitalism leads to enormous quantities of human waste) and 'wasted lives' are marked in contemporary times by redundancies, lifelong unemployment *and* social displacement – asylum seekers and refugees fleeing war, conflict, destruction of homes and livelihoods.

How might cultural criminologists research these issues? As defined in the introduction, cultural criminology is rooted in the Birmingham School of Contemporary Cultural Studies, critical criminology, as well as symbolic interactionist and ethnographic approaches to crime and deviance (Ferrell, 2006). There is a focus on the everyday meanings of crime and transgression, phenomenological analysis as well as methodologies that are predominantly ethnographic, participatory, textual and visual. 'Cultural criminology explores the many ways in which cultural dynamics intertwine with the practices of crime and crime control in contemporary society' (Ferrell, 2007). One methodology highlighted in the previous chapters for doing cultural criminology is participatory and arts-based methods.

Doing participatory and arts-based research with refugees and asylum seekers

This section documents one strand of a participatory action research project that also used participatory arts to examine the lived experience of asylum seekers, refugees and undocumented people. This is followed by a concluding section that discusses the radical democratic possibilities that cultural representations emerging from participatory research can offer. The conclusion suggests that creative and community arts, media representations and film cannot only be the means through which those labelled 'outsiders' might defy their marginalisation but might also be transformative, feed into public policy and offer an example of public scholarship.

O'Neill and Hubbard's (2010) *Sense of Belonging* arts/research project used both participatory action research and arts practice to examine: how the arts, defined in their broadest sense, might help mediate and represent the experience of arriving in a new country; what it means to feel a sense of belonging; and deliver cultural, social and economic benefits to new arrivals. The aim of the research (funded by the AHRC) was to understand the experiences of exile and displacement as well as facilitate processes and practices of inclusion and belonging with new arrivals by encouraging collaboration and exchange of ideas among artists, practitioners, academics, policymakers and new arrivals in the East Midlands. Working in partnership with four community arts organisations, the research explored a sense of belonging, place and place making with four transnational communities who were defined as refugees/asylum seekers, some of whom were undocumented. The project also commissioned work by five artists who are members of *The Long Journey Home* regional arts organisation.

The *Sense of Belonging* research project worked with migrant groups, including women, unaccompanied young refugees and asylum seekers and refugees from a rich variety of communities. The project was launched with a 'walking' event developed by internationally recognised artist and educator Misha Myers, who was consultant to the walks. The walks involved migrants to the East Midlands (in Nottingham, Derby, Loughborough and Leicester), drawing a map from a place they call home to a special place, and then walking that map with a co-walker in the new environment in which they find themselves. The walks took place simultaneously on Friday 16 May 2008 at 10 a.m., lasting for around two hours (See figures 7.3 and 7.4).

Post-walk discussions (held at Mount Fields Lodge Youth Centre and facilitated by Myers) led to the emergence of connecting themes for the development of the arts/research practice and workshops[1].

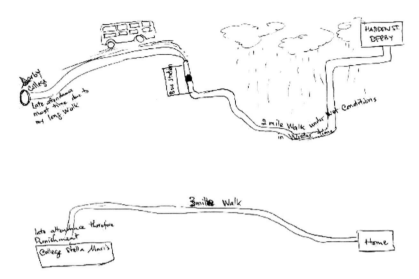

Figure 7.3 Sketch of a map. *Sense of Belonging* project of 2008

Figure 7.4 Sharing a walk
Photo: Aria Ahmed.

Following the walks, a series of arts/research workshops took place in each locale putting art at the heart of social research and further exploring themes raised by the walks. The arts/research workshops were led by the four community arts organisations, City Arts, Charnwood Arts, Long Journey Home, and Soft Touch, in collaboration with O'Neill and Hubbard. The artworks that emerged from the workshops and some of the narratives produced in the workshops were exhibited at the Bonington Gallery in Nottingham, January 2009.

This collaborative research project built upon the strong regional work of many artists, community arts organisations, voluntary and statutory sector agencies and researchers working with new arrivals, community groups and the region. It also built upon previous work (O'Neill, 2002, 2008) that explored the social role of the arts in processes of social change and the space between ethnographic, participatory research and arts-based work.

The research partners engaged in three strands of activity. First, they developed a website and a database of exhibiting artists to connect with each another as well as to programmers, schools and regional community and participatory arts organisations seeking artists for their projects and programmes in schools and community settings. This *raised* the impact of arts and cultural activity for social policy agendas in participation with new arrivals. Second, they held a 'diversity pool' event that focused upon bringing artists and programmers together, so that artists could showcase their work and that employment and employability were supported and fostered. Third, they conducted the research and arts project called *A Sense of Belonging* using participatory research and participatory arts-based methods. This led to an exhibition of work produced in arts/research workshops.

What emerges in the process of doing the participatory research is that the arts-based research communicates what belonging means to those participating in the research, exploring their experiences and feelings about home, dislocation, place making, belonging and friendship. A combination of photographs, art and narrative enables the reader/audience to understand what it is like to live in Nottingham, Derby, Leicester and Loughborough for new arrivals as well as highlighting the perilous journeys people make to seek freedom and safety from nations, including Zimbabwe, Congo, Iraq, Iran, Eritrea, Albania, Turkey and Afghanistan. The emotional and physical impact of these journeys, and the experiences of 'double consciousness' and being 'home away from home' are represented alongside the rich cultural contributions and skills migrants bring to the region's cities, towns, cultures and communities. Two of the workshops and their outcomes are documented and discussed next. The images are accompanied by some of the narrative, text and conversation around the issues of concern to this chapter.

'Belonging is not only a passport'

One key theme across all of the workshops was the movement across borders, fleeing, hiding and taking huge risks to seek freedom and safety.

> We had been packed inside the lorry, different people from different backgrounds. The lorry was carrying frozen foods. There was not enough space for us. They tried to push us in tightly, because more people meant more money. After ten hours we feel the lorry went inside the ship and we could feel the sounds of the ship moving on the sea. To keep the food ok in the lorry the driver turned on the refrigeration. It was so cold. When they turned it off it was so hot, there was a lot of people inside and there was not enough oxygen, we were desperate. Then the plastic around the fan was burnt and it began pouring smoke inside. Women and babies were crying. I thought this was the end. My last day in life. I lost hope. I thought the bottle of coke I have is half empty if I suck it I could get some oxygen. Also my bag I thought if I put my head inside to get some oxygen to survive. I am not sure I am alive or dead; it was like a dream, in a dream-like hallucination. We lost hope. We banged and shouted and were crying. The driver opened the air conditioner and we could feel him fix it and then it worked and we were so happy to be cold. When I see a lorry I go and check out to see if it has this. We were in the lorry for 57 hours each of us had drink, biscuits, chocolate. 20 or 25 people with no space to move or stand up. Boxes all around us. There are many, many stories and each person will have a different story.

When asked what belonging means to him, the artist quoted before said: 'Being here is about freedom. I can go anywhere. I am not stopped by the police. You can feel you are human here. People appreciate you.'

The same theme of travelling to safety is described by a mother who paid an agent to stow herself and her children onto a lorry travelling from France to the East Midlands in the UK:

> We waited almost two months at Calais with my two children. Some of the agents they care for us, they understand. A woman came to see me. She said 'we feel for you one month on your own with the children and we know a way that has not been tried'. We had to lie amongst packing boxes, six people, myself, my son and daughter and three others. We waited for five hours inside the lorry in the car park in the cold of winter. Then we left; five hours is like five days; my daughter was sleeping but she was only five years. My son had to pee. I said to do it in the corner. He said, 'I can't Mum.' I said, 'You have to just do it.' In the Manche tunnel we were in a queue for four hours. Then we travel to Loughborough, we thought we must be in Scotland! In the police station they bring us pot noodle, but we can't eat that. I said, 'Can we have bread?' The children were crying. I said to the police, 'Which camp are you taking us to?' He said, 'We don't put people in camps in England you will go to a hotel in Leicester.' We got there very late. I said, 'Can we have bread for the children?' 'No all the kitchen is closed up until morning'. So we slept. I woke with a start and ran into breakfast place crying, 'Please! Please, can I have breakfast for my children?' An Iraqi man said to me, 'It is ok, everyone is here for breakfast; you can have breakfast.' I had not changed my clothes or washed. The journey was hard, very painful.

'Home away from Home' (Fig. 7.5) was an installation made of wood, photographs, textiles, cigarette packets, water bottles and children's clothes. The work was accompanied by an explanatory text that told the reader that the textile pieces that covered the box-like structure were literally created from the stories of the participants. Pieces of thread, cloth and, in some cases, photographs had been woven into the squares, and the enclosed space depicted the refugees' experience of escaping their countries in containers and lorries. Exhibition visitors were able to climb into the box and feel the confined space. Their senses were engaged by the items the artists had included in the container, including a chocolate wrapper and an empty plastic bottle. The sounds of ports, stations, engines were mixed with the

Figure 7.5 Home away from Home
Photo: Aria Ahmed.

stories of those who had taken the journey, and included texts such as 'after twenty seven years I breathed in freedom air' and 'my home? It was one and now it is two. I have been divided into two places like two souls in one body'.

'Home-made'

The major theme and focus in the Nottingham-based workshop was on home and belonging. In the initial workshops, we spoke together about concepts and memories of home, belonging and place making. The workshops led by Heather Connelly focused upon language and communication as well as the sensory aspects of 'home'. Participants described a sense of home being found in colours, textures, smells and cooking. These were transitional phenomena that embody emotional experiences related to 'home', including a coffee pot, landscapes, sounds, fabric/textiles, photographs, music, the smells of spices and coffee, and objects like coffee pots, crockery, colours and fabrics. As symbols of 'home', they were incorporated into the art works that the women made.

As one of the women said, feelings of home were evoked when consuming 'traditional food, when we meet each other we make traditional coffee and feel at home.' For a woman from Eritrea home was 'here, where my children were born, are with me'; another woman mentioned 'being able to speak your own language at home'. To feel at home women would visit 'parks and green spaces, Nottingham, London, restaurants with traditional food and churches'. Another woman described a sense of home in relationships:

> Where I lived, to begin with, there were many British families and they didn't really bother me as they thought I was British. But when I spoke and asked teenagers to be quiet or something, they would say, 'Go back to your own country.' It is difficult everywhere with teenagers. Now I live in an area with lots of refugees and families from India/Pakistan and we can say anything to each other – we understand each other.

The women decided that they wanted to create a space in the gallery where visitors could experience something of the women's sense of home and belonging. It was agreed that a tent/gazebo would be decorated with silk screens, floor cushions and textiles that evoked 'home' for the women (See Fig. 7.6). People attending the exhibition would be invited to step into the women's world evoked in the silks screen drapes decorating the tent – a sensory, welcoming space that might elicit understanding of women's lives and cultures. Conversations with the women were recorded and the sound files were used as part of the exhibition. This allowed the public sitting in the installation space to hear fragments from the women's stories, enabling connection and attunement (Scheff, 2010) between the visitors and the women who created the installation.

A sense of 'attunement' (Scheff, 2010) was also experienced between the women in the workshops, for, as with walking, art making created the necessary space and facilitated connections through the creative process, stimulating movement between women's inner

Figure 7.6   Home-made
Photo: Aria Ahmed.

worlds and their social, external reality. As one of the participants noted,

> We are sewing and we are talking together about our problems ... For me I learn lots of things; now I am interested in art. I think all the ladies we have become friends. I make a joke and she understands me and she can come back with a joke. I feel we are friends.

Social displacement and managing risk: Laws, border controls and the age of camps

Our aim, in the exhibition, was to raise awareness about the routes people take to reach safety and how they create a sense of belonging, a sense of home in the new situation. In the storyboard documented in Figure 7.7, what becomes obvious is that transnational belonging involves mobility, multiple affiliations, hybridity as well as loss and dislocation. Lives and roles are transformed in the process; people labelled 'refugee' or 'asylum seeker' experience downward mobility, and are located often at the margins of the margins. Having a voice,

Figure 7.7   Escape to Safety. Storyboard from workshops with unaccompanied young asylum seekers
Photo: Paul Ghent.

a personal and political space to tell and share stories was documented as very important to the process of belonging and this can be facilitated in the process of participatory research. In turn, arts-based participatory research is not just a mimetic reflection on someone's origins but is constitutive; it brings something new into the world. The *Sense of Belonging* research project demonstrated that such work may generate (in both the participants and the viewers) a dialogical process of reflection and sensorial interaction and attunement that links the visual and the imaginary to other sensory registers (Buckley, 2006, p. 62), connecting inner and outer realities.

The counter-hegemonic role of participatory action research and participatory arts can lead to a radical democratisation of images and texts that can move us, pierce us, challenge identity thinking and bring us in touch with the micro-relational worlds, helping us to connect with our feeling worlds in a subjective reflexive relationship with the feeling worlds of the Other, destabilising the relation between us and them, self and Other into a subject-subject relationship. What emerges through the potential space and the attunement that occurs in and through participatory research projects can counter identity thinking and misrecognition, destabilise regressive discourses (O'Neill, 2008) and help us move towards what Lindner (2006) calls egalization and social justice. This kind of research runs counter to the negative and humiliating messages and images we sometimes find in the mainstream media that ultimately feeds into the public imagination and fuels racism and Othering. Arts-based and participatory methodologies can challenge exclusionary discourses and processes. They can also offer representational challenges that can be change causing, challenging identity thinking, helping the connectivity defined in 'attunement'. The work art engages us in is relational and it can also support the development of democratic spaces, imaginings and discourses.

Radical democratic imaginaries?

In the introduction we stated that the imaginary domain is a moral and psychic space that is necessary in order to keep open and rework the repressed elements of the imaginary (Cornell, 1995). We also agreed that criminologists must acknowledge that 'everyday life is lived in the imaginary'. And that the ways in which we imagine the 'outsider' are imbricated in the various measures of social control and sanction that society employs to deal with them (Rafter, 2006; Melossi, 2008), and these measures become particularly acute when outsiders are imagined to be dangerous or polluting.

Michael Winterbottom's powerful film *In this World* (2002) opens with the flight of two Afghan young men, cousins Enayat and Jamal, from a refugee camp in Peshawar, Pakistan. The film is about their journey and the movement of people across borders in search of safety and the opportunity to fulfil dreams and hopes. It presents a moving example of the yo-yoing, circuitous routes that migrants make (Marfleet, 2006); their journey broken up in nodal cities and way stations on the 'silk road' across Pakistan, through Iran, Turkey, Italy and France. Filmed in a grainy documentary style, it is a fictive tale using real footage of camps and the situations experienced by unaccompanied young asylum seekers. Darke, a film critic, writes:

> *In This World* shows migration and displacement, and the way it works on two human beings ... their seeping through the cracks in

checkpoints, breaching porous borders, stowing-away in the hold of global circumnavigation. It is this force that propels those forwards on the back of pick-up trucks, in the belly of sea-borne containers and, in one powerfully emblematic sequence, as two tiny figures wedged beneath the wheels of an HGV heading for the UK.

Darke (2003)

Roger Bromley (2007) writing in *Globalized People, Migration and Cinema* uses the film to articulate the way globalisation has impacted on migration to the EU through cinematic narrative. He states:

Both Jamal and Enyat experience pain and suffering throughout the journey and are forced to improvise, bribe, and 'fake' their way through the harsh, physical and human, landscapes. In some instances, details of their travel are shown in close up and at some length, at other times captions summarise the passage of hours or days. The camera is rarely at a distance from them, they are almost always subjects with primacy given to their point of view. It is never a film about 'victims' in any detached, liberal sense. The worst journey of all is the most subtly conveyed. We see Jamal, Enyat and a Turkish father, mother and child being secured in a freight container (a space designed to store the non-human), aware of them only through whispers, the cries of the child and the occasional flicker of a lighter. We also see the outcome of this stage of the journey – the death of Enyat and of the child – but the lack of food, airlessness and light deprivation, and the enforced silence is not narrated explicitly or melodramatically, but in a simple caption: '40 hours later'. Thus we are not shown, and only barely told about, this unendurable experience. It is in this way that the viewer is forced to imagine, empathise with and complete the 'missing' narrative – what illegal means in human terms, not only in this specific case but in the larger narrative of migration.

Bromley (2007, p. 20)

What we understand by radical democratic imaginaries includes the circulation, radicalisation and institutionalisation of democratic discourse (Smith, 1998, p. 7); the critical recovery of the hidden histories of the marginalised and repressed; ensuring the preservation of the space for democratic contestation against 'regulatory and governing authorities' techniques of neutralisation' (Walters, 2003) and the forces of authoritarianism; 'equal access to material resources necessary for self development and meaningful participation in social, cultural, political and economic decision making' (Smith, 1998, p. 31); anti-essentialism and resistance to all forms of domination and 'disciplinary normalisation' (ibid., p. 35) and inclusive, cultural citizenship[2]. Our work as cultural criminologists can not only highlight the importance of cultural representations of and reactions to crime and deviance, but might also be involved in thinking otherwise, of imagining differently and facilitating public scholarship, greater understanding and awareness and democratic discourses and imaginings.

In summary, this chapter has drawn upon a number of key themes in the available literature to examine the global, social and relational processes underpinning the production of refugees, the movement of people across borders, and the ways that cultural criminologists might engage with these topics. The tension between international human rights law and state-centric protection of 'porous' borders and the tension between humiliation and human dignity are important aspects of understanding globalisation and forced migration. Drawing upon Lindner (2006), the future directions for research, policy and practice in this area must surely be to focus upon the following as part of a radical democratic imaginary:

(i) accept the impact of migration both forced and free and the emergence of transnational communities and identities;
(ii) build decent institutions based upon justice, equality and global citizenship;
(iii) develop interventions based upon holistic concepts of social justice that will address humiliation, misrecognition and Othering.

The last chapter further consolidates themes of challenging misrecognition and Othering through a discussion of participatory action research carried out in Vancouver's Downtown Eastside (skid row).

8
Crime, Poverty and Resistance on Skid Row

This final chapter takes as its starting point the need to uncover the counter-narratives, the hidden histories of the people labelled as deviants and criminals in inner-city neighbourhoods. In doing so, the chapter draws upon community arts-based research conducted by O'Neill and Stenning (2011) in downtown eastside Vancouver (skid row) where 'community' is documented through the eyes of the inhabitants – the binners, sex workers, street vendors and artists struggling to make out in circumstances not of their choosing[1]. One dominant theme in the research – the struggle for recognition – emerges against depictions that categorise and record residents as abject, 'other' and 'different'.

Using Barthes' (1991) notion of the 'punctum', this chapter argues that certain photographs and social media are able to pierce us, bring us in touch with intractable reality in ways that we cannot forget. Using visual methodologies, photographs and social media, gathered through participatory and arts-based research, a picture emerges of the liveable lives of the residents made out in the margins of the city and the margins of legality, welfare and poverty. What emerges through their stories both reinforces and challenges some of the dominant tropes we find in fictive texts on crime in the inner city. What is clear is that the stories laid bare here offer oppositional discourses and representations to the rather simplistic message of the 'deviant' inhabitants and criminality of the residents of 'skid row' found in the mainstream media.

Visual methods

Given the growth of visual studies and the use of visual methodologies in social research, visual ethnography and visual data are often deployed illustratively using photographs, diagrams and sketches to help make or advance a point, or to elicit data from participants (photo elicitation). Rooted in a long-term project that connects the cultural analysis of the New Deviancy theorists and Birmingham School for Contemporary Cultural Studies in the UK with the North American focus upon ethnomethodology, Hayward and Presdee (2010) argue for a 'new methodological orientation towards the visual that is capable of encompassing meaning, affect, situation, symbolic power and efficiency and spectacle in the same "frame"' (p. 3). Hayward and Presdee's approach fuses phenomenological analysis of crime and transgression with theoretical analysis of late modern culture. This is the approach taken by O'Neill (2011a) in her long history of work with marginalised groups and is evident in the research conducted in Vancouver's Downtown Eastside (DTES) with the individuals who live there (O'Neill and Stenning, 2011).

DTES: A problem community

Dominant messages and discourses around skid row serve to identify it as a problem community par excellence (Campbell, Boyd and Culbert, 2009; O'Neill and Stenning, 2011), described variously as 'the poorest postal code in Canada' (Christoff and Kalache, 2007) and 'the most concentrated scene of human degradation in North America' (Wente, 2008 cited in O'Neill and Stenning, 2011). Messages from visitors posted on the Virtual Tourist website supports these descriptions urging people to keep away from DTES, unless you want to buy drugs. Here DTES is described as 'one of the worst ghettos in North America' and '[i]f you imagine a mixture of something like "Zombies: dawn of the dead", "Thriller" and "V the visitors" then you'll get the picture. Sad but who said life was perfect?' One thread is labelled 'Beggars, homeless & junkies, Vancouver':

> Supposedly, peaceful Vancouver Canada has a huge drug problem and one of the worst ghettos in North America. [*Describing addicts*

on the streets]: They look like animals; the way they move, the constant moving; you'd think that their bodies couldn't put up with that for too long. While Vancouver is undeniably pretty from a distance, up close it has become an appalling stew of junkies, beggars and scavengers that is unrivalled in the developed world.

Virtual Tourist, (2011)

The downtown eastside was once 'the heart of Vancouver's retail and banking district' and like many city centre spaces

economic conditions changed – retail stores and hotels moved West ... the streetcars and trams were displaced by the automobile ... the once-grand hotels became down-and-out beer parlours with single occupancy rooms housing people with a variety of difficulties ... By the 1990's, the Downtown Eastside seemed to be in a kind of free fall.

Campbell, Boyd and Culbert (2009, p. 1)

Crack cocaine and heroin abuse were added to the problem of alcohol abuse and the deinstitutionalisation if the mentally ill from hospitals, and with little or no housing support, since the 1960s, added to the decline of the neighbourhood, which had fast become a site of cheap single room housing. In 1993, 'the federal government stopped funding social housing, as part of its deficit cutting agenda. All this combined to produce a perfect storm' (Campbell, Boyd and Culbert, 2009, p. 2).

Campbell, Boyd and Culbert (2009) produce a rich history of the Downtown Eastside documenting the 'vulnerability and despair' as well as the 'hopefulness and resilience' in the community drawing upon historical archives, academic, journalistic and local residents' association reports. Portrayed as a risky and dangerous neighbourhood in the mainstream media, the authors set out to show that DTES is also a community of hope with people who care about its future and who are demanding urgent solutions. Indeed, a community in a long struggle of resistance to poverty, lack of social housing and more recently experiencing creeping gentrification.

Inner-city areas like the Downtown Eastside are always subject to media representation as well as the source of fiction, and this tends not to be constituted by the voices of the people who live and work there. The absence of an alternative voice in the media from the perspective of the denizens of DTES raises important ethico-political issues relating to the politics of representation and democracy as well as any attempts to address the poverty, welfare and gentrification issues (that effectively displace people and increase homelessness), through public policy. This chapter represents the voices and images of people who live in the community (See Figs. 8.1 to 8.5).

Re-presenting DTES: Alternative media

Strategies of representation, we argue, relate both to addressing the current lack of resident voices in mainstream media, as well as to developing specific strategies that take into account the complex realities of the residents' lives. Broadcast media are generally held to be the main contributors to the functioning of a public sphere in democratic societies, even if such an argument is used primarily to

Figure 8.1 Research participant taking a photograph of the Megaphone Office
Photo: April Smith, AHA Media.

point out the inadequacies of really existing television and radio in terms of their social roles. The main issue in terms of representation of lived lives is the provision of perspectival diversity that redresses the prevailing lack of representation from such communities as DTES in the mainstream media.

Low-cost social media offering alternative representations in contrast to the mainstream 'big' media provide the opportunity for communities to display their own narratives that highlight their experiences and concerns in complex and productive ways. Georgina Born (2004) suggests that the challenge, in an age of diversity, is to contribute to the formation of a more adequate communicative democracy than we have yet seen. Born argues for the existence of 'channels for counter-public to speak to counter-public as well as the integration into an (always imperfect) unitary pubic sphere' (p. 515).

Two of the organisations working with O'Neill et al. (2011) in DTES Vancouver are AHA Media (citizen journalists) and Megaphone, a street-level newspaper, both of which offer alternative representations rooted in the lives of citizens of DTES and offer local people a chance to develop training, skills, be employed and/or, in the case of Megaphone, supplement their welfare as street vendors.

AHA: Social media organisation

April Smith (AHAMedia.ca), a social media expert, describes herself as a 'citizen journalist', and resident of DTES[2]:

> I'm from the Downtown Eastside, a neighbourhood that has 20,000 residents, where 4,000 folks are homeless and 6,000 people have no phone, Internet or computers. This area is endemic to high levels of people who have addictions, mental illness and face poverty. It is a strong community with deep roots in Vancouver's history. Life is not easy in my area and it is a daily struggle to survive. It is one of the oldest neighbourhoods and I am proud to call it my home.

For the last three years April and her two colleagues who form AHA Media have documented life in DTES from the inside, and because they belong to the neighbourhood and communities who live there, the richness of the archives, blogs, photos and videos sharing stories of DTES presents a more compelling and complex depth than the social commentators and photographers who have documented the area over the decades – the social documentary or photographers who come into the DTES to film the street and alleyway scenes, the graffiti in public places.

> My interests are documentation of daily life in the Vancouver Downtown Eastside area, highlighting the positive while bringing to light the injustices that occur in the neighbourhood. I have filmed observations, both subversive and situational, over the last three years.

April goes in to say that

> We went online on November 11th 2008 – At the time, both Hendrik and I were living in the Astoria Hotel on Hastings Street. We were sitting there laughing at how the rats were jumping up to eat our food that we had hung up in bags to keep away from them! Those rats just didn't give up!
>
> Today on Canada's Remembrance Day 2008, AHA Media is born on WordPress! We're a group of Downtown Eastside residents that have been learning about technology from the Fearless City Mobile Project. We are trying to bridge the digital divide!

After a car accident, April found herself in DTES. 'Things happen in the blink of an eye.' When interviewed by a filmmaker working on a film in DTES, she had, indeed, that day been evicted. 'I just don't want to be a statistic. We are real people, we have needs, and we have wants'. (See April's story in the documentary film 'With Glowing Hearts' (2011) on http://wghthemovie.ca/.)

April states that as citizen journalists documenting the DTES using social media, they help to democratise the usual standard imagery of DTES. They also challenge the mainstream media-led constructions of DTES by subverting the dominant messages and images; this involves 'de-mystifying the folk devil'. AHA Media aim to be DTES' news and reporting site, challenging myths and stereotypes of the area and resisting the 'othering' of residents as 'zombies' or 'animals', as dehumanised and so undeserving of our interest and compassion.

Figure 8.2 April and Hendrik of AHA Media
Photo: AHA Media.

AHA Media have an enormous archive of stories, blogs and news items. They give public talks too and seek to be employed for this work. April states: 'Through this site, AHA Media is learning to use social media to help our neighbourhood's social justice, housing and economic issues.' They have covered 'the Women's Memorial March, Poverty Olympics and ... the Grand Housing March. We cover stories about Illegal Tenant Eviction from SRO Hotels and Downtown Eastside Pedestrian Safety Project'.

> Because we have personal relationships with people of our neigh-bourhood, we're able to get that close, inside angle that sometimes Traditional Media isn't always able to get. We've also developed a reputation in our community where local residents come see us for advocacy both online and offline. Through our work, we're helping to create social change by using social media.
> Social media has made a difference in my life and it's helping my community grow. Access to a simple cell phone is hard enough

Figure 8.3   AHA citizen journalist's media team Christmas 2011
Photo: AHA Media.

in the Downtown Eastside. It's so important in finding home or a job, being on call for work, connecting with doctors, employers, friends and family. Communication is certainly a tool for nurturing positive change. More access is the hand up solution for the Downtown Eastside.

Megaphone: Street-level newspaper

Megaphone is a street level newspaper similar to the Big Issue in the UK. Like the Big Issue, it is sold on the streets of Vancouver by homeless and low-income vendors. The aim described by the Executive Director, Sean Condon (who runs the newspaper, lives and works in DTES), is to 'provide economic opportunities to homeless and low-income people while building grassroots support to end poverty'. Vendors are or are not homeless, may have transited or are dealing with transiting drugs and/or alcohol abuse, and are involved in or have exited sex work. What criminal activity the residents of DTES are involved in revolves around economic need, crimes of poverty and/or are related to drug and alcohol addiction.

OUR MISSION *Megaphone's* goal is to provide economic opportunities to homeless and low-income people while building grassroots support to end poverty

The magazine comes out every two weeks. Vendors buy the paper for 75 cents and sell the magazine to customers for a $2 suggested donation. All money from the transaction goes into the pocket of the vendor.

Selling the paper gives our vendors a sense of pride and has helped some overcome homelessness, drug and alcohol addiction, and their mental or physical illnesses. By giving them a place and a voice in their community it helps raise their self-esteem

Street papers have a long and colorful history in Vancouver. The first street paper was named Spare Change and started in 1992. In 1998 the paper was renamed Street News. A few years later a second street paper was started by vendors named Street Corner. In 2007, both papers were brought back together and in 2008 it was renamed Megaphone.

Megaphone (2011)

In the May 2011 issue, key articles focus upon concerns at the heart of community needs: housing and the development of much-needed social housing; Cannabis culture (DTES is home to Canada's first public injection site); and a mixture of cultural and poetic articles from the creative writing workshops that Megaphone supports – *Voices of the Street*. The environment is a key issue too, for this is a community with recycling at its core. Clothes, bottles and cans are recycled to raise extra money and, as one Megaphone vendor said, it is a community that recycles people too. 'It's mostly about recycling the DTES ... there is a lot of recycling goes on here and a lot of people are recycled too and some just end up in the waste bin. There is a lot of real trauma here too.'

On the website, a number of Megaphone vendors describe something of their life and work. Two are reproduced next:

I worked construction all my life until I got arthritis. Now I can't work construction anymore, so I sell papers to supplement my

Figure 8.4 Patrick Doyle. Megaphone vendor
Photo: Megaphone.

income. I hurt my back, knees, and hips. I burnt my body out early. I started picking rocks early on the farm. Every spring you'd pick rocks. I'm from Ontario — St. Mary's, Mitchell area. I'd never been to B.C. But once I got here I never left. I'd been all over Canada. I mean, all over Canada. I haven't been to the Yukon yet; that's the only one place I haven't made. I was panhandling at Granville and Hastings for a couple years. I was sitting there, panhandling, when somebody walked up and told me about Megaphone. I like it because I've got a big mouth and you get to talk to people. You got a reason to approach people — you're not asking for money, you're selling them stuff. You're giving them a service. And a lot of people like the paper. I like the stories in Megaphone. There are all kinds of stuff you don't see in normal papers — like the guy who was getting roughed up by the cops, you don't see that in the news or nothing. And people should know about that. You make more money with the paper — and the extra money helps. If you read the paper and you know what you're talking about, you can sell. Selling makes me feel better, but I always feel good. I don't let

Figure 8.5 Levi Holland. Megaphone vendor
Photo: Megaphone.

myself get down. I like my customers. Having regulars means you have a bit of a regular income. Sometimes it can be sporadic. But you build up your regulars and it's a good thing.

I just started selling Megaphone this year. I've been pretty successful and have been getting some pretty good tips. I read the magazine first so I can talk to my customers about what's in it. I also learn a lot from the magazine myself.

What I like most about selling Megaphone is just getting out there, meeting people. It brings your spirits up. I also like going to different areas of Vancouver that I don't usually go to. I think that's important, because you should get to know other people from other communities and they should get to know you so they can get through the stereotypes of the Downtown Eastside.

I sell Megaphone and the Hope in Shadows calendar with my partner and two brothers. When one of us gets tired of standing on the corner, one of the others will take over. We call it a tag-team.

I was born and raised in Smithers. The Hudson Bay Mountain was part of my dad's clan. So that mountain was our hunting ground, our trapline and our fishing, before it got taken over. It's pretty racist around Smithers. I grew up with that racism from the day I was born until I left. Back in the '80s, there was a land claims case going on, and that's when the racism really reared its ugly head. People were going around beating up natives walking on the street.

It's still like that, maybe not as bad, but it's still there. That was one of the main reasons I left. There's no getting away from it in a small town, you run into the same idiots everyday. Plus all my friends were moving out of Smithers, looking for work.

I've been living in the Downtown Eastside off-and-on since 1985. I tell people when I'm selling Megaphone that everything the media portrays about the neighborhood is always negative. But there are a lot of women down here trying to help themselves. And not everybody is a drug addict, or a sex trade worker. There are healthy families down here and healthy people.

There's a lot of good people in Vancouver, a lot of generous people, and I just want to thank them. A lot of times I end up talking to my customers about whatever goes on down here and they give me their point of view and I learn from that. And they learn from what I have to say also.

What is clear from the material documented previously, the voices of people living in DTES, is the social struggle and the resistance involved in their everyday lives which is supported by resident-led social media and street-level news. Residents challenge hegemonic images that define them as abject and 'othered'. On the one hand disrespectful and dehumanising narratives and images are plenty, and on the other resistance to poverty, humiliation and disrespect and a struggle for recognition are palpable too. Welfare is set at $500 per month. The cheapest single room in DTES costs $375, leaving very little for food and other items. People survive by queuing up in food lines, provided by various organisations and programmes and getting free (recycled) clothing from agencies, such as the DTES Neighbourhood Centre and women's centres. Many people sleep in shelters or on the streets. Numbing the pain with alcohol, glue and drugs is a reality for many, as is survival sex work, panhandling and theft. Falling through the cracks in North America/Canadian welfare system can have devastating consequences as many of the participants in the research shared.

One of the 'binners' ('dumpster diver', 'scavenger'), a young man who took part in O'Neill and Stenning's (2011), research described it as follows:

> It is difficult for me to show how our community at the DTES is because of our life. I for one do not like my picture ever taken and like most of us down here are reasons of: family/friends looking for us, police warrants, not wanting employers to connect us to DTES.
>
> Now these reasons seem hardcore but most of us down here are downtrodden and poor and are drug addicts. But we are still humans and as humans we still develop a community, we are social beings. There are so many different communities going on in the DTES. There are the soup kitchens, the shelters, the help groups, community centers and even independent groups help with a hearing ear or food or clothes or even just standing on the street with a smile helps.
>
> Now for me I ended up down here after losing to a drug addiction and finally in jail for trafficking drugs. I was depressed and moved into single room occupancy [SRO]. I lost my finance, friends, and income, then too embarrassed to talk to family and close friends, I became an alien and just lived off the food and shelter. Some can say without the structure of the DTES I could have easily died, but because of the way things work down here I survived my depression and then eventually found a job at United We Can. They are a non-profit organization that recycles bottles. They employ the down and out people – that was me and give them a stepping stone to get back into the community and back into life. Even though it is only minimum wage, I was able to work 4 hour shifts. I was not able to hold down a job before cuz of the 8 hours/5 days, too depressing plus pay checks, could either start cuz of no money or ended up blowing all my check at once. At least here [UWC] I was able to just work 4 hours and 3–4 days

a week with cash pay at the end of the day. Give me a start to get my life back on track and out of my depression cuz of giving me direction to my life.

The community down here works where the longer you live here, the more people you recognize and vice versa recognize you that eventually you/we become comfortable with each other and start a dialogue and then the rest is human nature, we are all social beings.

Honeth's (2005) work on the struggle for recognition is helpful here to make sense of the complexities of the lives of the residents in DTES, and the social, ethico-political issues that motivate both AHA Media and Megaphone.

Disrespect, resistance and recognition

Honeth's work (2005) argues that social struggle emerges from violation of recognition and dignity (p. 160), and draws on Marx's concept of dignity, Sorel's concept of honour and Sartre's concept of recognition. Park and Burgess (1925, 1967) also refer to social conflict as a struggle for recognition. However, in the development of the social sciences, Honeth shows that 'social struggle' 'under the influence of Darwinian or utilitarian models' was defined 'in terms of competition, over material opportunities' (p. 160). Hence, in the Hobbesian history of the social sciences, social struggle and conflict have been defined as based around 'interests' linked to 'the objective inequalities in the distribution of material opportunities without ever being linked in any way to the web of moral feelings' (p. 161). Honeth argues that the conceptual analysis of Marx, Sorel and Sartre were forgotten 'fragments of an invisible underdeveloped theoretical tradition' (p. 180). He seeks to address this and reconstructs a theory of recognition using Hegel and Mead to link social struggle with moral disrespect and in so doing brings into high relief the relationship between disrespect and recognition.

Honeth (2005, p. 163) states that

[m]otives for social resistance and rebellion are formed in the context of moral experiences stemming from the violation of deeply rooted expectations regarding recognition ... If normative

expectations are disappointed by society; this generates precisely the type of moral expressed in cases where subjects feel disrespected. Hurt feelings of this sort can however, become the motivational basis for collective resistance only if subjects are able to articulate them within an intersubjective framework of interpretation that they can show to be typical for an entire group.

Hence personal experiences of hurt, humiliation and disrespect are interpreted not just as affecting the individual but the group, and shared semantics of the experiences facilitate social movement or struggle around the issues of concern. This is evident in the preceding chapter and is certainly evident in the history April documents of the development and work of AHA Media and the principles underpinning Megaphone street news. It is also present in the interviews with residents of DTES who took part in the participatory and arts-based research (a methodology based upon the principles of intersubjective recognition and participation, inclusion, valuing all voices). In their research report, O'Neill et al., 2011 and the community research team write:

> there is a lot of incredible people in this community;
> the unique attraction is the sense of community here;
> I have to resist things need to change.

Overwhelmingly, participants described DTES as a welcoming neighbourhood with an enormous amount of creative and artistic energy. 'I feel very intimate in this community and connected, people are accepted, here are people from all walks of life here.' Another person said, 'From the outside eye it looks dysfunctional and yet like any dysfunctional family we make it work ... But there is a strong community here.'

The report also found that relational dynamics are deeply implicated in experiencing, defining and understanding 'community' in DTES:

> Community involves the connections between people. We live our lives relationally and this involves networks of social relations. The media archive that AHA Media productions have amassed, the long history of activism and resistance, and Megaphone's archive all evidence the *relationship* aspect of community.
>
> O'Neill et al. (2011)

Honeth suggests that what people cope with privately 'can then become the moral motives for a collective "struggle for recognition"' (p. 164). In this way social struggle/social action tears people 'out of the crippling situation of passively endured humiliation and helping them, in turn, on their way to a new, positive relation-to-self' and in so doing 'feel that they have moral or social worth' (p. 164). 'This may, of course, be further strengthened by the recognition that the solidarity within the political groups offers by enabling participation to esteem each other' (p. 164). And this involves 'the inter-subjective conditions for personal integrity'. Honeth argues that 'the "struggle for recognition" is to be viewed as a critical framework for interpreting the processes by which societies develop' (p. 171). And, given the developments in and intersection of cultural anthropology and cultural sociology (*and we argue, cultural criminology*) we are able more carefully to recover the experiences of marginalised groups.

Drawing upon Hegel and Mead, Honeth argues that no fewer than three forms of recognition, love, rights and esteem constitute the social conditions under which human beings 'can develop a positive attitude to themselves' (p. 169). AHA Media and Megaphone are underpinned by a real understanding and focus upon intersubjective recognition. We argue here that genuinely participatory cultural criminological research can serve as the visual and semantic bridge between representations of community and the private experience of injury that enables the development of recognition, indeed intersubjective recognition. Such research can also document and explore the collective identity that emerges in the tension between resistance and the struggle for recognition – in this case the sense of community in DTES and the sense of belonging.

Community, recognition and belonging in DTES

One of the research participants, part of the writing group for the research report, wrote to O'Neill, in response to the first draft of the research report.

[T]here is another thing that contributes to the strong sense of community amongst us is that, whether this is a result of being poor, or whatever other dynamic is in operation here; (I say poor because that is my rationale) – so one of the reasons for the strong sense of community, for me, is that people who live in dtes (not counting gated communities (such as co-ops), the people who are out and about, there are not too many pretences; there is honesty and integrity to emotions, behaviour. there is a directness of approach and communication. a 'tell it as it is', and also the language, the sentence structure, is succinct, brief, quick, to the point, as a 'prick' a Jamaican friend said. sharp, lively, it's heavily based on street, rez (reservation), ghetto lingo. and i love it).

O'Neill found much evidence of the social issues and problems people experience: poverty, low income, violence, sex work outside residencies, needles and detritus, the drug dealers that prey on the vulnerable, disease and health problems that come with addiction, homelessness and lack of money, the need for money, feeling outside consumer society, feeling stigmatised and othered and judged, being seen and treated (as one person put it) like 'bears in a zoo'. There is also much evidence of resistance to these problems – the campaigning and advocacy that led to the public injection site, the poverty (alternative) Olympics, campaigns for social housing such as tent city and resistance to the 'creeping gentrification'. These demonstrate the need to claim a space for voices represented so well by *Megaphone* and *AHA Media* as well as by the long history of activism and advocacy in DTES.

Taking a phenomenological approach, O'Neill's arts-based research both documents and analyses the politics of community and resistance in DTES. Difference is visualised and other ways of seeing the spaces and places of 'community' through the eyes of some of the most marginalised inhabitants becomes possible. And, just as the trials, tribulations, joys and successes experienced by an individual become inscribed in his or her face, the same could be said of a community, and that the well-being (or otherwise) of a community can be read from visual images of it (O'Neill and Stenning, 2011). The picture that emerges contrasts with the hegemonic image and instead uncovers struggles for recognition in the rich multilayered stories and photographs by residents that speak of community, politics and resistance.

Postscript

Where might the kind of critical and cultural criminological research and analysis we undertake in *Transgressive Imaginations* take us[1]? In a recent talk at Durham University, Zygmunt Bauman (2011) offered the audience an invitation to develop an agenda for sociology. Drawing upon four of Bauman's key points, we close this book by offering an invitation to develop an agenda for cultural criminology and towards a public criminology – in the twenty-first century – that connects with the idea of a radical democratic imaginary. We argue here that through an examination of transgressive imaginations, popular culture and the everyday we can both (a) engage a wider audience and (b) work with different publics through critical, cultural and participatory methodologies.

For example, as discussed in Chapter 5, Janice Haaken's documentary is a great example of deeply engaged visual, participatory and performative film-making that engages the widest possible audience through its accessibility, storytelling and visuality. The film 'attunes' with the audience to the life stories of its participants – the inmates of Portland State Hospital who have pleaded 'guilty except for insanity'. In Chapter 5 we make an argument for the transgressive, transformative potential of Haaken's film in that it engages audiences in ways that pierce or puncture us into a deeper encounter, connection, attunement, recognition and understanding of the lives of those deemed absolutely abject – the criminally insane.

At one and the same time Haaken's film is a wonderful example of participatory film-making across a number of registers and with a number of publics, tensions and struggles. Haaken worked with inmates through the methodology of participatory film (even the sound track is developed using words and music from inmates), with staff and senior managers in the hospital, as well as with criminal justice agencies beyond the doors and boundaries of the institution, and with the families of some of the inmates. Hence, as a cultural text, the film is constructed from a multiplicity of knowledges and experiences (including dominant symbols and tropes from visual culture enshrined in the footage used from *One Flew Over the Cuckoo's Nest*) and the complex narratives that unfold are gripping, horrifying and demand action. The audience engages with the characters in Haaken's film as flesh and blood beings, not as ciphers of their 'condition' or as subject-objects of scrutiny. We engage with the everyday, ordinariness and extraordinariness of lived experiences in the psychiatric secure hospital in a respectful and dignified way, through what Scheff (2006) calls 'attunement'. The film challenges conventionally limited imaginings of madness and draws attention to mediated constructions of deviance, care and control. In doing so, it is a great example of a radical democratic imaginary in operation, both methodologically (through participatory scholarship, research, analysis and storytelling) and in the possibilities it creates for mobilising social and political engagement around the dire lack of community mental health support and lack of a welfare safety net in North America. For the people in the film, the only way they can get mental health support is by committing a crime.

The agenda we outline and invite readers to engage with for critical/cultural criminology in the twenty-first century involves thinking through what a public criminology looks like. The issue of public criminology has been taken up recently by Loader and Sparks (2011) and, like them, we do not present the 'one true path' (p. 115) to how we think this should be achieved. Rather, we discuss the tributary that we intend to follow. For us it includes the importance of the following four key points made by Bauman (2011) that sparked our criminological imagination.

First, 'de-familiarise the familiar and familiarise the unfamiliar'. Here Bauman made reference to Milan Kundera (2007) using the tear in the curtain to see through to reality, avoiding cheap convictions and stereotypes. Kundera calls for artists and the humanities and social sciences to join forces. For example, Haaken's film, *Guilty Except for Insanity*, utilises critical thinking and analysis as well as respect for the dignity of the people she participates with to make the film. Her skills as a film-maker enable her to defamiliarise the images and representations of 'mental illness', 'criminality' and 'insanity' in visual culture, while enabling the viewer to access and engage with the complex, psychosocial realities of the five people whose stories are told. Her scholarship and cultural practice and her 'attunement' to the individuals she works with guards against the representation of 'cheap stereotypes and convictions' that might facilitate the transformation of people's pain into enjoyment – for where suffering can simply be consumed/enjoyed, something of its horror is removed. Shriver's (2010) *We Need to Talk about Kevin*, discussed in Chapter 2, also does this work of defamiliarisation, bringing to the surface the usually unspoken terrors of motherhood. Its subject – a mass murder perpetrated by a 15-year-old boy as narrated by his mother – tears the curtain to provide us with a stark representation of a mother-son relationship. In doing so, the complexity of parenthood, cultural understandings of childhood and cultures of violence are made visible.

Second, Bauman called for what E. M. Forster (2000 [1910]) described in *Howard's End* as 'only connect': take up interaction with other spheres of human life, show the interconnections. Thus interdisciplinarity, what we might also call transdisciplinarity, that involves working across disciplines in participatory ways to develop knowledge with communities, with the stereotypical subjects of research, can make a difference. The participatory research in DTES Vancouver documented in Chapter 8 suggests that art and social media-based research can be a way of overcoming barriers, challenging stereotypes, producing more complex knowledge, as well as creating safe spaces for dialogue and for listening and communicating experience across linguistic and cultural divides. In participatory and arts-based research, findings can be made more accessible beyond academia and offer social and cultural impact. This is also the case for detailed historical archival research that connects across place and time with knowledges and contexts beyond the boundaries of mainstream 'criminology' as discussed in Chapters 3 and 4. Transdisciplinary scholarship (such as that promoted by the Leonardo Education and Art Forum, see Leonardo On-line (2011)) that connects cultural studies, critical theory and visual culture, history, feminist and gender studies and psychosocial analysis to a sociologically embedded criminology, is, for us, part of the very future of criminology – as an already unfinished 'discipline'.

Third, Bauman recommended 'unravelling doxa' – 'knowledge with which you think but of which you don't know'. Here he means the art of thinking consciously. This, for us, is synonymous with critical thinking, with dialectical thinking, with thinking otherwise, against the grain. As criminologists and researchers we need to concern ourselves not only with the art of thinking, but the art of listening and seeing too. Using innovative and multi-sensory methodologies in criminological research is vital to the art of thinking critically and creatively for developing and sustaining a criminological imagination. Bringing this approach to the analysis of cultural representations enables us to explore the consumption of visual and written representations of crime, to consider what constitutes 'popular criminology' (Rafter, 2007), while also acknowledging that culture is not found but made, by artists, film-makers and researchers as well as by the audience. So cultural representations can be read and interpreted in different ways, and audiences are also creators of culture.

Fourth, Bauman urged us to open and keep open dialogue, and to spread the art of sociology around through dialogue and participation. For us, it is important that this is dialogue that is unfinished, that opens and keeps open the spaces for critical thinking, resistance and reflection. We aspire to dialogue that is interdisciplinary/ transdisciplinary, that fosters mutual trust, and subject-subject relationships as far as possible – which values expertise in communities, uncovers hidden histories, shares knowledge and expertise and sets the horizon of our criminological endeavours against the highest quality of research and practice. Challenging and resisting dominant images and stereotypes of 'the school shooter', the 'female avenger', 'prostitutes' and 'asylum seekers', and making this work available to as wide an audience as possible can serve to raise awareness, challenge, as well as educate and create spaces for the voices of individuals and groups who are otherwise silenced. The dominant images, stereotypes and tropes that we often find in the public imagination and in the kind of 'zoo-keeping' (O'Brien, 2005) ethnography that exists within some contemporary criminology do not reflect the courage, resistance, or liveable lives of those on the margins of neoliberal capitalism. Nor do they reflect the kind of public scholarship we are advocating here, one that deals in complexity and connects with the constructed, performative nature of our social worlds and criminological knowledge production.

For ourselves, the importance of critical/cultural public scholarship cannot be overstated, not in didactic ways, but heuristically and creatively by defamiliarising the familiar and familiarising the unfamiliar, working together in interdisciplinary/transdisciplinary ways, using critical and dialectical thinking, and by opening and keeping open spaces for critical creative research, theory and practice in our criminological imaginations, endeavours and futures. This is our hope for the future of critical/cultural criminology – to move towards a public criminology for the twenty-first century attuned to understandings of transgression, protest and 'knowledges of resistance', especially in relation to sexual and social inequalities, and which makes possible a radical democratic imaginary.

Notes

2 Children as Victims and Villains: The School Shooter

1. 'Doli incapax' is the presumption that children are not responsible for their criminal actions. It was abolished in England and Wales for 10- to 13-year-olds in 1998. ASBOs, introduced in 1998, are civil measures that can be used to control non-criminal 'nuisance' behaviour, such as noise, truancy, intimidation and bullying. They can be applied to individuals aged 10 and over.
2. In Germany, there were school shootings in Erfurt in 2002 and in Winnenden in 2009. In Finland, they occurred in Tuusula in 2007 and in Kauhajoki in 2008.
3. Kevin's attachment to his water gun is an ironic foreshadowing, as he does not use a firearm to carry out his school attack.

3 Violent Female Avengers in Popular Culture

1. With thanks to Helen Cook for providing this information. Karen Leander worked for the Stockholm Centre for Public Health and led public awareness campaigns on violence against women in Sweden. See Leander (2006).

5 Madness and Liminality: Psychosocial and Fictive Images

1. Directed by Janice Haaken, professor of psychology at Portland State University and a documentary film-maker. Produced by Portland State University in association with Herzog and company Running time 90 minutes: http://www.guiltyexcept.com/.
2. Such as the turn to emotion (Karstedt, 2002), the narrative and biographical turn (Roberts, 2002; O'Neill, 2010b) and the cultural turn (Ferrell et al., 2004).

6 Serial Killers and the Ethics of Representation

1. John George Haigh, who was executed in England in 1949, dissolved his victims' bodies in acid. Neville Heath, executed in England in 1946, sexually assaulted and mutilated his female victims. Ed Gein, an American serial killer active in the 1950s, dismembered his victims.

2. Gacy murdered over 30 young men and boys in Chicago in the 1970s, most of whom he buried underneath his house. He appeared as a clown at local children's parties and at community fundraising events.
3. 'Torture porn' is a term that has been used to describe films which depict extreme, gory violence that is simultaneously shocking and titillating (Edelstein, 2006).
4. The killer's actions recall the 2001 murder of Peter Falconio, a British tourist, who was abducted at gunpoint on a remote highway in the Northern Territory of Australia.

7 Outlaws, Borders and Folk Devils

1. O'Neill (2011b) writes, 'Following Misha's model walks were led by residents who were seeking asylum or had gained refugee status or humanitarian protection. Their walking partners were local dignitaries, policy makers, community artists or other residents. They started off at a place viewed by individual residents as "home" and ended at a place he or she experienced as "special". During the walk, the resident talked about his or her life. The process of narrating aspects of one's past and present biography took place in a dialogic space between walker, co-walker and the environment. What Myers (2007) calls "making place through process" emerged – a performing of emplacement, not as linear process but a dialectical, complex process eliciting multiple modalities of experience – "between here and there and nowhere", not only for the new arrivals but also for the co-walkers.'
2. Lister's (2007, p. 58) body of work on citizenship and its intersections with poverty define 'citizenship' as a 'multi-tiered concept and practice' marked by the dynamics of inclusion/exclusion. Lister writes that Naila Kabeer's work on citizenship provides 'four values of inclusive citizenship that emerge from Kabeer's empirical work in the Global South'. These four values are justice, recognition, self-determination and solidarity. Lister writes that Kabeer articulates them as follows: justice involves 'when it is fair for people to be treated the same and when it is fair that they should be treated differently' (Kabeer, 2005, p. 3); recognition involves 'the intrinsic worth of all human beings, but also recognition of and respect for their differences' (p. 4); self-determination involves 'people's ability to exercise some degree of control over their lives' (p. 5); and solidarity is, 'the capacity to identify with others and to act in unity with them in their claims for justice and recognition' (Kabeer, cited in Lister, 2007, pp. 50–1).

8 Crime, Poverty and Resistance on Skid Row

1. This research project (O'Neill and Stenning, September 2010–September 2011 – is funded by the British Academy, the Wolfson Research Institute and the School of Applied Social Sciences, Durham University) sought to

explore, in partnership with local agencies, ways of seeing the spaces and places of community through the eyes of DTES residents and workers, using participatory action research (PAR) and participatory arts (PA). This research built upon Stenning's photographs of DTES in 2002 and 2008. The principles underpinning PAR and PA are inclusion, participation, valuing all local voices, community-driven and sustainable outcomes. Community co-researchers based in each organisation worked with Maggie to conduct the research and supported the creation of visual representations of 'community'. This group formed the research team and authored the report and articles.

2. From personal communication with April Smith.

Postscript

1. See a chapter by O'Neill (2012) 'Ethno-mimesis and participatory arts' in *Advances in Visual Methodology*.

References

Abrams, J. J., Lieber, J. and Lindelof, D. (2004–10) *Lost*, USA: ABC Studios.

Agamben, G. (1995) *Homo Sacer: Sovereign Power and Bare Life*, Stanford: Stanford University Press.

Aitken, S. C. (2001) 'Schoolyard Shootings: Racism, Sexism, and Moral Panics Over Teen Violence', *Antipode*, 33(4): 593–600.

Altheide, D. L. (2009) 'The Columbine Shootings and the Discourse of Fear', *American Behavioral Scientist*, 52(10): 1354–70.

Bakhtin, M. M. (1984) *Rabelais and his World*, Bloomington, IN: Indiana University Press.

Bakhtin, M. M. (1986) *Speech Genres and Other Late Essays*, Austin: University of Texas Press.

Ballinger, A. (2000) *Dead Woman Walking: Executed Women in England and Wales 1900–1965*, Aldershot: Ashgate.

Ballinger, A. (2007) 'Masculinity in the Dock: Legal Responses to Male Violence and Female Retaliation in England and Wales, 1900–1965', *Social and Legal Studies*, 16(4): 459–81.

Barthes, R. (1991) *Camera Lucida*, New York: Hill and Wang.

Bassett, C. (2007) *The Arc and the Machine: Narrative and the New Media*, Manchester: Manchester University Press.

Battersby, C. (1998) *The Phenomenal Woman*, Cambridge: Polity Press.

Bauman, Z. (2004) *Wasted Lives: Modernity and its Outcasts*, Cambridge: Polity Press.

Bauman, Z. (2007) *Liquid Times: Living in an Age of Uncertainty*, Cambridge: Polity Press.

Bauman, Z. (2011) 'Reflections on Economy and Society', Public Lecture given at Durham University, 16 February.

Belvaux R., Bonzel, A. and Poelvoorde, B. (1992) *Man Bites Dog*, Belgium: Les Artistes Anonymes.

Benjamin, J. (1993) *The Bonds of Love: Psychoanalysis, Feminism, and the Problem of Domination*, London: Virago Press.

Benjamin, W. (1983) *Charles Baudelaire: A Lyric Poet in the Era of High Capitalism*, London: Verso.

Bereswill, M., Morgenroth, C. and Redman, P. (2010) 'Alfred Lorenzer and the Depth-Hermeneutic Method', *Psychoanalysis, Culture & Society*, 15(3): 221–50.

Bertilsson, M. (1986) 'Love's Labour Lost? A Sociological View', *Theory, Culture and Society*, 3(2): 19–35.

Bigelow, K. (1989) *Blue Steel*, USA: Lightning Pictures.

Birch, H. (1993) 'If Looks Could Kill: Myra Hindley and the Iconography of Evil', in H. Birch (ed.) *Moving Targets: Women, Murder and Representation*, London: Virago.

Birnbaum, R. (2003) 'Lionel Shriver [Interview]', *identitytheory.com*, 24 July: http://www.identitytheory.com/interviews/birnbaum118.php (Accessed on 7 February 2011).

Born, G. (2004) *Uncertain Vision: Birt, Dyke and the Reinvention of the BBC*, London: Martin Secker & Warburg Ltd.

Boskin, J. (1997) *Rebellious Laughter: People's Humor in American Culture*, Syracuse, NY: Syracuse University Press.

Bradshaw, P. (2004) 'Elephant [Review]', *The Guardian*, 30 January: http://film.guardian.co.uk/News_Story/Critic_Review/Guardian_review/0,,1134158,00.html (Accessed on 7 February 2011).

Bradshaw, P. (2010) 'The Killer Inside Me [Review]', *The Guardian*, 3 June: http://www.guardian.co.uk/film/2010/jun/03/the-killer-inside-me-review (Accessed on 20 August 2010).

Brah, A. (1996) *Cartographies of Diaspora: Contesting Identities*, London: Routledge.

Bromley, R. (2007) *Between a World of Need and a World of Excess: Globalized People, Migration and Cinematic Narrative*, unpublished paper, from personal communication with the author.

Bronfen, E. (1992) *Over Her Dead Body: Death, Femininity and the Aesthetic*, Manchester: Manchester University Press.

Brotherton, D. and Barrios, L. (2004) *The Almighty Latin King and Queen Nation: Street Politics and the Transformation of a New York Gang*, New York: Columbia UP.

Brown, A. (2003) 'From Individual to Social Defences in Psychosocial Criminology', *Theoretical Criminology*, 7: 421.

Brown, E. (2008) 'Race, Space and Crime: The City, Moral Panics and "Risky" Youth', in C. Krinsky (ed.) *Moral Panics Over Contemporary Youth*, Farnham: Ashgate.

Buckley, L. (2006) 'Studio Photography and the Aesthetics of Citizenship in the Gambia, West Africa', in E. Edwards, C. Gosden and R. B. Phillips (eds) *Sensible Objects: Colonialism, Museums and Material Culture*, New York: Berg.

Burns, R. and Crawford, C. (1999) 'School Shootings, the Media, and Public Fear: Ingredients for a Moral Panic', *Crime, Law and Social Change*, 32(2): 147–68.

Butchard, S. (2010) *Five Daughters*, UK: BBC.

Butler, J. (1990) *Gender Trouble: Feminism and the Subversion of Identity*, New York and London: Routledge.

Butler, J. (1997) *Excitable Speech: A Politics of the Performative*, London: Routledge.

Cameron, D. and Frazer, E. (1987) *The Lust to Kill*, Cambridge: Polity Press.

Cameron, J. (1991) *Terminator 2: Judgment Day*, USA: Carolco Pictures.

Campbell, L., Boyd, N. and Culbert, L. (2009) *A Thousand Dreams: Vancouver's Downtown Eastside and the Fight for its Future*, Vancouver/Toronto: Greystone Books.

Caputi, J. (1987) *The Age of the Sex Crime*, London: The Women's Press.

Carlen, P. (2009) 'Review', *British Journal of Criminology*, 49(4): 574–77.

Carver, R. (2009) 'So Much Water So Close To Home', *What We Talk About When We Talk About Love*, London: Vintage.

Castles, S. (2003). 'Towards a Sociology of Forced Migration and Social Transformation', *Sociology-the Journal of the British Sociological Association* 37(1): 13–3.

Chesney-Lind, M. (2006) 'Patriarchy, Crime and Justice', *Feminist Criminology*, 1(1): 6–26.

Christoff, S. and Kalache, S. (2007) 'The Poorest Post Code', *The Dominion*, 12 January:. http://www.dominionpaper.ca/articles/909 (Accessed on 30 May 2011).

Clarke, J. (2001) 'The Pleasures of Crime: Interrogating the Detective Story', in J. Muncie and E. McLaughlin (eds) *The Problem of Crime*, London: Sage.

Clover, C. (1992) *Men, Women and Chainsaws: Gender in the Modern Horror Film*, Princeton: Princeton University Press.

Cohen, S. (1972) *Folk Devils and Moral Panics: the Creation of the Mods and Rockers*, London: MacGibbon and Kee.

Cohen, S. (2002) *Folk Devils and Moral Panics*, London: Routledge. 3rd edition.

Cohen, S. and Young, J. (1981) *The Manufacture of News*, London: Constable.

Connell, R. W. (1987) *Gender and Power*, Cambridge: Polity Press.

Connell, R. W. (1995) *Masculinities*, Cambridge: Polity Press.

Corbin (1990) 'Commercial Sexuality in Nineteenth-Century France: A system of Images and Regulations', in C. Gallagher and T. Laquer (eds) *The Making of the Modern Body: Sexuality and Society in the Nineteenth Century*, Berkeley: University of California Press.

Corbin, A. (1990) *Women For Hire: Prostitution and Sexuality in France after 1850*, Cambridge: Harvard University Press.

Cornell, D. (1995) *The Imaginary Domain: Abortion, Pornography and Sexual Harassment*, London and New York: Routledge.

Cornell, D. (2006) 'An Interview with Drucilla Cornell', in R. Heberle (ed.) *Feminist Interpretations of Theodor Adorno*, Pennsylvania: The Penn State University Press.

Coulthard, L. (2007) 'Killing Bill: Rethinking Feminism and Film Violence', in Y. Tasker and D. Negra (eds) *Interrogating Post-Feminism: Gender and the Politics of Popular Culture*, Durham: Duke University Press.

Creed, B. (1993) *The Monstrous-Feminine: Film, Feminism and Psychoanalysis*, London: Routledge.

Cresswell, T. (1996) *In Place/Out of Place: Geography, Ideology and Transgression*, Minneapolis: University of Minnesota Press.

Crossley, N. (2004) 'Not being Mentally Ill', *Anthropology & Medicine*, 11(2): 161–80.

Dahl, J. (1994) *The Last Seduction*, USA: Incorporated Television Company.

Dargis, M. (2006) 'In "Hard Candy", an Internet Lolita is Not as Innocent as She Looks', *The New York Times*, 14 April: http://movies.nytimes.com/2006/04/14/movies/14hard.html (Accessed on 16 June 2010).

Darke, C. (2003) 'The Underside of Globalisation: On Michael Winterbottom's *In this World*', http://www.opendemocracy.net/arts-Film/article_1120.jsp (Accessed on 30 April 2011).

Demme, J. (1991) *The Silence of the Lambs*, USA: Orion Pictures Corporation.

Ditmore, M., Levy, A. and Willman, A. (2010) *Sex Work Matters*, London: Zed.

Douglas, J. (and Olshaker, M.) (1995) *Mindhunter: Inside the FBI's Elite Serial Crime Unit*, New York: Schribner.

Eagleton, T. (1981) *Walter Benjamin: Towards a Revolutionary Criticism*, London: Verso.

Early, F. H. and Kennedy, K. (2003) 'Introduction', in F. H. Early and K. Kennedy (eds) *Athena's Daughters: Television's New Women Warriors*, Syracuse: Syracuse University Press.

Eastwood, C. (1992) *Unforgiven*, United States: Warner Brothers.

Edelstein, D. (2003) 'The Kids in the Hall', *Slate.com*, 24 October: http://www.slate.com/id/2090284/ (Accessed on 7 February 2011).

Edelstein, D. (2006) 'Now Playing at Your Local Multiplex: Torture Porn', *New York Magazine*, 28 January: http://nymag.com/movies/features/15622/ (Accessed on 16 July 2010).

Egger, S. A. (2002) *The Killers Among Us: An Examination of Serial Murder and its Investigation*, Upper Saddle River: Prentice Hall.

Ellis, B. E. (1991) *American Psycho*, New York: Vintage Books.

Enloe, C. (2007) *Globalization and Militarism: Feminists Make the Links*, New York: Rowman and Littlefield.

Fairweather, S. (2007) 'Ray Lawrence: Jindabyne', *Aesthetica*, 19: 48–9.

Ferrell, J. (1993) *Crimes of Style: Urban Graffiti and the Politics of Criminality*, New York: Garland Publishing.

Ferrell, J. (1995) 'Urban Graffiti: Crime, Control and Resistance', *Youth and Society*, 27: 73–92.

Ferrell, J. (1998) 'Freight Train Graffiti: Subculture, Crime, Dislocation', *Justice Quarterly*, 15(4): 587–608.

Ferrell, J. (1999) 'Cultural Criminology', *American Review of Sociology*, 25: 395–418.

Ferrell, J. (2001) *Tearing Down the Streets: Adventures in Urban Anarchy*, New York: Palgrave Macmillan.

Ferrell, J. (2005) 'Cultural Criminology', in E. McLaughlin and J. Muncie (eds) *The Sage Dictionary of Criminology*, London: Sage.

Ferrell, J. (2006) *Empire of Scrounge*, New York: New York University Press.

Ferrell, J. (2007) 'For a Ruthless Cultural Criticism of Everything Existing', *Crime, Media, Culture*, 3(1): 91–100.

Ferrell, J., Hayward, K., Morrison, W. and Presdee, M. (2004) 'Fragments of a Manifesto', J. Ferrell, K. Hayward, W. Morrison and M. Presdee (eds) *Cultural Criminology Unleashed*, London: Glasshouse.

Ferrell, J., Hayward, K. and Young, J. (2008) *Cultural Criminology: An Invitation*, London: Sage.

Ferrell, J., Milovanovic, D. and Lyng, S. (2001) 'Edgework, Media Practices, and the Elongation of Meaning', *Theoretical Criminology*, 5(2): 177–202.

Ferrell, J. and Sanders, C. R. (1995) 'Toward a Cultural Criminology', J. Ferrell and C. R. Sanders (eds) *Cultural Criminology*, Boston: Northeastern University Press.

Fincher, D. (1995) *Se7en*, USA: New Line Cinema.

Fleming, T. (2007) 'The History of Violence: Mega Cases of Serial Murder, Self-Propelling Narratives, and Reader Engagement', *Journal of Criminal Justice and Popular Culture*, 14(3): 277–91.

Forster, E. M. (2000 [1910]) *Howard's End*, London: Penguin.

Forman, M. (1975) *One Flew Over the Cuckoo's Nest [Motion Picture]*, United States: Fantasy Films.

Foucault, M. (1977) *Discipline and Punish: The Birth of the Prison*, London: Allen Lane.

Foucault, M. (2006) *Madness and Civilisation*, London: Vintage.

Fox, J. A. and Levin, J. (1998) 'Multiple Homicide Patterns of Serial and Mass Murder', *Crime and Justice*, 23: 407–55.

Frigon, S. (2006) 'Mapping Scripts and Narratives of Women Who Kill Their Husbands in Canada 1866–1954', in A. Burfoot (ed.) *Killing Women: The Visual Culture of Gender Violence*, Waterloo, ON: Wilfrid Laurier Press.

Frogatt, L. and Hollway, W. (2010) 'Psychosocial Research Analysis and Scenic Understanding', *Psychoanalysis, Culture & Society*, 15: 281–301.

Frost, V. (2010) 'Five Daughters was BBC Drama at its Best', TV&RadioBlog, *guardian.co.uk*, 28 April: http://www.guardian.co.uk/tv-and-radio/tvandradioblog/2010/apr/28/five-daughters-bbc-drama-best (Accessed on 26 August 2010).

Frymer, B. (2009) 'The Media Spectacle of Columbine: Alienated Youth as an Object of Fear', *American Behavioral Scientist*, 52(10): 1387–404.

Gadd, D. and Jefferson, T. (2007) *Psychosocial Criminology*, London: Sage.

Giddens, A. (1992) *The Transformation of Intimacy: Sexuality, Love and Eroticism in Modern Societies*, Cambridge: Polity Press.

Gillespie, C. (2007) *Lars and the Real Girl [Motion Picture]*, United States: Metro-Goldwyn-Meyer.

Gonick, M. (2006) 'Between "Girl Power" and "Reviving Ophelia": Constitution of the Neo-Liberal Girl Subject', *NWSA Journal*, 18(2): 1–20.

Grant, C. (2004) *Crime and Punishment in Contemporary Culture*, London: Routledge.

Greer, C. (2003) 'Sex, Crime and the Media: Press Representations in Northern Ireland', in P. Mason (ed.) *Criminal Visions: Media Representations of Crime*, Cullompton: Willan.

Greer, C., Ferrell, J. and Jewkes, Y. (2008) 'Investigating the Crisis of the Present', *Crime, Media, Culture*, 4(1): 5–9.

Greer, C. and Jewkes, Y. (2004) 'Extremes of Otherness: Media Images of Social Exclusion', *Social Justice: A Journal of Crime, Conflict and World Order*, 32(1): 20–31.

Greer, G. (2008) 'Burden of Guilt', *The Guardian*: http://www.guardian.co.uk/uk/2008/jan/25/ukcrime.germainegreer (Accessed on 1 March 2011).

Griffiths, R. (2010) 'The Gothic Folk Devils Strike Back! Theorizing Folk Devil Reaction in the Post-Columbine Era', *Journal of Youth Studies*, 13(3): 403–22.

Grixti, J. (1995) 'Consuming Cannibals: Psychopathic Killers as Archetypes and Cultural Icons', *Journal of American Culture*, 18(1): 87–96.

Haaken, J. (2008) 'Too Close for Comfort: Psychoanalytic Cultural Theory and Domestic Violence Politics', *Psychoanalysis, Culture & Society*, 13: 75–93.

Haaken, J. (2010) *Guilty Except for Insanity [Documentary]*, United States: Portland State University.

Haggerty, K. (2009) 'Modern Serial Killers', *Crime, Media, Culture*, 5(2): 168–87.

Hall, S. (1982) 'Cultural Studies: Two Paradigms', in T. Bennett, G. Martin, C. Mercer and J. Woollacott (eds) *Culture, Ideology and Social Process*, Milton Keynes: Open University Press.

Hall, S., Critcher, C., Jefferson, T. and Clarke, J. N. (1978) *Policing the Crisis*, London: Macmillan.

Hall, S. and Jefferson, T. (1976) *Resistance through Rituals*, London: Hutchinson.

Hall, S. and Winlow, S. (2007) 'Cultural Criminology and Primitive Accumulation', *Crime, Media, Culture*, 3(1): 82–90.

Hanson, C. (1992) *The Hand that Rocks the Cradle*, USA: Hollywood Pictures.

Harris, T. (1988) *The Silence of the Lambs*, New York: St Martin's Press.

Hawks, H. (1959) *Rio Bravo [Motion Picture]*, United States: Armada Productions.

Hay, C. (1995) 'Mobilization through Interpellation: James Bulger, Juvenile Crime and the Construction of a Moral Panic', *Social and Legal Studies*, 4(2): 197–223.

Hayward, K. J. and Presdee, M. (2010) *Framing Crime: Cultural Criminology and the Image*, London and New York: Routledge.

Hebdige, D. (1979) *Subculture: The Meaning of Style*, London: Methuen.

Heidensohn, F. (1996) *Women and Crime*, Basingstoke: Palgrave Macmillan. 2nd edition.

Hendrick, H. (1997) 'Constructions and Reconstructions of British Childhood', in A. James and A. Prout (eds) *Constructing and Reconstructing Childhood*, London: Routledge.

Herbst, C. (2004) 'Lara's Lethal and Loaded Mission: Transposing Reproduction and Destruction', in S. A. Inness (ed.) *Action Chicks: New Images of Tough Women in Popular Culture*, Basingstoke: Palgrave Macmillan.

Hirschman, E. C. and Stern, B. B. (1994) 'Women as Commodities: Prostitution Depicted in The Blue Angel, Pretty Baby, and Pretty Woman', *Advances In Consumer Research*, 21: 576–81.

Hitchcock, A. (1960) *Psycho*, USA: Shamley Productions.

Hollway, W. and Jefferson, T. (2000) *Doing Qualitative Research Differently: Free Association, Narrative and the Interview Method*, London: Sage.

Hollway, W. (2008) 'The Importance of Relational Thinking in the Practice of Psycho-social Research: Ontology, Epistemology, Methodology and Ethics', in S. Clarke, P. Hoggett and H. Hahn (eds) *Object Relations and Social Relations: The Implications of the Relational Turn in Psychoanalysis. Exploring Psycho-social Studies*, London: Karnac.

Holmes, R. M. and Holmes, S. T. (1998) *Contemporary Perspectives on Serial Murder*, London: Sage.

Holmlund, C. (1993) 'A Decade of Deadly Dolls: Hollywood and the Woman Killer', in H. Birch (ed.) *Moving Targets: Women, Murder and Representation*, London: Virago.

Honeth, A. (2005) *The Struggle for Recognition: The Moral Grammar of Social Conflicts*, Cambridge: Polity Press.

Hooper, T. (1974) *The Texas Chainsaw Massacre*, USA: Vortex.

Hubbard, P. (1999) *Sex and the City: Geographies of Prostitution in the Urban West*, Aldershot: Ashgate Press.

Irigaray, L. (1993) *Je, Tu, Nous: towards a culture of difference*, London: Routledge.

Inness, S. A. (2004) 'Boxing Gloves and Bustiers: New Images of Tough Women', in S. A. Inness (ed.) *Action Chicks: New Images of Tough Women in Popular Culture*, Basingstoke: Palgrave Macmillan.

Jackson, G. and Dube, D. (2006) *What am I Living For? Living on the Streets of Leicester*, Leicester: Diocese of Leicester.

Jamieson, J. (2005) 'Youth Justice and the Question of "Respect"', *Youth Justice*, 5(3): 180–93.

Jarvis, B. (2007) 'Monsters Inc.: Serial Killers and Consumer Culture', *Crime, Media, Culture*, 3(3): 326–44.

Jenkins, P. (1994) *Using Murder: The Social Construction of Serial Homicide*, New York: Aldine De Gruyter.

Jenkins, P. (2002) 'Catch Me Before I Kill More: Seriality as Modern Monstrosity', *Cultural Analysis*, 3: 1–17.

Jenks, C. (2003) *Transgression*, London: Routledge.

Jenks, C. (2007) *Childhood*, London: Taylor & Francis. 2nd edition (Kindle edition).

Jeremiah, E. (2010) 'We Need to Talk about Gender: Mothering and Masculinity in Lionel Shriver's "We Need to Talk About Kevin"', in E. Podnieks and A. O'Reilly (eds) *Textual Mothers/Maternal Texts: Motherhood in Contemporary Women's Literatures*, Waterloo, ON: Wilfrid Laurier University Press.

John, N. (1994) (ed.) *Violetta and her Sisters: The Lady of the Camellias Responses to the Myth*, London: Faber and Faber.

Jones, A. (1996) *Women Who Kill*, Boston: Beacon Press.

Jones, K. W. (2009) 'The Thirty-Third Victim: Representations of Seung-Hui Cho in the Aftermath of the "Virginia Tech Massacre"', *The Journal of the History of Childhood*, 2(1): 64–82.

Jouve, N. W. (1986) *The Street-Cleaner: The Yorkshire Ripper Case on Trial*, London: Marion Boyars Publishers.

Kabeer, N. (2005) 'The search for inclusive citizenship: meanings and expressions in an interconnected world', in N. Kabeer (ed.) *Inclusive Citizenship*, London: Zed Books.

Kaplan, J. (1988) *The Accused [Motion Picture]*, United States: Paramount Pictures.

Karpman, B. (1954) *The Sexual Offender and His Offenses*, New York: Julian.

Karstedt, S. (2002) 'Emotions and Criminal Justice', *Theoretical Criminology*, 6(3): 299–318.

Katz, J. (1988) *Seductions of Crime*, New York: Basic Books.

Katz, J. (1999) *How Emotions Work*, Chicago: University of Chicago Press.

Kaveney, R. (2006) *Teen Dreams: Reading Teen Film from Heathers to Veronica Mars*, London: I. B. Tauris.

Kermode, M. (2006) 'Hard Candy [Review]', *The Observer*, 18 June: http://www.guardian.co.uk/film/2006/jun/18/features.review (Accessed on 16 June 2010).

King, A. (2006) 'Serial Killing and the Postmodern Self', *History of the Human Sciences*, 19(3): 109–25.

King, N. and McCaughey, M. (2001) 'What's a Mean Woman Like You Doing in a Movie Like This?' in M. McCaughey and N. King (eds) *Reel Knockouts: Violent Women in the Movies*, Austin: University of Texas Press.

Kinton, M. (2008) 'Burden of Guilt', *The Guardian*: http://www.guardian.co.uk/commentisfree/2008/jan/30/comment.mentalhealth (Accessed on 30 January 2008).

Kishtainy, K. (1982) *The Prostitute in Progressive Literature*, London: Allison and Busby.

Kristeva, J. (1982) *Powers of Horror: An Essay on Abjection*, trans. by Leon S. Roudiez, New York: Columbia UP.

Kroger, J. (2004) *Identity in Adolescence: The Balance Between Self and Other*, Hove: Routledge. 3rd edition.

Kundera, M. (2007) *The Curtain: An Essay in Seven Parts*, London: Harper Collins.

Kushner, T. and Knox, K. (1999) *Refugees in an Age of Genocide*, London: Frank Cass.

Laclau, E. and Mouffe, C. (2001) *Hegemony and Socialist Strategy*, London: Verso. 2nd edition.

Lambert, A. and Simpson, C. (2008) '*Jindabyne*'s Haunted Alpine Country: Producing (an) Australian Badland', *M/C Journal: A Journal of Media and Culture*, 11(5): 81–7.

Larsson, S. (2008) *The Girl with the Dragon Tattoo*, London: Quercus.

Lavigne, A. (2011) *With Glowing Hearts*, Vancouver: Animal Mother Films.

Lawrence, R. (2006) *Jindabyne*, Australia: April Films.

Leander, K. (2006) 'Reflections on Sweden's Measures Against Men's Violence Against Women', *Social Policy and Society*, 5(1): 115–25.

Leavy, P. and Maloney, K. P. (2009) 'American Reporting of School Violence and "People Like Us": A Comparison of Newspaper Coverage of the Columbine Massacre and Red Lake School Shootings', *Critical Sociology*, 35(2): 273–92.

Lefebvre, M. (2005) 'Conspicuous Consumption: The Figure of the Serial Killer as Cannibal in the Age of Capitalism', *Theory, Culture and Society*, 22(3): 43–62.

Leonardo Education and Art Forum (2011) *Leonardo On-line*, http://www.leonardo.info/isast/LEAF.html (Accessed on 3 August 2011).

Lester, C. (2006) 'From Columbine to Red Lake: Tragic Provocations for Advocacy', *Journal of American Studies*, 47(1): 133–53.

Lewis, T. (2009) 'Risky Youth and the Psychology of Surveillance', in T. Monahan and R. D. Torres (eds) *Schools Under Surveillance*, New Brunswick, NJ: Rutgers University Press.

Lindner, E. (2006) *Making Enemies: Humiliation and International Conflict*, Westport, Connecticut and London: Praeger Security.

Lister, R. (2007) 'Inclusive Citizenship: realizing the potential', *Citizenship Studies*, (11): 49–61.

Loader, I. and Sparks, R. (2011) *Public Criminology?* Abingdon: Routledge.

Lorenzer, A. (1981, 2002) 'What is an Unconscious Phantasy?' trans. by T. Schaffrik. http://bidok.uibk.ac.at/library/schaffrik-lorenzer-work-e.html (Accessed on June 2010).

Lyng, S. (1990) 'Edgework: A Social Psychological Analysis of Voluntary Risk Taking', *American Journal of Sociology*, 95(4): 876–921.

Lyng, S. (1998) 'Dangerous Methods: Risk Taking and the Research Process', in J. Ferrell and M. S. Hamm (eds) *Ethnography at the Edge*, Boston: Northeastern University Press.

Machado, H. and Santos, F. (2009) 'The Disappearance of Madeleine McCann: Public Drama and Trial by Media in the Portuguese Press', *Crime, Media, Culture*, 5(2): 146–67.

Maguire, M. (1997) 'Crime Statistics, Patterns and Trends: Changing Perceptions and Their Implications', in M. Maguire, R. Morgan and R. Reiner (eds) *The Oxford Handbook of Criminology*, Oxford: Oxford University Press. 2nd edition.

Malle, L. (1978) *Pretty Baby [Motion Picture]*, United States: Paramount Pictures.

Marfleet, P. (2006) *Refugees in a Global Era*, Basingstoke: Palgrave Macmillan.

Marshall, G. (1990) *Pretty Woman [Motion Picture]*, United States: Touchstone Pictures.

Martin, G. (2009) 'Subculture, Style, Chavs and Consumer Capitalism', *Crime, Media, Culture*, 5(2): 123–45.

Masters, T. (2010) 'Tell Me About Your Daughter', *BBC News*, 23 April: http://news.bbc.co.uk/1/hi/entertainment/8637075.stm (Accessed on 26 August 2010).

Matheou, D. (2010) 'How The Killer Inside Me Got Inside the Mind of Michael Winterbottom', FilmBlog, *guardian.co.uk*, 26 January: http://www.guardian.co.uk/film/filmblog/2010/jan/26/the-killer-inside-me-sundance (Accessed on 20 August 2010).

McG (2000) *Charlie's Angels*, USA: Columbia Pictures Corporation.

McG (2003) *Charlie's Angels: Full Throttle*, USA: Columbia Pictures Corporation.

McRobbie, A. and Thornton, S. L. (1995) 'Rethinking "Moral Panic" for Multi-Mediated Social Worlds', *British Journal of Sociology*, 46(4): 559–74.

Megaphone (2011) 'Home Page', http://www.megaphonemagazine.com/legacy/content/about_megaphone.html (Accessed on 30 April 2011).

Melossi, D. (2008) *Controlling Crime, Controlling Society*, Cambridge: Polity Press.

Mitchell, E. (2003) 'Elephant Movie Review: "Normal" High School on the Verge', *New York Times*, 10 October: http://movies.nytimes.com/movie/review?res=980CEED6163FF933A25753C1A9659C8B63 (Accessed on 7 February 2011).

Miller, V. (2004) '"The Last Vestige of Institutionalized Sexism"? Paternalism, Equal Rights and the Death Penalty in Twentieth and Twenty First Century Sunbelt America: The Case for Florida', *Journal of American Studies*, 38(3): 391–424.

Moore, S. (2004) 'Elephant [Review]', *Film Quarterly*, 58(2): 45–8.

Morris, W. (2003) 'Cosmic "Elephant": High School Existential', *Boston Globe*, 14 November: http://www.boston.com/movies/display?display=movie&id=2847 (Accessed on 7 February 2011).

Morrissey, B. (2003) *When Women Kill: Questions of Agency and Subjectivity*, London: Routledge.

Muller, V. (2008) 'Good and Bad Mothering: Lionel Shriver's "We Need to Talk About Kevin"', in M. Porter and J. Kelso (eds) *Theorising and Representing Maternal Realities*, Newcastle Upon Tyne: Cambridge Scholars Press.

Muncie, J. (2009) *Youth and Crime*, London: Sage. 3rd edition.

Muncie, J. and Goldson, B. (2006) 'England and Wales: The New Correctionalism', in J. Muncie and B. Goldson (eds) *Comparative Youth Justice*, London: Sage.

Munroe, R. (1999) 'In Denial of What's Paid For It: A Review of Not All the Time… But Mostly…' in *Not All The Time… But Mostly…* – Exhibition Booklet, Nottingham: Nottingham Trent and Staffordshire Universities.

Murray, A. (1995) 'Mind your Peers and Queers: Female Sex Workers in the AIDS Discourse in Australia and Southeast Asia', *Gender, Place and Culture*, Sage.

Muschert, G. W. (2007) 'Research in School Shootings', *Sociology Compass*, 1(1): 60–80.

Muschert, G. W. (2009) 'Frame-Changing in the Media Coverage of a School-Shooting: The Rise of Columbine as a National Concern', *The Social Science Journal*, 46: 164–70.

Muzzatti, S. (2004) 'Criminalising Marginality and Resistance: Marilyn Manson, Columbine and Cultural Criminology, in J. Ferrell, K. Hayward, W. Morrison and M. Presdee (eds) *Cultural Criminology Unleashed*, London: Glasshouse.

Naylor, B. (2001) 'Reporting Violence in the British Print Media: Gendered Stories', *Howard Journal of Criminal Justice*, 40(2): 180–94.

Naylor, B. (1995) 'Women's Crime and Media Coverage: Making Explanations', in R. E. Dobash, R. P. Dobash and L. Noaks (eds) *Gender and Crime*, Cardiff: University of Wales Press.

Nelson, R. (2006) 'Not Another Teen Movie', *The Village Voice*, 4 April: http://www.villagevoice.com/2006-04-04/film/not-another-teen-movie/ (Accessed on 16 June 2010).

Neroni, H. (2005) *The Violent Woman: Femininity, Narrative, and Violence in Contemporary American Cinema*, New York: State University of New York Press.

Neuner, T., Hubner-Lieberman, B., Hajak, G. and Hausner, H. (2009) 'Media Running Amok after School Shooting in Winnenden, Germany!' *European Journal of Public Health*, 19(6): 578–9.

Newitz, A. (1997) 'White Savagery and Humiliation, Or a New Racial Consciousness in the Media', in M. Wray and A. Newitz (eds) *White Trash: Race and Class in America*, New York: Routledge.

Newman, M. (2009) 'Feminist or Misogynist?' *The F Word*, 4 September: http://www.thefword.org.uk/reviews/2009/09/larrson_review (Accessed on 1 July 2010).

Nicolson, D. (1995) 'Telling Tales: Gender Discrimination, Gender Construction and Battered Women Who Kill', *Feminist Legal Studies*, 3(2): 186–206.

Nispel, M. (2003) *The Texas Chainsaw Massacre*, USA: New Line Cinema.

O'Brien, M. (2005) 'What is Cultural about Cultural Criminology', *Brit. J. Criminology*, 45: 599–612.

O'Neill, M. (1997) 'Saloon Girls: Death and Desire in the American West' in Holliday, R. and Hassard, J. (eds) *Film and Organization*, London: Sage. pp. 117–130.

O'Neill, M. (1998) 'Organization Representation: Work and Organizations in Popular Culture' in J. Hassard and R. Holliday (eds) *Film and Organization*, London: Sage.

O'Neill, M. (2001) *Prostitution and Feminism: Towards a Politics of Feeling*, Cambridge: Polity Press.

O'Neill, M. (2002) 'Global Refugees: Ethno-mimesis as Performative Praxis', in M. Miles (ed.) *Divers(c)ities: Recoveries and Reclamations*, Exeter University, Bristol: Intellect Books.

O'Neill, M. (2004) Crime, Culture and Visual Methodologies: Ethno-Mimesis as Performative Praxis', in J. Ferrell, K. Hayward, W. Morrison and M. Presdee (eds) *Cultural Criminology Unleashed*, London: Glasshouse Press.

O'Neill, M. (2007) 'Ethno-mimesis, feminist praxis and the visual turn' in *Cultural Sociology* [ed] Tim Edwards. London: Sage.

O'Neill, M. (2008) 'Transnational Refugees: The Transformative Role of Art?' *Forum Qualitative Sozialforschung / Forum: Qualitative Social Research*, 9(2), Art. 59, http://nbnresolving.de/urn:nbn:de:0114-fqs0802590.

O'Neill, M. (2010a) *Asylum, Migration and Community*, Bristol: Policy Press.

O'Neill, M. (2010b) 'Cultural Criminology and Sex Work: Resisting Regulation through Radical Democracy and Participatory Action Research (PAR)', *Journal of Law and Society*, 37(1): 210–32.

O'Neill, M. (2012) 'Ethno-mimesis and participatory arts', in S. Pink (ed.) *Advances in Visual Methodology*, London: Sage.

O'Neill, M. and Campbell, R. (2001) *Working Together to Create Change*, http://www.safetysoapbox.com.uk (Accessed on 30 May 2011).

O'Neill, M. and Giddens, S. (2001) 'Not all the time...', *Feminist Review*, 67: 1–10.

O'Neill, M. and Harindranath, R. (2006) 'Theorising Narratives of Exile and Belonging: The Importance of Biography and Ethno-Mimesis in "Understanding" Asylum', *Qualitative Sociology Review*, 2(1): 39–53.

O'Neill, M. and Hubbard, P. (2010) 'Walking, Sensing, Belonging: Ethno-mimesis as Performative Praxis', *Visual Studies*, 25(1): 46–59.

O'Neill, M. and Stenning, P. (2011) 'Politics, Community and Resistance in Skid Row: A Photo Essay' (under submission), *Crime, Media, Culture*.

O'Neill, M., Numminen, J., Painchaud, L., Smith, A., Snider, G. and Wall, K. (2011) 'Cynthia and Community, Politics and Resistance in DTES', *Megaphone Magazine*, http://megaphonemagazine.com/communityreport.

Park, R. E. and Burgess, E. W. (1925, 1967) *The City: Suggestions for the Investigation of Human Behavior in the Urban Environment*, Chicago: University of Chicago Press.

Pearson, K. (2007) 'The Trouble With Aileen Wuornos, Feminism's First Serial Killer', *Communication and Critical/Cultural Studies*, 4(3): 256–75.

Peary, G. (2003) 'Gus Van Sant – Elephant [Interview]', *geraldpeary.com*: http://geraldpeary.com/interviews/stuv/van-sant-elephant.html (Accessed on 7 February 2011).

Peckinpah, S. (1969) *The Wild Bunch*, United States: Warner Brothers/Seven Arts.

Pheterson, G. (1989) (ed.) *A Vindication of the Rights of Whores*, Seattle: Seal Press.

Phillips, N. D. and Strobl, S. (2006) 'Cultural Criminology and Kryptonite', *Crime, Media, Culture*, 2(3): 304–31.

Phoenix, J. (2009) 'Frameworks of Understanding', in J. Phoenix (ed.) *Regulating Sex for Sale: Prostitution Policy Reform in the UK*, Bristol: Policy Press.

Picart, C. J. and Greek, C. E. (2007) 'The Compulsions of Real/Reel Serial Killers and Vampires', in C. J. Picart and C. E. Greek (eds) *Monsters In and Among Us: Toward a Gothic Criminology*, Cranbury: Associated University Press.

Pickering, S. (2005) *Refugees & State Crime*, Annandale NSW, Australia: The Federation Press.

Pike, S. M. (2009) 'Dark Teens and Born-Again Martyrs: Captivity Narratives after Columbine', *Journal of the American Academy of Religion*, 77(3): 647–79.

Presdee, M. (2000) *Cultural Criminology and the Carnival of Crime*, London: Routledge.

Presdee, M. (2004) *Cultural Criminology: The Long and Winding Road*, London: Sage.

Probyn-Rapsey, F. (2007) 'Complicity, Critique and Methodology', *Ariel: A Review of International English Literature*, 38(2–3): 65–82.

Prud'homme, A. (1991) 'Little Flat of Horrors', *Time*, 5 August: http://www.time.com/time/magazine/article/0,9171,973550-1,00.html (Accessed on 16 July 2010).

Rafter, N. (2006) *Shots in the Mirror*, Oxford: Oxford University Press. 2nd edition.

Rafter, N. (2007) 'Crime, Film and Criminology: Recent Sex-Crime Movies', *Theoretical Criminology*, 11(3): 403–20.

Read, J. (2000) *The New Avengers: Feminism, Femininity and the Rape Revenge Cycle*, Manchester: Manchester University Press.

Read, J. (2004) '"Once Upon a Time There Were Three Little Girls": Girls, Violence, and Charlie's Angels', in S. J. Schneider (ed.) *New Hollywood Violence*, Manchester: Manchester University Press.

Redhead, S. (1993) *Rave Off: Politics and Deviance in Contemporary Youth Culture*, Aldershot: Avebury.

Redhead, S. (1995) *Unpopular Cultures: The Birth of Law and Popular Culture*, Manchester: Manchester University Press.

Redhead, S. (2004) *Paul Virilio: Theorist for an Accelerated Culture*, Edinburgh: Edinburgh University Press.

Redman, P., Bereswill, M. and Morgenroth, C. (2010) 'Special Issue on Alfred Lorenzer: Introduction', *Psychoanalysis, Culture & Society*, 15: 281–301.

Refugee Action (2006) *The Destitution Trap: Research into Destitution Among Refused Asylum Seekers in the UK*, London: Refugee Action.

Ringrose, J. (2006) 'A New Universal Mean Girl: Examining the Discursive Construction and Social Regulation of the New Feminine Pathology', *Feminism and Psychology*, 16(4): 405–24.

Roberts, B. (2002) *Biographical Research*, Buckingham: Open University Press.

Roeg, N. (1973) *Don't Look Now*, UK: Casey Productions.

Romney, J. (2010) 'The Killer Inside Me [Review]', *The Independent*, 6 June: http://www.independent.co.uk/arts-entertainment/films/reviews/the-killer-inside-me-18-1992307.html (Accessed on 20 August 2010).

Ronson, J. (2002) *Them: Adventures with Extremists*, London: Picador.

Ronson, J. (2005) *The Men who Stare at Goats*, London: Picador.

Ronson, J. (2006) 'Bad Tidings', *The Guardian*, 23 December: http://www.guardian.co.uk/world/2006/dec/23/usgunviolence.usa (Accessed on 24 November 2010).

Sales, R. (2007) *Understanding Immigration and Refugee Policy Contradictions and Continuities*, Bristol: Policy Press.

Sanders, T., O'Neill, M. and Pitcher, J. (2009) *Prostitution: Sex Work, Policy and Politics*, London: Sage.

Self, H. (2003) *Prostitution, Women and Misuse of the Law: The Fallen Daughters of Eve*, London: Frank Cass.

Scheff, T. (2006) 'Silence and Mobilization: Emotional/Relational Dynamics', http://www.humiliationstudies.org/documents/ScheffSilenceand Mobilization.pdf (Accessed on 18 October 2008).

Scheff, T. (2007) ' Politics of Hidden Emotions: Responses to a War Memorial' *Peace and Conflict: Journal of Peace Psychology*, 13(2): 1–9.

Scheff, T. (2010) 'Normalizing as the Opposite of Labeling' http://www.soc.ucsb.edu/faculty/scheff/77.pdf (Accessed on 1 April 2010).

Schmid, D. (2005) *Natural Born Celebrities: Serial Killers in American Culture*, Chicago: University of Chicago Press.

Schubart, R. (2007) *Super Bitches and Action Babes: The Female Hero in Popular Cinema, 1970–2006*, Jefferson, NC: McFarland.

Schulian, J. and Tapert, R. G. (1995–2001) *Xena: Warrior Princess*, USA: MCA Television.

Scott, E. S. (2002) 'The Legal Construction of Childhood', in M. K. Rosenheim (ed.) *A Century of Juvenile Justice*, Chicago: University of Chicago Press.

Scott, R. (1991) *Thelma & Louise*, USA: Metro-Goldwyn-Mayer.

Scoular, J. and Sanders, T. (2010) 'Introduction: The Changing Social and Legal Context of Sexual Commerce: Why Regulation Matters', *Journal of Law and Society*, Special Issue: Regulating Sex/Work: From Crime Control to Neo-liberalism? 37(1): 1–11.

Scoular, J. and O'Neill, M. (2007) 'Regulating Prostitution: Social Inclusion, Responsibilization and the Politics of Prostitution Reform', *British Journal of Criminology*, 47(5): 764–78.

Scraton, P. (2008) 'The Criminalisaton and Punishment of Children and Young People', *Current Issues in Criminal Justice*, 20(1): 1–13.

Seal, L. (2010) *Women, Murder and Femininity: Gender Representations of Women Who Kill*, Basingstoke: Palgrave Macmillan.

Seltzer, M. (1998) *Serial Killers: Life and Death in America's Wound Culture*, London: Routledge.

Shapiro, A. (1996) *Breaking the Codes: Female Criminality in Fin-de-Siecle Paris*, Stanford: Stanford University Press.

Shriver, L. (2010) *We Need to Talk about Kevin*, London: Serpent's Tail (Kindle edition).

Simon, J. (2007) *Governing through Crime*, Oxford: Oxford University Press.

Simpson, P. L. (2000) *Psycho Paths: Tracking the Serial Killer Through Contemporary American Fiction*, Carbondale and Edwardsville: Southern Illinois University Press.

Slade, D. (2005) *Hard Candy*, USA: Vulcan Productions.

Smith, A. M. (1998) *Laclau and Mouffe: The Radical Democratic Imaginary*, London: Routledge.

Smith, D. (2006) *Globalization: The Hidden Agenda*, Cambridge: Polity Press.

Smith, J. (2008) 'The Girl with the Dragon Tattoo by Stieg Larsson', *The Times*, 20 January: http://entertainment.timesonline.co.uk/tol/arts_and_entertainment/books/fiction/article3202077.ece (Accessed on 1 July 2010).

Soothill, K. and Walby, S. (1991) *Sex Crime in the News*, London: Routledge.

Spencer, J. W. and Muschert, G. W. (2009) 'The Contested Meaning of the Crosses at Columbine', *American Behavioral Scientist*, 52(10): 1371–86.

Springhall, J. (2008) 'The Monsters Next Door: What Made Them Do It?' in C. Krinsky (ed.) *Moral Panics Over Contemporary Youth*, Farnham: Ashgate.

Stallybrass, P. and White, A. (1986) *The Politics and Poetics of Transgression*, London: Methuen.

Stanley, L. and Wise, S. (1993) *Breaking Out Again*, London: Routledge.

Sutcliffe, T. (2010) 'The Weekend's TV', *The Independent*, 26 April: http://www.independent.co.uk/arts-entertainment/tv/reviews/the-weekends-tv-five-daughters-sun-bbc-the-ricky-gervais-show-fri-channel-4-1954101.html (Accessed on 26 August 2010).

Tarantino, Q. (2003) *Kill Bill: Volume 1*, USA: Miramax Films.

Tarantino, Q. (2004) *Kill Bill: Volume 2*, USA: Miramax Films.

Tasker, Y. (1993) *Spectacular Bodies: Gender, Genre and the Action Cinema*, London: Routledge.

Tasker, Y. and Negra, D. (2007) 'Introduction', in Y. Tasker and D. Negra (eds) *Interrogating Post-Feminism: Gender and the Politics of Popular Culture*, Durham: Duke University Press.

Taylor, D. (2009) *Underground Lives: An Investigation into the Living Conditions & Survival Strategies of Destitute Asylum Seekers in the UK*, Leeds: Positive Action for Refugees and Asylum Seekers.

Taylor, I., Walton, P. and Young, J. (1973) *The New Criminology*, London: Routledge and Kegan Paul.

Theweleit, K. (1987) *Male Fantasies* Vol. 1, Cambridge: Polity Press.

Theweleit, K. (1989) *Male Fantasies: Male Bodies; Psychoanalyzing the White Terror* Vol. 2, Minneapolis, MN: University of Minnesota Press.

Thompson, A. (2010) 'Sundance: Winterbottom Defends The Killer Inside Me', *Indiewire*, 26 January: http://blogs.indiewire.com/thompsononhollywood/

2010/01/27/sundance_winterbottom_defends_the_killer_inside_me/ (Accessed on 20 August 2010).

Thompson, J. (2010 [1952]) *The Killer Inside Me*, London: Orion.

Thompson, K. (1998) *Moral Panics*, London: Routledge.

Tithecott, R. (1997) *Of Men and Monsters: Jeffrey Dahmer and the Construction of the Serial Killer*, Madison: University of Wisconsin Press.

Tonso, K. L. (2009) 'Violent Masculinities as Tropes for School Shooters', *American Behavioral Scientist*, 52(9): 1266–85.

Travers, P. (2010) 'The Killer Inside Me [Review]', *Rolling Stone*, 18 June: http://www.rollingstone.com/movies/reviews/17929/118419 (Accessed on 20 August 2010).

Tyler, I. (2006) 'Welcome to Britain: The Cultural Politics of Asylum', *European Journal of Cultural Studies*, 9(2): 185–202; 1367–5494.

United Nations Human Rights Commission (2011) http://www.unhcr.org/4c176c969.html (Accessed on 19 March 2011).

Van Sant, G. (2003) *Elephant*, USA: HBO Films.

von Sternberg, J. (1930) *The Blue Angel [Motion Picture]*, Germany: Universum Film.

Verhoeven, P. (1992) *Basic Instinct*, USA: Carolco Pictures.

Virtual Tourist (2011) 'Vancouver, British Columbia', http://www.virtualtourist.com/travel/North_America/Canada/Province_of_British_Columbia/Vancouver-903183/Warnings_or_Dangers-Vancouver-Downtown_Eastside-BR-1.html#ixzz1MnhtQCB9 (Accessed on 16 May 2011).

Walkowitz, J. (1977) 'The Making of an Outcast Group: Prostitutes and Working Women in Nineteenth Century Plymouth and Southampton', in M. Vicinus (ed.) *A Widening Sphere: Changing Roles of Victorian Women*, Lodnon: Methuen.

Walkowitz, J. (1980) *Prostitution and Victorian Society*, Cambridge: Cambridge University Press.

Walkowitz, J. (1982) 'Jack the Ripper and the Myth of Male Violence', *Feminist Studies*, 8(3): 542–74.

Walkowitz, J. (1992) *City of Dreadful Delight*, London: Virago.

Walters, R. (2003) *Deviant Knowledge: Criminology, Politics and Policy*, Cullompton: Willan.

'Wacquant'. Minneapolis, MN (2009) *Prisons of Poverty*, Minneapolis, MN: University of Minnesota Press.

Webber, C. (2007) 'Background, Foreground, Foresight: The Third Dimension of Cultural Criminology', *Crime, Media, Culture*, 3(2): 139–57.

Weigel, S. Z. (1996) *Body-and Image-Space: Re-Reading Walter Benjamin*, trans. by G. Paul, R. McNicholl and J. Gaines. London and New York: Routledge.

Wente, M. (2008) 'Meet Vancouver's Next Mayor', *The Globe and Mail*, 19 June 2008, p. 15.

Whedon, J. (1997–2003) *Buffy the Vampire Slayer*, USA: 20th Century Fox Television.

Whitford, M. (1991) *Luce Irigaray: Philosophy in the Feminine*, London: Routledge.

Williams, R. (2001 [1958]) 'Culture is Ordinary', in J. Higgins (ed.) *The Raymond Williams Reader*, Oxford: Blackwell.

Willis, P. E. (1978) *Profane Culture*, London: Routledge and Kegan Paul.

Wilson, D. (2007) *Serial Killers: Hunting Britons and their Victims, 1960–2000*, Winchester: Waterside.

Winterbottom, M. (2002) *In this World [Motion Picture]*, United Kingdom: The Film Consortium.

Winlow, S. (2001) *Badfellas: Crime, Tradition and Masculinities*, Oxford: Berg.

Winlow, S. and Hall, S. (2006) *Violent Night: Urban Leisure and Contemporary Culture*, Oxford: Berg.

Woolf, M. (2007) 'Six Months After Madeleine, Another 600 Are Still Missing', *The Independent*, 4 November.

Young, A. (1996) *Imagining Crime: Textural Outlaws and Criminal Conversations*, London: Sage.

Young, A. (2008) 'Culture, Critical Criminology and the Imagination of Crime', in T. Anthony and C. Cuneen (eds) *The Critical Criminology Companion*, Sydney: Hawkins Press.

Young, A. (2009) 'The Screen of the Crime: Judging the Affect of Cinematic Violence', *Social and Legal Studies*, 18(1): 5–22.

Young, A. (2010) 'Is there Such a Thing as "Just Looking"?' in K. J. Heyward and M. Presdee (eds) *Framing Crime: Cultural Criminology and the Image*, London: Routledge.

Young, J. (1999) *The Exclusive Society: Social Exclusion, Crime and Difference in Late Modernity*, London: Sage.

Young, J. (2004a) 'Crime and the Dialectics of Inclusion/Exclusion', *British Journal of Criminology*, 44(4): 550–61.

Young, J. (2007) *The Vertigo of Late Modernity*, London: Sage.

Young, J. (2011) *The Criminological Imagination*, Cambridge: Polity Press.

1oXHayendoX (2009) School Shooting et Violence, Youtube: www.youtube.com (Accessed on 12 October 2010).

Index

Page numbers in **Bold** represent figures.

abjection 1–7, 13, 37–44, 138, 149;
  and madness 87–99; and sex
  workers 65–82
The Accused (Kaplan) 47
Agamben, G. 108, 121
AHA Media (citizen
  journalists) 142–5, **145**
Aitken, S. 25–7
Alba, Jessica 112
Alien (Scott) 46–50
Altheide, D. 26–8
Amelio, Sonia 73–6
American Psycho (Harron) 105–6,
  110
androgyny 58–63
Anti-Social Behaviour Orders
  (ASBOs) 21–3
Arts and Humanities Research
  Council (AHRC) 126
Asperger's Syndrome 58
asylum seekers 13–18, 119–37, 158,
  161; and migration 119–24
attunement 94–9, 132–3, 156

Bad Tidings (Ronson) 20, 30–2,
  39–41; Christmas fantasy 30–2;
  shootings plot 30; topics
  explored 30
*Badfellas: Crime, Tradition and
  Masculinities* (Winlow) 14
Bakhtin, M. 3
Ballinger, A. 43
Barrios, L.: and Brotherton, D. 15
Barthes, Roland 92, 138
BASE jumping 3–4
Basic Instinct (Verhoven) 46
Bassett, C. 34
Baudelaire, Charles 71

Bauman, Z. 123–5, 155–8
BBC News 112
Becker, H. 14
Behavioural Sciences Unit,
  Quantico 103
Benjamin, J. 81
Benjamin, Walter 69–71
Bereswill, M.: Morgenroth, C. and
  Redman, P. 93, 98
Bernardo, Paul 44
biographical analysis 90–2
Birch, H. 43
Birmingham Centre (School)
  for Contemporary Cultural
  Studies 9, 125, 139
Blue Steel (Bigelow) 48
Bobbitt, Lorena 56
Bonington Gallery
  (Nottingham) 128–35
borders 6, 65, 74, 87, 91, 161;
  integration mechanisms 121–4;
  outlaws and folk devils 119–37;
  and sovereignty 119–24
Born, G. 142
Boskin, J. 39
Boston Globe 32
Boyd, N.: Culbert, L. and
  Campbell, L. 140
Bradshaw, P. 111
Brady, Ian 43
Bromley, R. 136
Bronfen, E. 75
Brotherton, D.: and Barrios, L.
  15
Brown, A. 84–6, 97
Buffy the Vampire Slayer
  (Whedon) 46–7
Bulger, James 22–5, 36–7

bullying 25–41; and madness 90–9; and the school shooter 25–41
Bundy, Ted 106
Burgess, E.: and Park, R. 151
Burns, R.: and Crawford, C. 24
Bush, Pres. George W. 39, 110
Butchard, S. 112–14
Butler, J. 79–80

Campbell, L.: Boyd, N. and Culbert, L. 140
Campbell, R.: and O'Neill, M. 77
Canada: Virtual Tourist website (Vancouver) 139–40, *see also* Downtown East Side, Vancouver (DTES)
cannibalism 103–6
capitalism 11–13, 65, 77, 82, 102, 106, 121; human waste 125
captivity narratives 26
Caputi, J. 103
Carmen (Merimee) 75–6
carnivalesque acts/events 2–7
Carver, R. 114–16
castration 56–7
Chadwick, Edwin 70
Charlie's Angels (McG) 47–50
Chesney-Lind, M. 44
childhood 6, 75, 82, 157; folk devil representation 21–3; the school shooter 20–41; victims and villains 20–41, 160
Cho, Seung Hui 29
citizen journalism 142, 145
citizenship 13, 137, 161
Clarke, J. 7
Clover, C. 48, 55
Cohen, S. 14, 23
Colet, Louise 66
Columbine High School Massacre 23–35; Cho, Seung Hui 29; media footage 34–5
community 27–31, 57, 87–98, 105, 113–16, 126–8, 138–54, 161–2; relationship aspect 152–4

Condon, S. 145
Connelly, H. 131
constructive rationality 82
Contagious Diseases Acts 66–9, 72
Corbin, A. 68
Cornell, D. 8
Coulthard, L. 49
Crawford, C.: and Burns, R. 24
Creed, B. 48, 55
Cresswell, T. 4
crime 1–2, 20–4, 27–8, 54–60, 84–9, 98, 101–3, 113–18, 125; and deviance 7–17; Downtown East Side Vancouver 138–54; and sex workers 73–82
criminology 2, 92, 125; correctionalism and conservatism 84–6; critical 9–10, 125, 156–9; cultural 8–18, 153–9, 155–9; feminist 18, 44–53; popular 7, 158; psychosocial 84–6; public 155–9; sociological 17
Culbert, L.: Campbell, L. and Boyd, N. 140
cultural denigration 108, 115
cultural history 6
cultural representations 1–2, 7, 16–20, 29, 39–41, 65, 126, 137, 158; popular, female avengers 42–63

Dahmer, Jeffrey 100–4; cannibalism 104; media representation 102–3
Dargis, M. 56
Darke, C. 136
Darwin, Charles 151
deadly dolls 46–50
demystify 18; folk devil 39–41, 143–5
depth-hermeneutic method 93
deviance 1–2, 7–12, 16–17, 52, 83–7, 92–8, 125, 137, 156; crime and poverty 138–54; double 42–5; imagining 2; and insanity

90–9; and sex workers 67–9;
sexuality 5
*Diagnostic and Statistical Manual
of Mental Disorders* (American
Psychiatric Association) 89; five
axes 89–92
Ditmore, M.: Levy, A. and
Willman, A. 64
Douglas, J. 103
Downtown East Side,
Vancouver (DTES) 15–19,
161; binners 138, 149–54;
community, recognition and
belonging 153–4; crime,
poverty and resistance 138–54;
and the media 141–51, **141**;
Pedestrian Safety Project 144;
problem community 139–42;
welfare 149–54
Drummond, Edward 88–92

edgework 2–5, 10, 15
Egger, S. 107–8, 113
Elephant (Van Sant) 20, 32–41;
explanations and affects of
screen violence 33–5; fictional
Columbine-style shooting
32–5
Ellis, Brett Easton 105–6
Empire of Scrounge (Ferrell) 10–11
Engels, Friedrich 70
equivalence 80–2
estrangement 25–41; and the
school shooter 25–41
ethnography 9–10, 14–16, 139,
158; and BASE jumping 3–4;
and sex work 64–82; zoo-
keeping 158–9
existential autonomy 15

facework 94–9
fear 18–21, 48, 54, 85, 91, 107,
121; and the folk devil 26–41
female avengers 16–19, 158–60; in
popular culture 42–63
female heroes 46–50, 57–63

feminism 18, 61–2, 75, 108;
appropriate 43–63; post
50–3; and sex workers 80–2;
stereotypes 58–63, 78–82; and
violent female avengers 42–63
Ferrell, J. 9–11, 14; Milovanovic, D.
and Lyng, S. 3; and Sanders, C. 9
Five Daughters (TV drama) 108–9,
112–18
Flaubert, Gustav 66, 70–1
folk devils 2, 14–18, 118–37, 143,
161; children as victims and
villains 21–3; demystifying
39–41; outlaws and borders
119–37; school shooters 20–41;
serial killers 100–18
folk heroes 2; *femme fatale* 46–7
Forman, Milos 83
Forster, E.M. 157
Foucault, M. 3, 68, 84
Fox, J.: and Levin, J. 101
Framing Crime (Hayward and
Presdee) 13–14
Frankfurt School 93
Frigon, S. 48
Frymer, B. 26
Fuller, R. 94

Gacy, John Wayne 104–5
Gadd, D.: and Jefferson, T. 85–6
Gein, Ed 102
gender boundaries 50–3
Giddens, S.: and O'Neill, M. 78–82
The Girl with the Dragon Tattoo
(Larsson) 57–63; character
backgrounds 58–61; Lisbeth
Salander character 57–63;
storyline 58–60
girlhood 55, 62
globalisation 1, 9, 72, 120–5,
136–7; negative 124–5
*Globalized People, Migration and
Cinema* (Bromley) 136–7
GMB union 72
Goffman, Erving 94
goths 25–32

governing through crime   28
Grand Central Station (New
   York)   4
Grand Housing March   144
Grant, C.   23
Greek, C.: and Picart, C.   104
Greer, C.   12
Greer, Germaine   88
Grier, Pam   46
Griffiths, R.   29
Grixti, J.   106
The Guardian   30, 111
Guilty Except for Insanity
   (Haaken)   83–99, 155–7
Guterres, High Commissioner
   António   124

Haaken, J.   83–99, 155–7
Haggerty, K.   102
Haigh, John George   102
Hall, S.   14–15; and Winlow, S.   11,
   14
The Hand That Rocks the Cradle
   (Hanson)   46
Hard Candy (Slade)   54–7, 62–3;
   Hayley Stark character   54–5;
   revenge fantasy   55–7; and
   victimhood   53–7
Harris, Eric   23–35
Harris, T.   102–6
Hay, C.   22
Hayward, K.: and Presdee, M.
   13–14, 139
Hazelwood, R.   103
Heath, Neville   102
Hebdige, D.   14
Hegel, Georg   151–3
Heidensohn, F.   42
Hendricks, H.   21
Herbst, C.   48–9
Hindley, Myra   43–4, 101
historical analysis   8, 65, 73, 76
Hobbes, Thomas   151
Hogan, John   88–9
Hollway, W.   85
Holmlund, C.   46–8

homelessness   13–19, 141, 146,
   154
Homolka, Karla   44
Honeth, A.   151–3
Howard's End (Forster)   157
Hubbard, P.: and O'Neill, M.
   125–35
Human Rights Convention
   (1951)   120
human waste (capitalist
   society)   125
human/monster hybrids   103–16

identity   4–14, 21, 45, 51,
   102, 106, 110, 135, 153;
   authentic motherhood   35–41;
   deviant   66–82, 100–18;
   disruption of   6
imagination   17–18, 81–2,
   119–21, 135–7, 155–9; radical
   democratic   1–2, 7–9, 17–18, 119,
   126, 135–7, 155–9
In This World (Winterbottom)   135
The Independent   111–13
Independent Asylum
   Commission   124
Indiewire   111
inequality   11, 53, 107, 117
Inness, S.   49
The Insanity Defence   88–92
Insanity Defence Reform Act
   (1984)   88
inter/trans disciplinary   157–8
International Monetary Fund   120
Ipswich Murders   112–18; *Five
   Daughters* (TV drama)   112–14
Irigaray, L.   81–2

Jack the Ripper   101–4
Jefferson, T.: and Gadd, D.   85–6
Jenkins, P.   101, 103, 106
Jenks, C.   3–5, 83–4
Jindabyne (Lawrence)   108–9,
   114–18
John, N.   66
Jones, A.   44

Jouve, N. 107
joyriding 4

Katz, J. 9
Kaveney, R. 33
Kill Bill (Tarantino) 47–50
killer beauties 46–50
The Killer Inside Me
 (Thompson) 108–18
King, A. 106
King, N.: and McCaughey, M. 50
Kinton, M. 88–9
Klebold, Dylan 23–35
Knox, K.: and Kushner, T. 121
Koch, Mayor Ed. 4
Kretschmer, Tim 29
Kristeva, J. 6
Kundera, M. 156
Kushner, T.: and Knox, K. 121

labelling 94–9
Lambert, A.: and Simpson, C. 115
Lars and the Real Girl
 (Gillespie) 94–9
Larsson, S. 57–63
The Last Seduction (Dahl) 46
Lawrence, R. 115
Leander, K. 60
Leavy, P.: and Maloney, K. 27
Lefebvre, Henri 105
Leonardo Education and Art
 Forum 157
less dead 107–8, 113–18; social
 types 108
Levin, J.: and Fox, J. 101
Levy, A.: Willman, A. and
 Ditmore, M. 64
liminality 6; children who kill 6,
 20–41; and madness 83–99; and
 sex workers 69–71
Lindner, E. 135, 137
Lister, R. 161
Loader, I.: and Sparks, R. 156
The Long Journey Home arts
 organisation 126–35
Lorenzer, A. 83, 93–9

Lost (TV drama) 50–3, 61–3;
 Kate Austen character and
 behaviour 50–3
Lyng, S. 3, 9; Ferrell, J. and
 Milovanovic, D. 3

McCann, Madeleine 12–13;
 parents' trial by media 12
McCaughey, M.: and King, N. 50
McNaughton rule - Insanity Defence
 case (1843) 88–92
McRobbie, A.: and Thornton, S. 23,
 29
madness 14, 18, 109, 156–7, 160;
 biographical narratives 90–2;
 criminal justice *vs.* mental
 health care 89–90; film and
 fiction 86–99; guilty except
 for insanity (GEI) plea 83–99,
 155–6; labelling, normalising
 and attunement 94–8; and
 liminality 83–99; psychosocial
 criminology 84–6
male violence myth 112–14
Maloney, K.: and Leavy, P. 27
Man Bites Dog (Belvaux) 112
Manson, Charles 100
Manson, Marilyn 25, 30–2
marginalisation 2, 10–15, 64, 118,
 126
Martin, G. 11
Marx, Karl 151
Marxism 9–10, 93
Mayhew, Henry 70
Mead, Ruth 151–3
media analysis 10; prostitution
 and film 73–82; social issue
 representation 12
Megaphone 145–51; *Hope in the
 Shadows* calendar 149; mission
 statement 146; vendors 146–9,
 147, 148; *Voices of the Street* 146
Merimee, Prosper 75–6
methodology 15, 86, 152, 156;
 cultural and sex workers 73–82;
 ethno 15, 125, 139

Metropolitan Police Act (1839)   66
Millennium Trilogy (Larsson)   57
Milovanovic, D.: Lyng, S. and
   Ferrell, J.   3
mimesis   82
misogyny   58–63
modernity   11, 72, 102, 106, 123–5
Moore, S.   33
moral culpability   26, 54–7
moral panics   2; folk devil
   representation   21–3, 39–41
Morgenroth, C.: Redman, P. and
   Bereswill, M.   93, 98
Morris, W.   32
Morrissey, B.   44
Muller, V.   38
Munroe, R.   80–1
murderabilia   100
Murray, M.   82
Muschert, G.: and Spencer, J.   25–6
musculinity   46–7
Myers, M.   126

National Deviancy Conference   9
nationality   5, 17
Naylor, B.   43
neo-liberalism   72, 98
New Deal welfare   28
The New York Times   56
Nicolson, D.   43
Nilsen, Dennis   105
normalising   94–9, 137–8
Not all the time... but mostly (O'Neill
   and Giddens)   78–82

O'Hara, Maureen   73–6
One Flew Over the Cuckoo's Nest
   (Forman)   83–99, 156
O'Neill, M.   8, 14–16, 139–42,
   152–4, 161; and Campbell,
   R.   77; and Giddens, S.   78–82;
   and Hubbard, P.   126–35; *Saloon
   Girls*   73–6; and Stenning, P.
   138
Oregon State Hospital   83–99
O'Sullivan, J.   82

Othered peoples   18, 100–18,
   138–54; asylum seekers and
   refugees   119–37; children who
   kill   40–1; Insanity Defence   90–9
outlaws, borders and folk
   devils   119–37, 161; asylum and
   migration   119–24; identification
   and experiences   121–37; media
   representation   121–4, **122**, **123**;
   negative globalisation   124–5;
   participatory and arts-
   based research   125–9;
   social displacement and risk
   management   133–5; workshop
   key themes   129–35
outsiders   1, 8, 13, 62, 103, 106–7,
   135; sex workers   64–82; Trench
   Coat Mafia   25

paedophilia   54–7
Page, Ellen   55
Parent-Duchâtelet, A.   64
Park, R.: and Burgess, E.   151
participatory action research   8, 15,
   77–82, 92–3, 119, 152–7, 161–2;
   refugees and asylum seekers
   125–9, *see also* Downtown East
   Side, Vancouver (DTES)
Pearson, K.   45–6
Peel, Sir Robert   88
phenomenology   10, 14, 125;
   arts-based research   138–54
Phillips, N.: and Strobl, S.   12
Picart, C.: and Greek, C.   104
Pike, S.   26
popular culture   7, 16, 42–63, 76,
   155, 160
post-modernism   9
poverty   18, 27, 69–71, 77, 82, 98,
   113, 138–54, 161
Poverty Olympics   144, 154
power   3–16, 21, 38–9, 48–9, 54–5,
   59–60, 68–71, 84, 101–4, 111,
   124, 139
Presdee, M.   3–4, 73; and
   Hayward, K.   13–14, 139

prisons of poverty   98–9
prostitution   6–7; cultural
   construction   13, 64–82; and film
   (media analysis)   73–82
Prud'homme, A.   104
psychiatry   84
Psycho (Hitchcock)   102
psycho-social analysis   7, 14,
   17–18, 121, 157–8, 160;
   madness   83–99
Psychoanalysis, Culture and Society
   (Lorenzer)   93–9
punctum   138

radical democratic imaginary   1–2,
   7–9, 17–18, 155–9; refugees and
   asylum seekers   119, 126, 135–7
Rafter, N.   7
rampage attacks   23–41
rape-revenge   57–63
Read, J.   50, 61
Reagan, Pres. Ronald   88
recuperation   44
Red Lake School shootings   27–9
Redman, P.: Bereswill, M. and
   Morgenroth, C.   93, 98
Refugee Action   122
representation   12–24, 69–72,
   140–2, 157–61; asylum seekers
   and refugees   121–4; gender,
   women who kill   5–7; of
   prostitutes (whore stigma)   6–7,
   64–82; serial killers   100–18; via
   media   12–13; violent female
   avengers   42–63; young person as
   folk devil   20–41
resistance   1–17, 50, 91, 137, 158–9,
   161–2; knowledge of   8, 15;
   and sex workers   71–82, *see also*
   Downtown East Side, Vancouver
   (DTES)
Ressler, R.   101–3
revenge fantasy   54–63
Ridgway, Gary (Green River
   Killer)   108
Rio Bravo (Hawks)   73–6

Romney, J.   111–12
Ronson, J.   20, 30–2

Saloon Girls (O'Neill)   73–6
Sanders, C.: and Ferrell, J.   9
Sartre, Jean-Paul   151
Scheff, T.   83, 93–9, 132–3, 156
school shooters   6, 14–18,
   158–60; children as victims
   and villains   20–41; and the
   media   23–9
Schubart, R.   46–7, 61–3
Se7en (Fincher)   105, 110
Seal, L.   5
Seltzer, M.   109
Sense of Belonging arts/research
   project   126–34, **127**, **131**,
   133, **134**; key themes   129–35;
   workshops and exhibitions
   128–35
serial killers   12, 16–19,
   160–1; characteristics and
   portrayal   103–16; ethics of
   representation   100–18; evil
   genius   103–4; in film and
   fiction   57–63, 102–18; mass in
   person   104–6; as transgressive
   outsiders   106–7; as upholders of
   social order   107–9
*The Sewer, the Gaze and
   Contaminating Touch* (Stallybrass
   and White)   70
sex workers   13–19, 43, 108, 112–13,
   138; ethnography, film and
   fiction   64–82; history of   65–9;
   issues and images   68–9; and
   liminality   69–71; as outcast
   group   65–9; and resistance
   71–82; stereotypes   78–82
sexual pathology   101–3, 109–12
Shipman, Harold   101, 108
Shriver, L.   20, 35–9, 157
The Silence of the Lambs
   (Demme)   102–6
Simon, J.   28
Simpson, C.: and Lambert, A.   115

Simpson, P. 107
skid row 15–19, 138–54,
161–2; crime, poverty and
resistance 138–54
Smith, A. 8, 142–5
So Much Water So Close to Home
(Carver) 114–16
social control 1–2, 8, 11, 39, 42,
76, 107, 135
sociology 85, 158; cultural 9–10,
153–4
Solanas, Valerie 56
Sorel, Georges 151
Sparks, R.: and Loader, I. 156
Spencer, J.: and Muschert, G. 25–6
Stallybrass, P.: and White, P. 3–6,
70–1
Stenning, P.: and O'Neill, M. 138
Stern, D. 96–9
Street Offences Act 69
Strobl, S.: and Phillips, N. 12
sub-culture 9–11, 17, 30
Sundance Film Festival 110–11
super predators 26–7
Sutcliffe, Peter (Yorkshire
Ripper) 107
symbolism 9–14, 20–4, 45,
108, 114, 122, 125, 139; and
childhood 39–41; deadly, glutted
empire 38–40; and images
14–16; and sex workers 65–82

Tasker, Y. 46, 49
Terminator (Cameron) 46–50
The Texas Chainsaw Massacre
(Hooper / Nispel) 102
Thelma and Louise (Scott) 46–50
Thompson, J. 108–18
Thompson, Robert 22–5
Thornton, S.: and McRobbie, A.
23, 29
threshold dwellers 69–71
Time magazine 38, 104
Tithecott, R. 104
Tomb Raider (computer game): Lara
Croft 34, 48–50

torture porn 110
Town Police Clauses Act (1847) 66
transgression 1–18, 20, 51, 65–82,
84, 98–9, 106–8, 125, 139, 159;
cultural constructions
13–14; ethnography 14–16;
gendered 18; media construction
and analysis 11–13; sub-
culture 10–11
Trauerspeil tragedy 72
Tyler, I. 121

Unforgiven (Eastwood) 73–6
United Kingdom Borders and
Immigration Agency 120–2
United Nations: Human Rights
Commission 123–4
United Nations (UN) 120;
Convention on Refugees
(1951) 122
United We Can (UWC) 150–1
urban 9, 22, 26–8, 57, 102
US News and World Report
(magazine) 25

Vagrancy Act (1824) 66
Van Sant, G. 20, 32–5
Vancouver: Virtual Tourist
website 139–40, *see also*
Downtown East Side, Vancouver
(DTES)
Venables, Jon 22–5
victims 12, 20–41, 101,
105–17, 124, 136, 160; female
avengers 43–63
Victoria, Queen of England 88
Violent Nights (Winlow and Hall) 14
violent women 42–63, 101;
development in popular
culture 46–7
Virginia Tech Massacre 29; media
footage 34–5

Wacquant, L. 98–9
Walkowitz, J. 66–7, 111
Walsall Art Gallery 77

Walsall South Health Action Zone 77
Walters, R. 15
Wayne, John 73–6
We Need to Talk About Kevin
(Shriver) 20, 35–41, 157;
behaviour perceptions
37–41; reflection on authentic
motherhood 35–9
Weise, Jeff 27–9
White, P.: and Stallybrass, P. 3–6,
70–1
Whitford, M. 82
The Wild Bunch (Peckinpah) 73–6
Williams, R. 16
Willman, A.: Ditmore, M. and
Levy, A. 64
Wilson, D. 108

Winlow, S. 14; and Hall, S. 11, 14
Winnenden School shootings 29
Winterbottom, M. 111, 135
Wolfenden Committee 69
Women For Hire (Corbin) 68
Women's Memorial March 144
World Bank 120, 123
World Trade Centre 28, 35; war on
terror 28
Wright, Steve 112–14
Wuornos, Aileen 45–6, 62–3, 101,
104

Xena: Warrior Princess (Tapert) 46

Young, A. 7, 33–5, 47
youth crime 22